Orpheus and Eurydice in Myth, History, and Analytical Psychology

This fascinating study shows how the minor Greek story of Orpheus and Eurydice came to have a more persistent and varied impact on Western culture than any other Greek myth. In the last 2,000 years, it has captivated the imagination of successive ages. Writers and other artists have turned to it to explore unexpectedly diverse concerns, from classical philosophy, through Christian values, to challenges involving individual psychology and societal well-being.

Dawson's study of the mythic imagination traces how these concerns unfold in poems, plays, novels, films, paintings, operas, ballets, and sculptures. It charts a history of responses to the experience of loss and longing and the need to grow in self-awareness. And it illustrates how responses to this myth anticipate many of the claims associated with analytical psychology.

This book will be of interest to analysts, scholars, and students working with Jung's ideas, and to all those interested in adaptations of myth and the implications they harbour.

Terence Dawson is an independent scholar, following a career teaching English and European literature at universities in Brazil, the United Kingdom, and Singapore.

Orpheus and Eurydice in Myth, History and Analytical Psychology

lessons of loss with gratitude that we have this unique but paradoxical opportunity to love what does not endure and cannot be perfected'.

Polly Young-Eisendrath, *PhD, Jungian Analyst and Psychologist, author of The Present Heart: A Memoir of Love, Loss, and Discovery*

'The focus of Dr Dawson's excellent, interdisciplinary analysis of the metaphors of loss, longing, and self-awareness at the heart of the myth of Orpheus and Eurydice is not centred on the 'story' but on how each generation defines these issues differently as a specific 'concern.' Using C.G. Jung's definition of myth as belonging to the collective unconscious and 'feeling toned complexes', this innovative re-evaluation of the collective and individual concerns expressed through the myth emphasises its international, interdisciplinary nature and offers unique, creative perspectives that simultaneously unravel specific time-based societal concerns'.

Dr Elizabeth Brodersen, *accredited Jungian Analyst and Supervisor, CGJIZ, editor of Jungian Dimensions of the Mourning Process, Burial Rituals and Access to the Land of the Dead: Intimations of Immortality (Routledge, 2024)*

'According to Malinowski, myth is the re-arising of a primordial reality in narrative form; and in this book, Terence Dawson offers a fresh and insightful demonstration of what this really means in the case of Orpheus and Eurydice. Combining an extensive range of topics with his usual remarkable depth of interpretative analysis, Dawson moves with ease from ancient classical sources to modern texts, including cinema. With an innovative thesis and written with lucidity yet passion, this book shows us what it truly means to say that a myth is alive'.

Paul Bishop, *University of Glasgow, author of On the Blissful Islands with Goethe & Jung (Routledge, 2017)*

'In this magisterial history of the myth of Orpheus and Eurydice, Terence Dawson traces the story's variants through the centuries, always with a keen eye for the political and social concerns embedded in each narrative, boldly showing how this atypical Greek tale has become one of the most important myths of our time'.

Craig E. Stephenson, *author of Anteros: A Forgotten Myth (Routledge, 2011)*

Orpheus and Eurydice in Myth, History, and Analytical Psychology

Loss, Longing, and Self-Awareness

Terence Dawson

Routledge
Taylor & Francis Group

LONDON AND NEW YORK

Designed cover image: Odilon Redon, Orpheus, crying 'Eurydice! Eurydice! (c.1903–10), detail. The Cleveland Museum of Art.

First published 2025
by Routledge
4 Park Square, Milton Park, Abingdon, Oxon OX14 4RN

and by Routledge
605 Third Avenue, New York, NY 10158

Routledge is an imprint of the Taylor & Francis Group, an informa business

British Library Cataloguing-in-Publication Data
A catalogue record for this book is available from the British Library

ISBN: 978-1-032-85731-2 (hbk)
ISBN: 978-1-032-85730-5 (pbk)
ISBN: 978-1-003-51958-4 (ebk)

DOI: 10.4324/9781003519584

Typeset in Times New Roman
by codeMantra

Contents

Acknowledgements and Abbreviations

This study was begun in the 1990s, then shelved for many years, and finally completed in the 2020s. Over these years, I have accumulated many debts of gratitude: to all my ex-colleagues and students from the Department of English Language and Literature at the National University of Singapore, and especially to Susan Ang, without whom the study might never have been begun; to all my ex-colleagues and students from the Division of English at Nanyang Technological University, especially to Neil Murphy, for his support through many years. Also to the work and encouragement of countless Jungian analysts and gifted writers, especially to Andrew Samuels (in the United Kingdom) and Polly Young-Eisendrath (in the United States); to the work and inspiration of numerous scholars, past and present, who have shown how the claims of analytical psychology are deeply embedded in European and world literature, especially Paul Bishop (University of Glasgow) and Susan Rowland (Pacifica Graduate Institute); and to the encouragement of countless other scholars working in various fields across the arts and humanities, especially Robert Scott Dupree (University of Dallas), George Landow (Brown University), and Leslie Gardner, without whom I might never have remembered the project or brought it to completion.

Also, a very big thank you to the three anonymous reviewers who helped to secure the book's acceptance; at Routledge, to Katie Randall and Manon Berset for steering me so ably and good-humouredly through the obstacle course of the editorial process; and lastly to the patience and support of family members, especially my two daughters, Ynaiê and Beatrice, to whom this study is dedicated.

I am grateful to Jane Turney, managing editor of the *JAP*, for permission to revisit concerns which I first explored in 'The Orpheus Complex', *Journal of Analytical Psychology*, 45.2, April 2000, pp. 245–266; and to Max Noak, editor of *Harvest: International Journal for Jungian Studies* for permission to revise the argument which I first tested in 'Sliding Doors, Orpheus, and the Spanish Inquisition', *Harvest*, 49.1, 2003, pp. 40–57. Also, to Routledge for permission to reuse (as Chapter 1) a slightly revised version of 'Virgil, Epicureanism, and Unseemly Behaviour: The Epyllion in Georgics 4 and Its three Katábases', in *The Descent of the Soul and the Archaic: Katábasis and Depth Psychology*, ed. P. Bishop, T. Dawson, and L. Gardner, pp. 52–72, © 2023. Reproduced by permission of

Taylor & Francis Group; and to James Kohler of the Cleveland Museum of Art for permission to use on the front cover a detail from Odilon Redon's pastel on brown paper, *Orpheus*, crying 'Eurydice! Eurydice! (*c.*1903–1910; 27.2 × 22.9 in.), a gift to the museum from J.H. Wade 1926.25.

Abbreviations

Unless otherwise specified, references to the work of Jung are to *The Collected Works of C.G. Jung*, ed. Herbert Read, Michael Fordham, Gerhard Adler, and William McGuire, tr. R.F.C. Hull (vol. 2, Leopold Stein), 20 vols, London: Routledge & Kegan Paul, 1953–1976, which is abbreviated *CW* (+ vol. and page no.).

Introduction

Conventional wisdom identifies a myth with its earliest surviving version: the one summarised in every anthology (the 'classic' version). But however brilliant this might be—whether Sophocles' tragedy, *Oedipus the King*, or Virgil's account of the myth of Orpheus and Eurydice—no *version* of a myth should ever be confused with the *myth* itself. A version is *only* a version, and every version invites reformulation. For as long as a myth continues to attract the interest of writers and other artists, every new version represents a new concern pertinent to the time of its formulation.

And here's the surprise: over the last 2,000 years, writers and other artists have turned to the myth of Orpheus and Eurydice more *often* than to any other myth, and they have done so to explore a broader *range* of concerns that have been attached to any other myth: collective and personal concerns, religious and philosophical concerns, socio-political and psychological concerns, even theoretical concerns. In some versions, the concern represents a tendency pertinent to its time (Christian belief, in the Middle Ages) or to a social or political problem (sexual abuse in the seventeenth century; dysfunctional aspects of society in the twentieth); in other versions, it represents an emphatically personal challenge, whether how to cope with a personal loss, or the need to produce a significant work of art, or the challenge to adjust better to one's social reality.

The purpose of this study is to explain why the myth of Orpheus and Eurydice has been so endlessly adaptable; to trace the gradual evolution of the difficulties and concerns that writers and other artists have explored in versions of the myth from the time of Augustus to the early twenty-first century; to identify their psychological implications; and to illustrate how they represent typical human problems with which individuals continue to struggle today.

The myth of Orpheus and Eurydice first arose toward the end of the Greek Archaic period (750–480 BCE)—that is, at a time when the foundations of Western civilisation were being laid.[1] The economic and political advances of these years include the first use of coins, a rapid growth of trade, the dynamic expansion of the well-organised city-states, their establishment of colonies (*apoikia* = 'away-homes') around the coasts of the Mediterranean and the Black Sea, and the first experiment with democracy, by Solon, in Athens. The cultural advances are

DOI: 10.4324/9781003519584-1

no less impressive. They include the transformation of a rudimentary Phoenician script into early written Greek, the beginnings of Western science and philosophy, the earliest surviving literary works by a historical author (Hesiod), the rapidly increasing use of stone in temple architecture—and, not least importantly, the continued vibrancy of their *oral* culture.

The Greek myths—some of which date from the Mycenaean Age (1750–1050 BCE)—were of an astonishing variety: of different length, tone, and complexity. And yet they all represented an aspect of both the collective imagination and the ever-changing concerns of the various societies in which they arose and circulated. They reflected religious, social, and political concerns. Above all, they invited discussion. They fostered civic and cultural identity. They helped to give otherwise disparate societies a shared set of values and concerns. They were the beating heart of ancient Greece.

A myth, however, is not born fully formed and unchanging. It exists in a process of constant revision, modification, and reformulation. With every generation, the stories told gradually evolve and slowly change, for in an oral culture, a myth does not belong to the storyteller. It *belongs* to their audience, including the young storytellers of the next generation who, inevitably, will tell the story their own way. While some bards might have sought to tell or recite the story as well as they could remember it, the *vitality* of Greek oral culture would have come from its more original bards: those who liked to add something new to the story every time they told it, or to adjust an episode in the light of a recent communal issue, or to expand on a theme or concern that had caught their imagination.

Although most of the Greek myths first emerged in an oral culture (*mythos* = a *spoken* account or narrative), it is only after the invention of *writing* that, today, we can have any confidence in the possible significance we attribute to them. By the end of the Archaic period, writing was fast developing.[2] One might have assumed that this new skill would put an end to the great age of myth.

Instead, it triggered complex, closely argued new versions, which now also reflected the concerns and interests of their respective *authors*. As the concerns of a society evolve, so too do the concerns of its writers, and as a result, so too do its myths. Some stories are gradually forgotten. Others evolve to reflect changes in a society's attitudes, ideas, and concerns. In Aeschylus' *Oresteia* (458 BCE), Orestes is *acquitted* of matricide; only fifty years later, in Euripides' version of the myth (408 BCE), he is found *guilty*. Every such change signals a new attitude toward a significant socio-cultural concern.

The importance of the mythic imagination to the evolution of both the collective and the personal ideas that define Western culture can hardly be exaggerated. Without the vitality of Greek oral culture, we might never have had the great Athenian tragedies, or the histories of Herodotus and Thucydides (*historiê* = enquiry), or even the philosophy of Socrates, Plato, and Aristotle.[3] That is, without the vitality of Greek myth, there might never have been the fifth-century Athenian miracle, still widely regarded as the cornerstone of Western civilisation.

The myth of Orpheus and Eurydice both *is* and *isn't* a Greek myth. Although it arose in ancient Greece, it has little in common with the great myths of ancient Greece, such as those surrounding the Trojan War, or those associated with Thebes (the Oedipus cycle) or Athens (Theseus). In ancient Greece, it is unlikely that it was ever regarded as a major myth.

And yet, as this study will frequently have occasion to demonstrate, the history of a myth harbours many surprises.

The first of these occurred as the Roman Republic metamorphosed into the Roman Empire. The poet Virgil remembered the myth, and he very cleverly adapted it to serve as a tongue-in-cheek conclusion to a poem he was writing, in Latin, about farming (*Georgics* = On Agriculture, 29 BCE). Owing to the accidents of time, his is the earliest surviving account of the myth. It pokes fun at the myth that existed before him. That is, it does not 'represent' the Greek myth. And yet his *parody* of the Greek myth gradually triggered a fascination with the myth which has lasted for over 2,000 years.

Although scholars *know* that there is no such thing as a 'classic' version of a myth, they *continue* to identify a myth with its earliest surviving version (its 'classic' version). They describe other versions written in antiquity as *variants*. They describe later (post-classical) versions as *adaptations*. Myth critics interested in *later* adaptations compare the 'adaptation' against the 'classic' version. In similar fashion, Jungian critics are interested in the original implications of a myth (*archetype* = earliest-form), which, in their view, represent its timeless and thus ongoing significance.

But the 'classic' version of a myth represents only *one* aspect of a society at a specific moment of its evolution. As the concerns of a society evolve, so too do the concerns of its authors, and thus also the concerns found at the heart of every new version of the myth. Some concerns are gradually forgotten, while new concerns come to the fore. And at any given moment, inevitably, the myth is most strongly identified with the most *recent* concerns.

The purpose of this study is to show that the myth of Orpheus and Eurydice is not represented by any single version. It is defined and represented by *all* the different concerns that writers and other artists have associated with it over the last 2,000 years. The fascination which it continues to exercise on writers and readers today is derived from the psychological implications of all these concerns. They represent some of the ways in which individuals have engaged with an overwhelming feeling of loss and longing, and with the challenge to translate this into greater self-awareness—that is, with concerns with which individuals are still wrestling in the twenty-first century.

The Greek Myth of Orpheus and Eurydice

Orpheus is one of the most problematic figures in Greek mythology. In antiquity, he embodied such radically different notions that one wonders how they ever came to be projected into a single figure. Although he shares some attributes with his 'father' Apollo (both play a lyre, are unhappy in love, and keep others at bay), he was never regarded as a god. He is sometimes described as a demi-god. But most often, he is referred to as a 'hero', even though he has nothing in common with other Greek heroes (who were men of *action*, even violence). Orpheus is the only Greek hero whose essential characteristics can be conveyed by representing him in a static and *peaceful* pose: seated, playing a lyre, with wild animals and birds gathered around him. The lyre (*kíthara*) has a delicate, soothing beauty. It is the instrument of Apollo, whose primary attributes are the bow (to punish, to send pestilence) and the lyre (to calm, to regenerate). The lyre is also associated with Pythagoras, a mathematician and philosopher, and one of the first to write about musical scales and intervals.[4]

The origins of the myth of Orpheus and Eurydice are obscure, but the story is widely thought to have arisen as a response to the motifs at the heart of two very different traditions with which Orpheus was associated.

One is the story of the Argonauts. Pelias has seized the throne of Thessaly (mainland Greece) from Aeson. When Jason, his son, turns twenty, he is commanded by Hera to recover the Golden Fleece from Colchis (which lies on the eastern shores of the Black Sea, in modern Georgia) and to reclaim his kingdom. The myth of the Argonauts is about loss, longing, and the difficult recovery of something perceived as crucial to an aspect of the collective identity of ancient Greece.

The other is an aspect of Greek religion. Greek religious practices centred on the temples of a *pólis* (city-state), and they involved *communal* prayers and sacrifices to one or more of the Olympian gods.[5] But there was another aspect to Greek religion: the 'mystery' religions, so-called because they involved a concept which played no part in the Olympian religion: *individual* 'initiation' (Greek *mysteria* = Latin *initia*, a process also referred to as *teleté* = arriving at one's goal).[6] The rituals of the mystery religions took place at specific cult centres such as Eleusis (an independent *pólis* about twenty kilometres to the northwest of Athens). That is, rituals began with a 'pilgrimage' to the cult centre. They involved lengthy rites (sacrifice, purification), which often referred to both Dionysos and Orpheus. They required the initiate to embark on an imaginal 'descent' into an *underworld*, the purpose of which was to obtain the promise of salvation and eternal life.[7] In short, they imply a desire to *recover* a lost sense of individual wholeness. At Eleusis, at the heart of the ritual, the initiate was expected to have an imaginal experience of Kore/Persephone, the 'Divine Maiden': that is, to *recover* an image of her from the underworld/unconscious.[8]

The myth of Orpheus and Eurydice was almost certainly born of a combination of the key concerns of these two traditions: that is, of loss, longing, and a descent into darkness undertaken with the purpose of recovering/experiencing something important to collective identity and individual spiritual well-being.

In ancient Greece, the myth was first told toward the end of the Archaic period (about 500 BCE or earlier), and it circulated for the next 500 years or so. The earliest references to it refer to Orpheus and his *wife* (Greek *gyne*, which means both woman and wife). In the early third century BCE, in a fragment attributed to Hermesianax, she is called 'Thracian Agríope' (Wild Eyes).[9] The earliest extant reference to the name Eurydíke is in a pastoral poem by Moschus ('Lament for Bion', 150 BCE). And *Eurydíke* (= wide-law, wide-custom) suggests an epithet of Persephone, the queen of the underworld and goddess of vegetation/growth.[10]

And yet, despite the rich personal and religious implications of the *motifs* that define the myth, no ancient Greek version of it has survived. The extant references to it are all brief and inconclusive. We do not know *where* or *why* the myth first arose, or whether Orpheus returned from the underworld with or without 'Eurydice'.[11] We do not know how the myth either began or ended. We do not know how it evolved. The *paucity* of the surviving ancient Greek references to it suggests that it was never an important myth. By the first century BCE, it may have been on its way to being forgotten.

Then, one day, Virgil was reminded of it and, owing to the accidents of time, his version, in Latin verse, is the earliest surviving account of the myth. As a result, the myth of Orpheus and Eurydice has come to be widely identified with the *story* he tells.

A Redefinition of Myth

As a society evolves, so too do the concerns of its authors. Every fresh version of a myth represents a new concern pertinent to the society in which it emerges and to the interests of its author. Echoes of the implications attached to earlier versions, including the earliest, may continue to inhabit later versions, but with the passage of time, such echoes may grow faint or even disappear entirely. The predominant concern of later versions will almost always represent a new concern.

Although no ancient Greek versions of the myth have survived, it is as certain as it can be that Virgil made major changes to the story he inherited:

- His account of the myth *parodies* the Greek myth.
- He changes the *character* ascribed to Orpheus.
- He probably devised the *opening* of the myth (the death of Eurydice by a snake bite).
- He was probably the first to introduce the famous 'condition'.
- And almost certainly, he gave the myth a new ending: the violent death of Orpheus at the hands of women (which he adapted from a *separate* tradition about Orpheus).

In other words, his version of the myth differs not just in its details: it represents a *radically new account* of the story. This begs the question: How do we explain the fact that he transformed a minor Greek myth into a Roman myth that has fascinated the Western imagination ever since?

This study argues that the influence of Virgil's version stems not from its story, but from the specific *combination of affect-charged metaphors* that the story harbours.

Myth as a Combination of Affect-Charged Metaphors

A metaphor is a word used in a non-literal fashion. Writers turn to metaphor to express *succinctly* an association of ideas which it would be either long-winded, pedantic, or even impossible to clearly express in literal language. For example, the phrase 'All the world's a *stage*' suggests that *everything* in the world unfolds as if in a theatre in which everyone *acts or performs*.[12] The crucial point, however, is that metaphors can be understood in surprisingly different ways. For some, *performance* is an inevitable and necessary part of social manners; for others, it represents insincerity, deception, and fraudulence.

Myths are characterised by their concentrated use of a specific kind of metaphor: *abstract concepts* (= words which denote something which has neither a physical existence nor a single, fixed definition). Jung held that myths are composed of archetypes, that 'archetypal content expresses itself in metaphors', and that an archetype is defined by the 'feeling value' it has for the subject.[13] Similarly, Lakoff and Johnson argue that abstract concepts often reflect powerful *feelings*.[14]

The affect-charged abstract concepts (metaphors) implicit in Virgil's rendering of the story fall into six clusters:

- A feeling of *unbearable loss*, together with an *impossible longing* for what has been lost (Orpheus cannot imagine life without his lost Eurydice; he thinks of her constantly).
- A *determination* to bring Eurydice back to life—which involves a *misplaced sense of entitlement* (Orpheus assumes he has a 'right' to recover Eurydice from death).
- A belief in the persuasive power of *music* (Orpheus tries to persuade Aidoneus with his song, which he accompanies on a lyre).
- A *descent* into a *gloomy and dispiriting underworld* (the world of the dead) in which a 'condition' is imposed.
- Following his failure to observe this condition, Orpheus returns alone to the upper world, where he is overcome by *despair* and a *paralysing fixation* with his own loss. His *rejection* of all human society results in his death and *dismemberment*.
- His tragic end implies another, perhaps unexpected metaphor, for it is only implicit—and yet, as we shall see, it is central not only to Virgil's account of the myth, but also to most subsequent versions: Orpheus' lack of *self-awareness*.

The 'classic' version of the myth is defined less by its story than by the combination of core metaphors which it harbours: that is, by the motifs of *unbearable loss, impossible longing, inappropriate entitlement, a descent into darkness, despair,* and *self-awareness*. And the last of these is crucial. Whereas the Greek myth may have been associated with notions about collective identity and individual spiritual well-being, no account of the Greek myth survives which might have allowed the reader to have a clear idea what these notions referred to. Virgil shows greater interest in 'self-awareness'—and (as we shall see in Chapter 1), his text illustrates exactly what he means by this.

The important point here, however, is that in a text or other work of art, wherever one finds a combination of *most* of the feeling-charged metaphors listed above, there is the myth of Orpheus and Eurydice. Every subsequent response to this combination of metaphors represents a version of the myth. And because every writer interprets this combination of metaphors differently, they inevitably tell the story differently.

In short, writers and other artists turn to a myth to explore the affective charge that its combination of abstract metaphors suggests *to them*—and this is always an important *concern* which they have at the time of writing.[15]

Myth as the Expression of a Concern

The myth of Orpheus and Eurydice is unusual in that the combination of metaphors that define it can stir a surprising range of associations. That is, its key metaphors can trigger surprisingly different concerns—and often, they are concerns which carry a strong affective charge.

For example, the metaphors of *unbearable loss* and *impossible longing* might stir memories not only of the death of a beloved *person* (wife, parent, child, friend), but also the loss of *something* which the individual highly values (a moral system, a social value, a political value, a religious faith, or trust placed in another person). In the reader, all the metaphors that define the myth, of Orpheus and Eurydice can stir an unusual *range* of associations.

Every version of a myth expresses concerns pertinent (1) to the *society* and/or culture in which it is produced and (2) to a specific challenge facing its author at the time of writing. Moreover, every version of a myth tacitly *invites* the reader's response. If the reader is also a writer, the myth invites reformulation, and their response will reflect not only their personal associations with its metaphors, but also their personal concerns. This can be illustrated by the two earliest extant versions of the myth of Orpheus and Eurydice.

Everyone knows the story that Virgil tells, but many readers might be surprised not only by its context and its tongue-in-cheek humour, but also by its *primary* concern. His account of the myth forms part of his conclusion to a poem about the challenges that face a *farmer*. As we shall explain in Chapter 1, its primary concern is to illustrate how a farmer—and, by extension, all other responsible adults—should *not* behave.

A generation later, Ovid produced an equally witty version, which both pokes fun at and develops the implications of Virgil's account. It appears in his *Meta-morphoses* (8 CE), in a section about inappropriate love. Virgil defines Orpheus by an *excess* of affect. Ovid defines Orpheus by his emotional *apathy*. And yet, as we shall see in Chapter 2, his version of the myth implies that Orpheus needs to awaken to his dormant sexual needs: that is, to *forget* Eurydice and find a new partner.

Both poets wrote from within the same culture: the sophisticated literary culture of Augustan Rome which had a strong interest in moral philosophy-cum-psychology. Both are drawn to the same myth. Inevitably, their versions reflect this contemporary interest. But in each of them, its combination of metaphors stirs different associations related to their individual interests. Virgil is interested in how human beings respond to the challenges with which life presents them. Ovid is interested in the complexities of love. Each poet adjusts the story they inherit to reflect their own concern.

The implications are clear. For as long as a myth continues to trigger new versions, it is being constantly reformulated. The myth is not to be identified with Virgil's slightly earlier version. *Both* Augustan versions represent the myth—for at any given moment, the myth is represented by the 'sum' of all the *concerns* associated with the myth up to that moment.[16] And every new version will alter the 'sum' of these concerns. Every living myth exists in a process of constant *evolution*.

A Myth and Its Evolution

During the last fifty years, both authors and scholars have shown a keen interest in adaptations of earlier works—of plays, novels, operas, musicals, films, television programmes, even video games.[17] And yet, surprisingly little of the academic debate surrounding 'adaptation' refers to far and away the most obvious example of the tendency: the adaptation of Greek myths.

We have seen how the different concerns at the heart of the two Augustan versions of the myth of Orpheus and Eurydice reflect the different interests of Virgil and Ovid. But every so often, owing to a major shift in the concerns of a society, a new version of the myth will appear which reflects a significantly different *kind* of concern.

Over the last 2,000 years, the myth of Orpheus and Eurydice has been associated with very different kinds of concern. During classical antiquity, it was associated with *moral philosophy*. In the Middle Ages, it became associated with *Christian values*. Beginning with the Renaissance, for 300 years it became associated with the exploration of *love*. During the seventeenth century, for the first time, it became associated with a specific *social* issue (predatory sexual abuse). By the eighteenth century, two new concerns began to feature in versions of the myth: the refusal of women to be subject to male authority (the beginnings of *feminism*) and as a metaphor for political tyranny. With the advent of romanticism, writers began to see myths as the representation of deep-rooted tendencies in the human imagination. Many identified with Orpheus—sometimes producing intriguing accounts of their *inner experience*; at other times, revealing only the inadvisability of identifying with mythic figures.

In the last 120 years, the myth has become associated with a surprising range of new concerns. During the modernist years, they include *social marginalisation*, *self-transformation* through art, and the first version to explore the myth—or rather, to explore the myth of Eurydice and Orpheus—from an emphatically *female perspective*. The late 1930s and the Second World War introduced the first versions to explore the effect of *dysfunctional societies on individuals*, the first to reflect the *challenges of war*, and the first versions based on the work of Jung, including the first in which the author consciously explores *her* 'personal myth'. In the 1950s, writers explored the tension between *tradition and modernity*, the relation of Orpheus to the *creative impulse* (from both a male and a female perspective), and a film in which the director explores *his* 'personal myth'.

Between the 1960s and 1990s, the most intriguing versions represent the genres of science fiction and fantasy—and they span several new concerns: the frustration of feeling 'trapped' inside the myth, *the threat that AI poses* to both culture and individuality, and two versions strongly influenced by Jung: one about *the need to engage with the myth*; the other, a poignant analysis of misplaced *archetypal longings*. Versions of the myth produced between 1995 and 2020 bring the story full circle: they are all about the difficulty of accepting and responding to reality—and they reveal an intriguing and perhaps telling difference related to gender. Whereas versions written by men explore the difficulty that 'Orpheus' has in understanding the needs of 'Eurydice', the versions written by women illustrate how 'Eurydice' faces up to a harsh reality she would have preferred not to have had to confront.

In short, no other Greek myth has been reformulated more often. And no other Greek myth has been reworked to explore a more unexpected range of concerns—and, remarkably, they span the entire history of Western civilisation: from the significance of the Biblical Creation, Fall, and Redemption of humankind (Calderón), through the significance of the Renaissance and the beginnings of modernity (Ficino), to the damage that pathological dissociation does to *modern* societies (Malipiero, Salman Rushdie), and the threat to culture and individuality posed by AI (Poul Anderson).

Orpheus and Eurydice in Myth, History, and Analytical Psychology

A great many specialist scholarly studies have been written about the implications of the *figure* of Orpheus.[18] Either in passing or in greater detail, most refer to the story of his attempt to recover Eurydice from the underworld; they almost always consider Virgil's account of the myth to be the 'classic' version; and all-too-often they *assume* not only that it harbours the resonance that *may* have belonged to Greek versions of the myth, but also that it harbours concerns that were first found in the myth long after the death of Virgil. This tendency to relate later 'adaptations' of a myth to its 'classic' version results in a focus on 'sameness'. In contrast, this study argues that the defining characteristic of every major version of a myth is its 'difference'—that is, its *specific* concern.

This is the first major study to focus solely on the myth of Orpheus and Eurydice. There have, of course, been far more versions of the myth than could be covered in a book of this length. Selection, sometimes regrettable, has been inevitable—and the selection has been dictated by the argument. The study is transdisciplinary.

It discusses versions of the myth belonging to a range of art forms, including poems, plays, novels, films, paintings, operas, ballets, sculptures, even sociological and other theories. Its focus is on the implications of form and narrative structure, on metaphors and images, and—above all—on the specific concern at the heart of each version of the myth considered.

Throughout, the study is indebted to the work of Carl Jung, who is best known for suggesting that myths belong to the collective unconscious, that the collective unconscious is composed of archetypes, and that archetypes are composed of autonomous (*inherited*) dispositions which reveal themselves as numinous images encountered in dreams.[19] In contrast, this study argues that myths, especially post-classical versions, are more fruitfully explored in relation to his claims about how deep-rooted 'feeling-toned complexes' are responsible for many of the difficulties that face otherwise well-balanced individuals.[20]

Freud argued that dreams reflect mistaken sexual attitudes that develop in early childhood, that affect everyone, and from which it is impossible for individuals to completely free themselves. In contrast, Jung held that dreams and fantasies represent the nature of a difficulty facing their subject in the present (at the time of the dream), that these difficulties span a spectrum of concerns, and that they often imply a possible way to resolve this difficulty. As this study demonstrates, most versions of the myth of Orpheus and Eurydice—beginning with those by Virgil and Ovid—anticipate this claim. And by following the history of the *concerns* found at the heart of the myth, it sheds light on another of Jung's major concerns: his interest in the evolution of consciousness.

A striking aspect of versions of the myth of Orpheus and Eurydice is how many of them were written either in times of crisis or at a critical moment in their author's life. Virgil wrote as a civil war was moving toward a ruthless confrontation; Boethius, in prison while awaiting execution; Haydn, during the French Revolution; Nerval, toward the end of a mental breakdown; Rilke, as he was wrestling with writer's block; Cocteau, as he was struggling with self-confidence; H.D., as she was trying to process a devastating betrayal; Charlotte Salomon, as she awaited almost certain deportation to a concentration camp; Anouilh, to reflect on France's unpreparedness for the Second World War; Kathy Acker, to record how she felt on being diagnosed with terminal cancer; and Salman Rushdie, to expose the dysfunctionality at the heart of modern societies.

This is also the first study of the myth to trace the growing importance of Eurydice. Early versions give her little individuality. During the Middle Ages, she became identified with the Biblical figure of Eve, and thus became associated with the temptations that can lure a man into sin and perdition. From the early fourteenth century, she gradually came to be given a distinct personality. Even so, it was not until the early twentieth century that women writers began to re-imagine the myth in relation to an experience specific to women. Caroline Gordon refers to it as the myth of 'Eurydice and Orpheus'. This is the first study to explore some of the concerns at the heart of versions of the myth of Eurydice and Orpheus—and to identify how they differ from versions of the myth written by men: examples include versions by H.D., Muriel Rukeyser, Charlotte Salomon, Kathy Acker, and Sarah Ruhl.

The purpose of this study is to explain how Virgil's story about a young man with an overblown sense of entitlement and a shocking absence of self-awareness became a vehicle for the exploration of some of the defining concerns of Western culture. This suggests that writers and other artists who turned to this myth to explore intuitions about human nature gradually discovered that they were exploring aspects of their own *social* concerns and *psychological* difficulties. And to show how the history of the myth of Orpheus and Eurydice represents a history of a surprising range of the psychological, social, and political concerns with which individuals and societies are still wrestling today.

Notes

1 See H.A. Shapiro (ed.), *The Cambridge Companion to Archaic Greece*, Cambridge: Cambridge University Press, 2007; also, B.B. Powell, *Homer and the Origin of the Greek Alphabet*, Cambridge: Cambridge University Press, 1991.

2 See F.G. Kenyon, *Books and Readers in Ancient Greece and Rome*, Oxford: Clarendon Press, 1932.

3 See F. Graf, *Greek Mythology: An Introduction*, tr. T. Marier, Baltimore, MD: Johns Hopkins University Press, 1993, esp. pp. 68–78.

4 See C.H. Kahn, *Pythagoras and the Pythagoreans: A Brief History*, Indianapolis, IN: Hackett, 2001.

5 See W. Burkert, *Greek Religion: Archaic and Classical*, tr. J. Raffan, Oxford: Blackwell, 1985; J. Larson, *Understanding Greek Religion: A Cognitive Approach*, Abingdon, Oxon: Routledge, 2016.

6 See M.W. Meyer (ed.), *The Ancient Mysteries: A Sourcebook of Sacred Texts*, Philadelphia: University of Pennsylvania Press, 1999.

7 See, for example, the 'Hymn to Demeter' (lines 480–482), from the *Homeric Hymns*; also, with reference to the Eleusinian mysteries, see Sophocles, fragment 837, 'Fragments Not Assignable to Any Play', in *Sophocles: Fragments*, tr. H. Lloyd-Jones, Cambridge, MA: Harvard University Press, 1996.

8 K. Kerényi, *Eleusis: Archetypal Image of Mother and Daughter*, tr. R. Manheim, New York: Bollingen Foundation, 1967; also, P. Dronke, 'The Return of Eurydice', *Classica et Mediaevalia* 23 (1962), pp. 198–215 (p. 204).

9 Hermesianax of Colophon, fragment from Leonteon, bk.3, in *Hellenistic Collection*, tr. J.L. Lightfoot, Cambridge, MA: Harvard University Press.

10 Moschus, 'Lament for Bion' (line 124), in *Theocritus, Moschus, Bion*, tr. N. Hopkinson, Cambridge, MA: Harvard University Press.

11 F. Graf, quoted in J. Bremmer (ed), *Interpretations of Greek Mythology*, London: Routledge, 1988, pp. 81–82.

12 Jacques, in Shakespeare's *As You Like It* (c.1599/1623), Act 2, scene 7.

13 See C.G. Jung, 'The Psychology of the Child Archetype' (1940), *CW*, vol. 9.i, p. 157; and 'On the Nature of the Psyche' *CW* 8, 1947/1954, p. 209. For metaphor in dreams, see M. Winborn, *Interpretation in Jungian Analysis: Art and Technique*, Abingdon, Oxon: Routledge, 2019.

14 G. Lakoff and M. Johnson, *Metaphors We Live By*, Chicago, IL: University of Chicago Press, 1980.

15 See C.G. Jung, 'Studies in Word Association' (1906-1909), *CW* 2, pp. 1–479.

16 C. Lévi-Strauss, *Structural Anthropology*, New York: Basic Books, p. 217.

17 For example, L. Hutcheon, *A Theory of Adaptation*. London: Routledge, 2012, J. Bruhn et al. (eds.), *Adaptation Studies: New Challenges, New Directions*. London: Bloomsbury Academic, 2013, T. Leitch, *The Oxford Handbook of Adaptation Studies*. Oxford: Oxford University Press, 2014.

18 Book-length studies of the Orpheus of antiquity include: W.K.C. Guthrie, *Orpheus and Greek Religion* (1935), Princeton: Princeton University Press, 1993; I.M. Linforth, *The Arts of Orpheus*, Berkeley: University of California Press, 1941; R.G. Edmonds III, *Redefining Ancient Orphism: A Study in Greek Religion*, Cambridge: Cambridge University Press, 2013.

On Orpheus in the Middle Ages and Renaissance, see D.P. Walker, 'Orpheus the Theologian and Renaissance Platonists', *Journal of the Warburg and Courtauld Institutes* 16, 1953, pp. 100–120, and J. Friedman, *Orpheus in the Middle Ages*, Cambridge, MA: Harvard University Press, 1970.

Seminal theoretical works on Orpheus include M. Blanchot, 'Le regard d'Orphée', in *L'Espace littéraire*, Paris: Gallimard, 1955; M. Detienne, 'The Myth of the Honeyed Orpheus' (1971), in R.L. Gordon (ed.), *Myth, Religion and Society*, Cambridge: Cambridge University Press, 1981, pp. 95–109; also, M. Detienne, *L'Écriture d'Orphée*, Paris: Gallimard, 1989.

Studies of the influence of Orpheus on literature, music, and painting include E. Kushner, *Le Mythe d'Orphée dans la littérature française contemporaine*, Paris: A. G. Nizet, 1961; W.A. Strauss, *Descent and Return: The Orphic Theme in Modern Literature*, Cambridge, MA: Harvard University Press, 1971; W. Mellers, *The Masks of Orpheus: Seven Stages in the Story of European Music*, Manchester: Manchester University Press, 1987; C. Segal, *Orpheus: The Myth of the Poet*, Baltimore, MD: Johns Hopkins University Press, 1989; D. Kosinski, *Orpheus in Nineteenth-Century Symbolism*, Ann Arbor, MI: UMI Research Press, 1989; J.E. Bernstock, *Under the Spell of Orpheus: The Persistence of a Myth in Twentieth-Century Art*, Carbondale: Southern Illinois University Press, 1991; E. Henry, *Orpheus with His Lute: Poetry and the Renewal of Life*, London: Bristol Classical Press, 1992; and A. Wroe, *Orpheus: The Song of Life*, London: Jonathan Cape, 2011.

For a collection of essays from a post-Jungian/archetypal point of view, see *Orpheus* (Spring 71), New Orleans: *Spring Journal*, Fall 2004.

19 For recent introductions to Jung's ideas, see R. Williams, *C.G. Jung: The Basics*, Abingdon, Oxon: Routledge, 2019; P. Bishop, *Carl Jung*, London: Reaktion, 2014.

20 See C.G. Jung, 'Studies in Word Association' (1906-1909), *CW* 2, pp. 1–479; and 'A Review of the Complex Theory' (1934), *CW* 8, pp. 92–104.

Part I

Orpheus, or Impossible Longing

Chapter 1

The Myth of Orpheus and Eurydice as Moral Philosophy

Virgil's Epyllion

Political events don't often represent the best of a culture. The classic version of the myth of Orpheus and Eurydice was written while the Roman Civil War was grinding toward an uncertain showdown. And yet, these sixty years of brutal conflict coincide with a Golden Age of Latin culture. Its poetry is characterised by wit (whether playful or scathing) and a delight in referencing other works (including myths). Behind every allusion and analogy, readers were expected to recognise and appreciate the work's often serious purpose—for these same years also witnessed a revival of interest in two great schools of Greek moral philosophy: Stoicism and Epicureanism.[1] Virgil took a keen interest in the latter.

Epicurus (341–270 BCE) is best known today from the adjective *epicurean* (devoted to sensory pleasure, especially fine food and drink). This seriously misrepresents his teaching. His importance stems from four claims: (1) that everything in the world is composed of indestructible atoms; (2) that knowledge rests on sensory perceptions; (3) that religious beliefs express human tendencies; and (4) that human beings should seek a balanced life. He distinguishes between 'passing pleasures' (self-indulgence, wordly ambitions) and 'fixed pleasures' (friendship, the pursuit of philosophy). He insists that the best life is one lived in obscurity and which seeks equanimity (*ataraxia* = free from confusions): that is, a freedom from all worries and an unshakeable peace of mind.[2]

In the middle of the Civil Wars, his claims were expounded and further developed by the Roman poet, Lucretius. *On the Nature of Things* (*De Rerum Natura*, 60 BCE) is a philosophical poem. It argues that belief in gods can lead to unpardonable violence (such as that inflicted on Iphianassa/Iphigenia); that the gods have no interest in the prayers and entreaties of humans; and that the characters of myth are symbolic representations of human tendencies.[3] It circulated widely.

Virgil (Publius Vergilius Maro, 70–19 BCE) was about ten when the poem began to circulate. At fifteen, his father sent him to Rome to study law and rhetoric; instead, he spent his time studying philosophy and literature, and he became so interested in Epicureanism that he went to Naples to study with Siro, a famous teacher. All his life, he remained a convinced Epicurean.[4]

He wrote slowly, carefully weighing every phrase and its implications. In his mid-thirties, he began a new work ostensibly about farming, and he worked at it for

DOI: 10.4324/9781003519584-3

seven years. David Slavitt has described the *Georgics* (On Agriculture, *c.*29 BCE) as 'probably the most literary work of all classical poetry'.[5] It is in four 'books' (= parts, chapters), each of about 550 lines. The first looks at how to till the soil and care for crops. The second, how to look after trees and vines. The third, how to care for farm animals. And the fourth is devoted to beekeeping (because honey was the primary sweetener).

The first three and a half books are about the husbandry of a smallholding: about the rhythms of nature, the cycle of the seasons, and, above all, about the grit and determination needed to deal with the setbacks that nature and life present (storms, fire, plague, mishaps, etc.).[6] They illustrate an Epicurean moral philosophy. The second half of book four brings the *Georgics* to a conclusion. It consists of an *epyllion* (a little epic) composed of two interrelated myths.[7] The first is about Aristaeus, a beekeeper who has lost his bees (201 lines). To help him find them, he is told the myth of Orpheus and Eurydice (77 lines).

The story of Aristaeus is about a young man who breaks into helpless tears when his bees abscond: that is, he behaves in an inappropriate and unseemly fashion. Virgil cleverly modifies the Greek myth of Orpheus and Eurydice to comment on the challenge he ascribes to Aristaeus. On the one hand, his version of the myth pokes fun at the notion that the gods help human beings. On the other, it also illustrates how a myth (= the mythic imagination) might help an individual to resolve a problem facing them. As we shall see, however, Aristaeus lacks the self-awareness to understand this.

This chapter argues that Virgil's epyllion demonstrates the importance of having an unshakeable personal philosophy by *illustrating its opposite* (i.e. its absence). The purpose here is to show how Virgil anticipates Jung's later view: that dreams often harbour an implicit challenge, and yet they also indicate the possible consequence of a failure to engage with this challenge.[8]

Aristaeus and Cyrene: Unbearable Loss (1)

Every spring, to avert over-crowding, a part of each colony of bees will swarm; that is, they will leave their hive to start a new colony. It is unusual for a whole colony to abscond. When it does, it usually settles quite close by and is easy to find. Virgil, however, is writing tongue in cheek, and he underlines this from the outset.

The epyllion begins with Virgil discussing what a beekeeper should do if all his bees abscond and they cannot be recovered. He should engage in a practice called *bugonia*. That is, he must wait until the early spring; beat a two-year-old bullock to death; then, without breaking the skin, pound its flesh to pulp; cover the carcass with thyme and cassia, and leave it in an enclosed space. After nine days, from the fermenting flesh, a new swarm of bees will emerge. Various possible explanations have been offered for this belief, none of them persuasive. It is unlikely that Virgil gave them *any* credence. He was poking fun at human gullibility.

He was also preparing a question: 'Which of the gods devised this custom?'[9] It is an unexpected question, for as a committed Epicurean, he regarded not only the gods, but all mythological figures, as embodiments of human tendencies. He suggests that Aristaeus devised the custom.

Aristaeus is one of the more curious figures of Greek mythology. Hesiod mentions him in the *Theogony* (*c*.690 BCE), but the earliest substantial reference to him is in Pindar's ninth *Pythian Ode* (*c*.474 BCE).[10] Aristaios is fed on ambrosia and nectar (the food and drink of the gods); he is destined to be a new 'Zeus and holy Apollo' and to become 'the best god' (*aristos* = best). No one seems to have developed this claim. He slips from myth into folklore. Diodorus of Sicily (who wrote about a generation before Virgil) tells us that he 'learned from the Nymphs' how to make cheese and *bee-hives*, and that he was 'the first to instruct men in these matters'.[11] Virgil would have expected his readers to smile at the wit with which he re-imagines the new Zeus and Apollo as an adolescent beekeeper who breaks into tears on discovering that his bees have absconded.

As Charles Segal has shown, Virgil's story about Aristaeus is composed of episodes borrowed and adapted from other myths.[12] They all harbour the same metaphors as the myth of Orpheus and Eurydice: loss, yearning, despair, descent, and determination. Unable to find his bees, Aristaeus wanders up the Peneus to its source, *not* because bees usually build their colony close to water (which they do), but because the gorge of Tempe is where Apollo killed the Python, after which he purified himself in the river Peneios. From its banks, he cut a branch of laurel (*daphne*), which he took back to his shrine at Delphi and planted. Every four years, the winner in each event at the Pythian Games was crowned with laurel wreaths made from its leaves. The reference to the Peneus thus harbours an implicit contrast between heroism and athletic prowess with the comically *un-heroic* quest of Aristaeus.

On arriving at the source of the Peneus (a metaphor for where he hopes to find help), Aristaeus starts whining to his mother, who (*selon* Virgil) lives at the bottom of its pool of water. This, of course, is a witty parody of one of the most poignant and yet comical episodes from the first book of the *Iliad*. Agamemnon has demanded that Achilles surrender the 'rosy-cheeked Briseïs' to him. Burning with wounded pride, Achilles goes to the seashore and prays to his mother. When Thetis rises from the sea and asks him why he is crying, he begs her to persuade Zeus to help the *Trojans* push the Greeks back onto the beaches. He wants Agamemnon to regret the way he has treated 'the best of the Achaians'. His mother, of course, agrees—indeed, her name, *Thetis*, suggests 'one who pledges' ($\theta\acute{\epsilon}\tau\eta\varsigma$).

With carefully constructed irony, Virgil models the behaviour of Aristaeus ('the best god') on the whining of Achilles, 'the best of the Achaians' (*Aristos Achaiōn*). Indeed, the parody stretches to the entire Trojan War. Just as Menelaos wakes one morning to find that his wife Helen has left with Paris, so Aristaeus wakes one morning to learn that his bees have absconded (and Orpheus will learn that Eurydice has died of a snake bite). To recover his bees, Aristaeus must engage in a struggle which, tongue in cheek, is equated with the Trojan War. And just as the Trojan leaders, smitten by Helen's beauty, are reluctant to return her to the Greeks, so Aidoneus will impose a condition which prevents Orpheus from recovering Eurydice. Virgil would have expected his readers to enjoy the audacity and wit of his carefully calculated allusions.

The reader is invited to laugh at Aristaeus and his teary helplessness, but also to appreciate that the story is about a shattering human experience: the loss of something so highly valued that the subject cannot imagine life without it.

There follows the first 'downward journey' (*katábasis*, descent) of the epyllion. Cyrene invites Aristaeus inside, whereupon he plunges *into* the pool.[13] Virgil is contrasting two *kinds* of reality: a 'social' reality (beekeeping) and a 'mythic' reality (an imaginal realm, conceived as *deeper*). As an Epicurean, Virgil believed that one finds the solutions to one's problems through self-possession and self-awareness. As a poet, he believed in the reality of the imagination, especially in the reality of a 'deeper', more authentic level of the imagination. He is *playing* with motifs that are at once mythic, literary, *and* psychological.

Inside the pool, Aristaeus finds himself in a huge underground cavern through which flow *all* the rivers of the world. That is, he must recognise that his own imagination is boundless and endlessly fecund. This recognition prepares him for his next experience.

Cyrene's name is suggestive of 'something that will happen', or 'one who grants'.[14] But, ironically, Cyrene is unable to help her son directly. She tells Aristaeus that he must pay his dues to Ocean—and the Ocean is a metaphor for the unfathomable nature of Aristaeus' *inner* resources. That is, by propitiating Ocean, he confirms that he has come to the end of his *conscious* resources and undertakes to find the solution to his problem within himself, in his *subconscious*.

Having done this, Cyrene tells him that he must seek the help of Proteus, the Old Man of the Sea, who happens to be at Pallene. For Robert Graves, this was the last straw.

Aristaeus and Proteus: Determination and Intuition

For Graves regards Virgil's epyllion as 'mythologically absurd', as illustrating 'the irresponsible use of myth'. He objects to the story of Proteus being dragged in 'by the heels'.[15] He *knows* that Proteus does not live at Pallene, for Homer tells us that he lives on the low-lying island of Pharos, which is just off the Nile Delta.[16] It is difficult to understand why an eminent classicist with a keen sense of humour of his own should take such exception to Virgil's wit. The creations of mythology can be introduced wherever a poet chooses: the only question is whether the location is appropriate for the author's purpose. And opposite the estuary of the Peneus is the perfect site for Virgil's purpose.

It allows him to introduce his second 'downward journey'. Cyrene wraps Aristaeus in a mist and takes him down the river Peneus to its estuary, opposite which lies the peninsula of Pallene (modern-day Kassandra). Metaphorically, she takes him into a 'deeper' imaginal reality. As soon as they arrive at Pallene, she places him in a recess of a cave in which Proteus likes to rest from the noonday sun.

The encounter with Proteus is composed of two motifs: an ambush and determination. Virgil borrowed the episode from book four of the *Odyssey*, in which

Menelaos tells Telémakhos how, on his journey home from Troy, his ship was becalmed near Pharos. He sank into despair, whereupon Eidothea, a sea-nymph, rose from the sea and told him how to capture her father Proteus, who is a seer, and compel him to answer his question. In Virgil's poem, the part of the helpful, even if somewhat un-filial Eidothea is taken by Cyrene. But the description of Aristaeus' struggle with Proteus is surprisingly faithful to Homer.

In English, Proteus is widely associated with his ability to change form (*protean* = prone or able to change form). In ancient Greece, he was associated with *origin* (his name is probably an archaic form of *protogonos* = first-born). In both the *Odyssey* and the *Georgics*, the crucial aspect of the encounter with Proteus is not *his* ability to change form, but the determination of the *subject* (Menelaos and Aristaeus) to prevent this: that is, to hold onto him through whatever forms he assumes until he reverts to the one in which they *first* saw him emerge from the sea. Only if they can do this will he help them with their immediate problem.

Both Menelaos and Aristaeus are 'stuck'. Proteus represents the possibility of finding a solution to their impasse. He has the form of a seal on a beach, surrounded by other seals, because, as soon as disturbed, a basking seal will slip back into the sea with ungainly, but surprising agility. That is, Proteus is a metaphor for a kind of intuition which all-too-easily slips back into the unconscious. His transformations represent the instability of intuitions: that is, the tendency of a potentially useful intuition to be swiftly replaced by other notions which have no bearing on the subject's immediate predicament. Aristaeus must hold onto 'Proteus' until he reappears in his *original* form. Only then will the seer tell him what he needs to know.

Virgil, however, makes a significant amendment to his source. In Homer, Proteus is an all-seeing and helpful minor deity: he gives Menelaos a direct answer. As an Epicurean, Virgil did not believe that deities take any interest in human beings. His Proteus does not tell Aristaeus where to find either his lost bees or another colony to replace them. He gives him an indirect answer. He tells him the myth of Orpheus and Eurydice.

And Virgil cleverly reformulates this myth to represent the nature of the problem-cum-challenge facing Aristaeus and, more surprisingly, the possible consequences of *not* engaging with this problem-cum-challenge. The question it invites is: Will Aristaeus recognise the relation between his own situation and the myth—*and* adapt accordingly?

Orpheus and Eurydice: Impossible Longing

Aristaeus is *excessively* upset by the loss of his bees; he wants to find them again. Virgil remembered the myth of Orpheus and Eurydice, which he reworks to underline its hero's equally excessive distress. He makes no mention of the love that Orpheus and Eurydice enjoyed before her death, for his account of the myth is not about love. It is about an *excessive* attachment and an *impossible* longing to recover something without which his life holds no meaning for him. Orpheus has lost Eurydice, who is his 'wide-ranging' or guiding 'law' (*eur* = broad; *díke* = law, deep-rooted custom, that which is unquestionably right). He has lost his sovereign good. He cannot imagine life without her.

The links between the myth of Aristaeus and Orpheus include an intriguing series of associations and allusions which the reader today might easily miss, but which Virgil's intended reader would have recognised and relished.

Aristaeus learns how to keep bees from dryads, that is, from wood-nymphs who were the companions of Artemis, one of whose primary symbols is the bee.[17] Virgil tells us that, before her marriage to Orpheus, Eurydice was a dryad. In the Graeco-Roman world, bees were not only identified with dryads; they were also associated with *purity*. The priestesses of Apollo at Delphi were called *melissae* (= bees or honey): so too were the priestesses of Demeter, presumably because young women dedicated to a god or goddess were considered 'pleasing to the soul'. The verb *melítzo* means to strum or to play an instrument, or else to sing a song. That is, Orpheus' double musical talent (he both sings and plays the lyre) is also related—both phonetically and metaphorically—to the sweetness of honey. In Orphic teaching, the bee is a symbol of the soul and in a late Orphic or neo-Pythagorean tradition—a tradition possibly known to Virgil and his Epicurean friends—Eurydice is identified as Orpheus' *soul*.[18] The entire epyllion is built on an unexpected series of playful associations. By carefully choosing his words, Virgil fuses a story about the loss of a colony of *bees* with a myth about the loss of Orpheus' *soul*. His epyllion invites the reader to smile, even to laugh out loud—and yet never to forget that it is about a serious concern.

Proteus begins by telling Aristaeus that Orpheus is angry with him because Aristaeus tried to seduce Eurydice. It was while fleeing from his unwelcome advances that she was bitten by a snake and died. Virgil was probably the first to give this explanation of her death.

Following the loss of his bees, Aristaeus seeks help from an 'underworld'. Following the death of Eurydice, Orpheus sings of her for as long as he can bear. Then, as if this were a perfectly natural course of action, he determines to recover her from the lord of death.

He sets off on the third, and the best-known downward journey of the epyllion: a descent into the underworld. The episode is described not with reverential awe, but with gently mocking irony. The best known of the Greek heroes to descend into the underworld is Herakles.[19] Virgil parodies the heroism implicit in the determination to outface death by conjuring a deliberately *un-heroic* metaphor. He likens the approach of Orpheus through the gloom of the underworld to that occasioned by someone rambling past shrubbery at the approach of evening, unwittingly disturbing the small birds which had settled there for the night. With deadpan humour, he imagines the effect that the sound of Orpheus' lyre and voice has on some of the best-known residents of the underworld. As he advances, not only the Furies, but even the snakes writhing in their hair fall silent. The wheel of Ixion stops turning so it can listen. And all three of Cerberus' mouths fall open 'in wonder'. Virgil was clearly enjoying himself!

In myth, a *downward* journey is rarely problematic. As Virgil later notes in the *Aeneid*, 'The way down to Avernus is easy'.[20] The challenge facing Orpheus will come at the nadir—the deepest point of his descent.

Orpheus Alone: Unbearable Loss (2)

In myth, every 'downward journey' (*katábasis*) supposes two corollaries: (1) an *implicit challenge* to recover (or *learn*) something from the deeper reality; and (2) an *upward journey* (*anábasis*); that is, an attempt to return to one's habitual or social world.

Orpheus wants to persuade Aidoneus to release Eurydice to him *and* to be allowed to return to his social world with her. Virgil does not describe the scene of Orpheus pleading with Aidoneus. But he does tell us the condition that the latter imposes. No mention of such a condition has survived from either Greek or Hellenistic times. Most scholars believe that Virgil devised it.

Orpheus has no sooner entered the underworld than he is on his way out. And just as he is about to re-emerge into the light of day, for no clear reason, he looks back at Eurydice. She immediately cries out, 'What madness caused you to destroy us both?' Even as she speaks, she is drawn back into the underworld for ever. She has died a second death.

The condition teases the reader into believing that the impossible (to come back from the dead) is possible. That is, Virgil is tempting the reader to conclude that if only Orpheus had not turned, he would have succeeded in returning to his social world with her. His intended readers would have realised that no one can 'turn back Time'; no one who has died can return to their social reality.

Orpheus has achieved nothing by his descent. More importantly, he has *learned* nothing. From the outset, his sense of entitlement was misplaced. He had no right to expect to be successful. But instead of reflecting on the implications of his experience, he sinks deeper into his self-indulgent grief. Virgil was almost certainly the first to underline this.

Orpheus needs to return to his social reality. Instead, he sets off on a mistaken *anábasis*: a journey *up* the river Strymon (into modern-day Bulgaria): that is, *away* from Greece (his *social* reality) and into lands at that time imagined as bleak and backward. He has returned to the 'upper' world—but *not* to his 'social' world. He sinks further into self-absorbed and paralysing despair. He loses his grip on reality.

In ancient Greek culture, one of the oldest and most resonant images of Orpheus is that of a semi-divine musician who can make all nature, even wild animals, stop to listen to his singing and playing.[21] His lyre represents the power of music to remind human beings of the natural harmony of the world and, by extension, the relation between music, transformation, and regeneration. He personifies the mastery of inferior passions and desires, and the beginning of civilisation.

Virgil *parodies* this image. He transforms an image of Apollonian regeneration (the ability to calm all nature with the *joy* engendered by his playing and singing) into an image of excessive and self-indulgent *grief*. Orpheus is likened to a nightingale endlessly and *uselessly* lamenting the theft of her chicks by an uncouth ploughman. While wandering aimlessly around the north coast of the Black Sea to the estuary of the Don, and then back again to Thrace, he thinks of nothing but his own unbearable loss.

There is no evidence to suggest that the violent death of Orpheus at the hands of women ever formed part of the Greek myth of Orpheus and Eurydice.[22] It belonged to *other* traditions associated with Orpheus. It is frequently illustrated on Attic red-figure vases: for example, the *stamnos* (large jar used to store liquids) by Hermonax of Nola (460 BCE), which shows female figures attacking Orpheus with a roasting spit, pestle, and rock.[23] Surviving fragments referring to a lost play by Aeschylus, the *Bassarai*, suggest that Orpheus rejected Dionysos in favour of the sun/Apollo, for which the followers of Dionysos then killed and dismembered him. Despite occasional scholarly suggestions that there is a relation between this myth and the myth of Orpheus and Eurydice, the evidence so far proposed is unpersuasive.[24]

In short, Virgil was probably the first to *end* the story of Orpheus' desire to recover Eurydice from the underworld with the story of his brutal *death*. To the 'traditional' Greek myth of Orpheus and Eurydice, he added and adapted the scene from Euripides' *Bacchae*, in which the Maenads (female followers of Bacchus) become so angry with Pentheus for refusing to join them in their Dionysian frenzy that they attack and kill him.

After dismembering Orpheus, the Maenads throw his head into the Hebrus. There are few more poignant images in literature than that of his head floating down the Hebrus, still singing plaintively, 'Eurydice! Eurydice!' And yet, this *tragic* moment is a *comic* parody of a tradition central to Orphism, in which Orpheus was regarded as a prophet and, curiously, this association was often with his *severed head*—as on the Attic red-figure *kylix* (broad, shallow drinking cup) on which the *head* of Orpheus is shown prophesying to a scribe.[25]

Proteus has finished his story—and without offering *any* explanation why he told it, he slips back into the sea.

Aristaeus has no idea why Proteus told him the myth of Orpheus and Eurydice. He cannot see any parallels between the myth and his own desire to recover his bees. He does not even appear to consider himself responsible for Eurydice's death. In short, he is no further advanced than he was *before* consulting his mother. He has 'had the experience but missed the meaning'.[26] He has learned nothing.

What, then, can the *reader* learn from Virgil's account of the myth?

A Tragic Narrative with a Two-Part Structure

The key to Virgil's version of the myth of Orpheus and Eurydice lies in its repeated use of two-part narratives. The *Georgics* is divided into two parts (the first three and a half books and the epyllion). The epyllion is in two parts (the frame story about Aristaeus and the embedded myth about Orpheus and Eurydice). And both these stories have a two-part structure. And in tragic narratives with a two-part structure, the first part often faces the protagonist with an *implicit challenge*; and if it does, the second part usually illustrates the consequences of failing to meet this challenge.

This two-part structure can be found in many Greek tragedies.[27] But Virgil may be the first to relate such a two-part tragic structure to the myth of Orpheus and Eurydice. The first part of the story of Aristaeus *appears* to present him with a challenge to recover his lost bees. But this is a tease, for a myth is never about its story. The bees are not the issue. Virgil's focus is on Aristaeus' attitudes and behaviour. At the outset of the epyllion, he over-reacts to his loss. The challenge facing him is to stop behaving in an unseemly fashion: in other words, to borrow or buy a colony of bees from a neighbour—and to get on with his life.

As an embedded story, the first part of the myth of Orpheus reflects and comments on Aristaeus' unseemly behaviour. Orpheus over-reacts to the death of Eurydice. The challenge facing him appears to be to recover Eurydice from the underworld. But a myth is never about its subject. The challenge facing Orpheus is to recognise that his sense of entitlement is misplaced: he needs to accept that Eurydice is dead—and to reset his life.

The key to Virgil's account of the myth of Orpheus and Eurydice lies in the implications of the second part of the myth, which illustrates the possible consequences of *Aristaeus'* persistent self-indulgence. It describes how, on emerging from the underworld, Orpheus becomes ever more fixated on his loss and slips into a self-absorbed and paralysing depression. He rejects the 'social' world, and when he slights the Ciconian women, they attack him, kill him, and dismember him.

In the light of this potent warning, the question is: will Aristaeus adjust his attitude?

The *second* part of the story of Aristaeus is ingeniously ambivalent. Although Cyrene overheard Proteus tell Aristaeus that Orpheus is angry with him, she now tells her son that it was the dryads who caused his bees to swarm. They are angry with him for having caused the death of their friend, Eurydice. This is another tease. Virgil is inviting his readers to ask irrelevant questions (Which suggestion is true? Why does Virgil not tell us more about the dryads?).

The poet then obfuscates the issue further. Cyrene tells her son that if he wants to recover his colony of bees, he must offer the dryads the sacrifice of a bull and a heifer on each of four separate altars. In addition to which, he must offer a black ewe to Orpheus, at whose shrine he must also leave funeral dues. And even though she will already have been appeased, he must make a further offering of a calf to Eurydice.

Aristaeus makes his sacrifice—and it has long been assumed that he is *rewarded* for doing so. Charles Segal speaks for many when he refers to 'the success of Aristaeus' atonement'.[28]

There are, however, good reasons to doubt this success. The sacrifice is a further tease. In Greek religion, sacrifices were communal rites performed on behalf of a *community*. A priest or leader offered a sacrifice to one or more of the Olympian gods in exchange for a *hope* of divine favour (gift exchange). In the *Odyssey*, we learn that the ancient Greeks offered sacrifices to dryads—but this is poetic license, as the *same* text makes clear only a few lines later. If the Greeks wanted to foster the good-will of dryads, they left them *modest gifts* in front of a small wayside altar.[29] No ancient Greek would ever have offered the dryads such an extravagant sacrifice as Aristaeus offers them—and least of all to atone for a *personal* shortcoming.

The ending of the myth is *burlesque*. Virgil is lampooning the very practice he so vividly describes. He is poking fun at the idea that the gods can be persuaded, by means of sacrifices and offerings, to take an interest in human beings.

This suggestion is corroborated when Aristaeus discovers bees rising from the rotting cattle to form 'grape-like clusters' in the trees. The reader is teased into believing that he has appeased not only the dryads, but also Orpheus and Eurydice. And the reference to grapes invites the reader to think this might be owing to Dionysos, with whom Orpheus is related in the Greek mystery traditions. Virgil encourages the reader into thinking that *bugonia* is a useful way to recover one's bees when they abscond. It is unlikely that Virgil thought so. He is playing with his reader's hopes and gullibility.

The ending of the epyllion is a tease. The reader learns that Aristaeus has done as instructed, and that he has won a new colony of bees. This *appears* to represent a 'happy ending'. But does it? The reader still has the *tragic* ending of the myth of Orpheus and Eurydice echoing in their mind.

A happy ending would suggest that Aristaeus has learned something—but there is no indication that Aristaeus has learned *anything* from his experience. He does not understand why Proteus told him the myth of Orpheus and Eurydice. He does not acknowledge responsibility either for his part in the death of Eurydice or for his unseemly response to the loss of his bees. In short, he remains as he was at the outset: a representation of a human *type*. He personifies someone who is sufficiently competent in their everyday life, but who becomes flustered and helpless at the first sign of a difficulty. The implication is clear: that come the next mishap in his life, he will once again fall apart and go crying to his mother. The tragic fate of Orpheus suggests that if Aristaeus fails to mend his ways, life might be very unkind to him.

The brief coda underlines the topical relevance of the epyllion. Virgil tells his readers that he wrote the *Georgics* while Octavian was engaged in the events leading up to the Battle of Actium. Virgil might have *hoped* that Octavian would restore peace and political stability to Rome and its 'empire', but he could not have known that Octavian would become the emperor Augustus and achieve this. The final envoi to the *Georgics* suggests that Virgil was keenly aware that the political situation was still highly precarious.

Conclusion

Virgil's version of the myth of Orpheus and Eurydice illustrates how misleading it is to identify a classical myth with its *story*. Every version of a myth represents a *concern*—and this concern reveals itself through the metaphors and implied analogies which the story harbours. The poet has adapted the myth not only to amplify the *challenge* facing Aristaeus, but also to suggest the possible *consequences* of his inability to make any connection between himself and the myth that Proteus tells him. And by underlining the relation between the challenge and the outcome, he invites his readers to reflect on the importance of *self-awareness*.

Virgil's reworking of the myth of Orpheus and Eurydice may be the first version of a myth to represent an emphatically *personal* concern of its author.[30] Virgil's dominant concern in the *Georgics* is to illustrate how, if one is to meet the inevitable upheavals that occur in both the natural and the political worlds, one needs an unshakeable (Epicurean) moral philosophy: a personal ethic measured not by competence in normal circumstances, but by the ability to face an unforeseen disaster with equanimity. Virgil's epyllion is a tease. It is designed to corroborate a claim (about the value of good husbandry) by illustrating its *opposite* (Aristaeus' overexcitability and his inability to deal with the loss of his bees, which is only a minor mishap). And it plays with something of a paradox. On the one hand, it suggests that the gods (Cyrene, Proteus) cannot provide 'direct' help. On the other, it also suggests that a person's 'deeper' imagination (their private imagination, which may feature figures from myth) might harbour an 'indirect' answer to the difficulty facing them—but only *if* they can decipher the metaphors of which it is composed.[31]

Virgil wrote within an Epicurean-Lucretian tradition which suggested that mythic characters embody *allegories* of moral aspects of human behaviour. And yet, his version of the myth of Orpheus and Eurydice is *not* an allegory, nor even allegorical. In effect, he explores what amounts to a *psychological process*. His epyllion represents a landmark in our understanding of the nature of myth.

Owing to the accidents of time, Virgil's rendering is our earliest surviving account of the myth of Orpheus and Eurydice. As a result, its combination of abstract concepts defines the myth, not only *unbearable loss*, *impossible longing*, and *descent* (concepts which probably belonged to the Greek myth), but also *despair* and *self-awareness* (which probably represent Virgil's changes to the myth).

And if Virgil can adapt the myth, so too can others. A generation later, Ovid produced an equally memorable version of the same myth—and its very different psychological implications are equally audacious.

Notes

1 Their founders (Epicurus, 341–270 BCE; Zeno of Citium, 334–262 BCE) were contemporaries. Their views have much in common, and yet also differ significantly. See T. O'Keefe, *Epicureanism* (2010), Abingdon, Oxon: Routledge, 2014; B. Inwood, *Stoicism: A Very Short* Introduction, Oxford: OUP, 2018.
2 See G.K. Strodach, 'Introduction' to Epicurus, *The Art of Happiness*, tr. G.K. Strodach (1963), London: Penguin, 2012, pp. 26–27; also, J. Warren (ed.), *The Cambridge Companion to Epicureanism*, Cambridge: Cambridge University Press, 2009.
3 Lucretius, *De Rerum Natura* (1: 84-101; 2: 649-650; 3: 978-994), tr. W.H.D. Rouse, rev. M.F. Smith. Loeb Classical Library. Cambridge MA: Harvard University Press, 1992, pp. 8–11, 144–147, 266–267.
4 P. Levi, *Virgil: A Life*, London: Duckworth, 1997.
5 D. Slavitt, *Virgil*, New Haven, CT: Yale University Press, 1991, p. 50.

6 See C. Segal, *Orpheus: The Myth of the Poet*, Baltimore: Johns Hopkins University Press, 1989; also, K. Johnson, 'Introduction' to her translation: *Virgil's Georgics: A Poem of the* Land, London: Penguin, 2009.

7 Virgil, *Georgics* (4: 281–558), in *Eclogues, Georgics, Aeneid 1-6*, tr. H.R. Fairclough. Loeb Classical Library. Cambridge MA: Harvard University Press, 1994, 281–558.

8 For a contemporary take on Jung's view, see G. Amundson (ed.), *Psychological and Philosophical Studies of Jung's Teleology: The Future-Orientation of Mind*, London: Routledge, 2024.

9 Virgil, *Georgics* (4: 315), in *Eclogues, Georgics, Aeneid 1-6*, tr. H.R. Fairclough. Loeb Classical Library. Cambridge MA: Harvard University Press, 1994, 218–219.

10 Hesiod, *Theogony* (*ll.* 975–978), ed. G.W. Most. Loeb Classical Library. Cambridge MA: Harvard University Press, 2018, pp. 80–81; Pindar, 'For Telesicrates of Cyrene, winner, race in armor, 474 BCE', in *Olympian Odes, Pythian Odes*, tr. William H. Race (1997). Loeb Classical Library. Cambridge MA: Harvard University Press, 2012, pp. 356–359.

11 See Apollonius of Rhodes, *Argonautica* (4: 1128–1133), ed. W.H. Race. Loeb Classical Library. Cambridge MA: Harvard University Press, 2009, pp. 418–421; and Diodorus of Sicily, *Library* (4: 81), in *Library of History*, tr. C.H. Oldfather. Loeb Classical Library. Cambridge MA: Harvard University Press, 1939, vol. 3, pp. 73–75.

12 See C. Segal, *Orpheus: The Myth of the Poet*, Baltimore, MD: Johns Hopkins University Press, 1989, esp. pp. 36–53 and 73–94; also M. Owen Lee, 'The Epyllion', in *Virgil as Orpheus: A Study of the Georgics*, New York: State University of New York Press, 1996, pp. 101–126.

13 Cf. Iris diving down to tell Thetis that Achilles is about to be killed: see Homer, *Iliad*, tr. A.T. Murray, 2 vols. (bk. 24, *ll.* 77–99). Loeb Classical Library. Cambridge MA: Harvard University Press, 1999, vol. 2, pp. 568-571.

14 Virgil probably derived the motif of a hero being *granted* something by a water-goddess from a contemporary of Pindar: see Bacchylides, *Dithyramb* 17 ('The Young Athenians or Theseus for the Ceans to Perform in Delos'), in *Greek Lyric IV*, tr. D.A. Campbell. Loeb Classical Library. Cambridge MA: Harvard University Press, 1992, pp. 216–227.

15 R. Graves, 'Aristaeus', section 5, *Greek Myths*, 2nd ed., London: Cassell, 1958, pp. 280.

16 Homer, *Odyssey* (4, 351–425), tr. A.T. Murray, rev. G. Dimock. Loeb Classical Library. Cambridge MA: Harvard University Press, 1919, pp. 144–149.

17 See M. Detienne, 'The Myth of "Honeyed Orpheus"', in R.L. Gordon (ed.), *Myth, Religion, and Society: Structuralist Essays by M. Detienne, L. Gernet, J-P. Vernant, and P. Vidal-Naquet* (1981), Cambridge: Cambridge University Press, 2009, pp. 95–110.

18 See A.D. Nock, 'The Lyra of Orpheus', *The Classical Review* 41 (5), 1927, pp. 169–171; and I. Julia Jesnick, *The Image of Orpheus in Roman Mosaic*, Oxford: British Archaeological Reports, 1997, p. 27.

19 Herakles must bring Cerberus up from the underworld: see, Homer, *Iliad*, vol. 1 (8: 366–369), tr. A.T. Murray. Loeb Classical Library. Cambridge MA: Harvard University Press, 1999, pp. 378–379; this myth was later identified as his 'twelfth' labour; see also, the black-figure *hydria* (water-jar, jug), by the Peintre de l'aigle, *Hercule et Cerbère*, hydrie, 550-500 BCE, in the Musée du Louvre (E 701); and the 'Cerberus metope' from the Temple of Zeus, Olympia (*c*.460 BCE).

20 Virgil, *Aeneid* (6: 126), Virgil, *Aeneid* 1-6, tr. H.R. Fairclough. Loeb Classical Library. Cambridge MA: Harvard University Press, 1916/1994, pp. 514–515.

21 See for example, Antipater of Sidon, in *The Greek Anthology: Books VII and VIII*, tr. W.R. Paton, Cambridge, MA: Harvard University Press, 1917, pp. 6–7; also, Diodorus of Sicily, *The Library* 2, 35–34, 58.

22 For an opposite suggestion, see Martin L. West, 'The Lycurgus Trilogy', *Studies in Aeschylus*, *Beiträge zur Altertumskunde* 1. Stuttgart: De Gruyter/B.G. Teubner 1990, pp. 26–50.

23 Hermonax of Nola, *stamnos* in the Louvre (G. 416).
24 Martin West has suggested that it was after descending into the underworld in search of 'his wife' and 'seeing what things were like there', that Orpheus rejected Dionysos in favour of the sun/Apollo. See Martin L. West, 'The Lycurgus Trilogy', *Studies in Aeschylus. Studies in Aeschylus, Beiträge zur Altertumskunde* 1. Stuttgart: De Gruyter/B.G. Teubner 1990, pp. 26–50.
25 The Painter of Ruvo, *Young Man Writing Down an Oracle Pronounced by Head of Orpheus, while Apollo Looks On* (420–410 BCE), in Cambridge, Fitzwilliam Museum, on loan from Lewis Collection, Corpus Christi College.
26 Cf. T.S. Eliot, 'Dry Salvages, ii', from *Four Quartets*, in *The Complete Poems and Plays of* T.S. Eliot, London: Faber, 1969, p. 186.
27 For example, Sophocles' *Antigone*: see T. Dawson, 'Gender and the Political in *Antigone*: The Need to Listen to *Others*', in L. Gardner and C. Miller (eds), *Exploring Depth Psychology and the Female* Self, London: Routledge, 2021, pp. 94–112.
28 C. Segal, *Orpheus: The Myth of the Poet*, Baltimore: Johns Hopkins University Press, 1989, p. 53.
29 Homer, *Odyssey* (13: 349–355 and 356–360), tr. A.T. Murray, rev. G. Dimock. Loeb Classical Library. Cambridge MA: Harvard University Press, 1919.
30 When exactly authors began to express their personal concerns is of course still hotly debated. For a recent assessment of this issue, see M.J.O. Verheij, 'Selves in Conflict: Gill vs. Sorabji on the Conception of Selfhood in Antiquity: A Reconciliatory Review', *The Classical World* 107 (2) winter 2014, pp. 169–197.
31 This anticipates/illustrates Jung's later claim that the unconscious 'compensates' (serves to adjust or correct) a misguided attitude. See C.G. Jung, 'Definitions', in *Psychological Types*, *CW* 6, 1921, p. 419.

Chapter 2

The Myth of Orpheus and Eurydice as Psychological Process

Ovid's 'Song of Orpheus'

Ovid (Publius Ovidius Naro) was a generation younger than Virgil. He was in his early fifties when he completed the work which is widely regarded as his master-piece. *Metamorphoses* (about 8 CE) takes the form of a history of the world from its creation to the death of Julius Caesar. It is in fifteen 'books' (parts) and consists of an idiosyncratic retelling of over 250 myths, most of which end with a transformation—and many of which are about desire.

A major purpose of books 6–11 is to explain how the amorous desires of gods, mythological figures, and human beings are often accompanied by mental suffering.[1] Ovid writes about figures driven by powerful desires before they become aware of them. He describes the disruptive confusion produced by the awakening of erotic love. He writes about how love can become obsessive, how it can take complete possession of the individual, and about the helplessness of the individual when it does. He shows how, in their desires, even the greatest gods make fools of themselves (Apollo, the god of distance, is constantly thwarted in his intimate relationships). But no matter how misguided human love might be, he usually treats it with empathy. He understands that desire is an almost irresistible force which sweeps aside all other concerns and considerations.

Ovid's version of the myth of Orpheus and Eurydice is placed toward the end of this sequence, between myths about forbidden and inappropriate love.[2] The poet naturally borrowed from Virgil's recent rendering. He knew it, he admired it, and he used it as his base text. He then parodied it mercilessly. Virgil's Orpheus is characterised by an *excess* of affect. Ovid's Orpheus, by an *absence* of affect: he never expresses any feeling.

Ovid had a gift for describing compulsive desires, and yet in the *first* part of his rendering of this myth, he *chooses* not to exercise it. He describes the wedding of Orpheus and Eurydice with expressionless objectivity. The guests are not enjoying themselves; Hymen's torch keeps sputtering; the hall fills with smoke. Then, while 'the bride is walking on the grass, a snake bites her in the ankle, and she falls dead'. After mourning Eurydice 'enough' in the upper world (how much is 'enough'?), Orpheus decides to brave the Stygian world below. His plea to Persephone and Aidoneus consists of a sequence of deadpan clichés: 'I have come about my wife.

DOI: 10.4324/9781003519584-4

Her youth was stolen by the bite of a snake. I struggled hard to find the courage to bear her loss, but the God of Love got the better of me'.

His appeal is successful, but Orpheus turns and 'she dies a second death, but without complaint—for what had she to complain of, except that she was loved too much?' The reader, however, is given no indication of this love. Ovid's Orpheus goes through the motions of love required by Virgil's account of the myth, and yet, it is unclear whether he feels anything for Eurydice. Unsurprisingly, even some of the poet's greatest admirers have thought that his outrageous nonchalance undermines his version of the myth.[3]

This chapter focuses on the *second half* of Ovid's version: that is, following Orpheus' unsuccessful return from the underworld, on the implications of the song he sings to the trees and animals. Its purpose is to show how Ovid develops the suggestion that myths both harbour an *implicit challenge* and indicate the *possible consequences* of not engaging with this challenge.

Virgil's Orpheus sang only of Eurydice. Ovid's Orpheus never even mentions her. His song is about the loves of eight other mythic figures, and they all describe the pains of love. Just as Virgil turned to the myth of Orpheus and Eurydice to amplify the challenge facing *Aristaeus*, so Ovid turns to eight separate myths to amplify the challenge facing *Orpheus*. The 'Chinese box' structure of the two versions illustrates this:

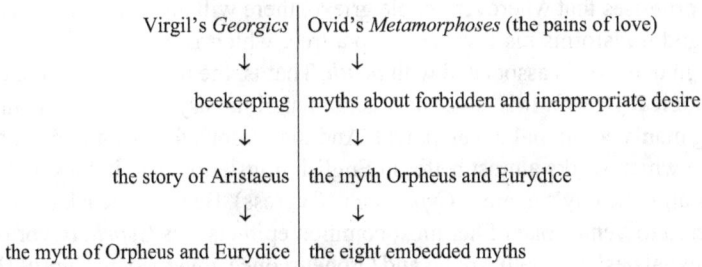

Virgil's *Georgics*	Ovid's *Metamorphoses* (the pains of love)
↓	↓
beekeeping	myths about forbidden and inappropriate desire
↓	↓
the story of Aristaeus	the myth Orpheus and Eurydice
↓	↓
the myth of Orpheus and Eurydice	the eight embedded myths

Figure 2.1 Virgil's *Georgics* and Ovid's *Metamorphoses*: Parallel Structures.

Virgil implies that, on returning from the underworld, Orpheus would have done better to forget Eurydice. Ovid first suggests that Orpheus feels no strong desire for Eurydice, and then takes *Virgil*'s suggestion to its logical conclusion. He implies that Orpheus ought not just to *forget* Eurydice: he needs to embark on a *new* relationship.

From the 1920s, Jung argued that it was impossible to interpret a single dream with complete certainty; that an analyst can be confident of an interpretation only when a series of dreams repeats motifs often enough for the *client* to recognise the concern to which they refer.[4] Ovid's 'Song of Orpheus' anticipates this suggestion. Each of its component myths identifies a different aspect of the ever-more insistent challenge implicitly facing Orpheus. Although endlessly witty, the purpose of the sequence of myths that make up the song of Orpheus is to prompt him to (re) discover his dormant sexual desire.

Orpheus: A Dormant Sexual Desire

Upon returning to the upper world without Eurydice, Orpheus rejects the advances of women who fall in love with him. Instead, he teaches Thracian men to give their love to boys so they can enjoy the springtime of their youth. He retires to a plateau where there are no trees, and there is no shade. The altitude suggests that he places himself 'above' others; the barrenness, that he has lost touch with reality.

As Orpheus begins to play his lyre, Ovid's version of the myth comes to life. The nonchalance continues, but it now harbours a clear purpose.

Seventeen different species of trees and seven different kinds of shrubs start to edge their way up the mountain so they can hear Orpheus better. The image is *contra naturam*. It suggests that Orpheus is no longer living a natural life. And one of the trees which edge closer to him defines the nature of the challenge facing him. The tale of Cypress is told by the narrator (Ovid).

Cypress and Apollo: A Maudlin Self-Absorption

Cypress is a young teenager loved by Apollo. He spends his time with a tamed and bejewelled deer, which he likes to ride. One day, by accident, he kills his pet, and his grief is so excessive that he wastes away and dies. Distraught by his death, Apollo promises that wherever people grieve, there will always be a cypress.

The god transforms his favourite into a tree, which is a symbol of *growth*, but the tree in question is associated with *death*. That is, the myth is about the *death* of psychological *growth*. It is about how sentimental fantasy leads to the paralysis of a young man's emotional development. And the reasons for this are explained in a tacit pun which works almost better in English translation than it does in the original. In Latin, the boy's name is *Cyparissus* (Cypress). Because the island of Cyprus was sacred to Venus, one of her most common epithets was *Cypria* (Cyprus). That is, the sexual desire of both Apollo and Orpheus, once governed by Cyprus (Venus), has become invested in Cypress (an adolescent boy).

Ovid gives Orpheus a very different character from Virgil, and yet, when adapting the embedded myths, he relates his argument to *Virgil's* version of the myth: for example, the excessive and mawkish grief (of Cypress, for the stag; and of Apollo, for Cypress) parodies the excessive grief of Orpheus for Eurydice in Virgil's version.

Orpheus now begins his song.

The Song of Orpheus

Each of the seven myths which compose his song explores a different facet of desire. Each has a different *subject*: two are about homosexual love; five are about a man's need to honour Venus. And their overarching purpose is to urge Orpheus to (re)discover his sexual desire.

The first song is about another young teenager.

Ganymede and Jove: Inappropriate Fascination

Virgil's account of the myth of Orpheus and Eurydice expresses only Orpheus' point of view. In contrast, Ovid exploits the fact that a myth often harbours two or more very different points of view.

When Jove developed a passion for Ganymede, he took the form of an eagle, seized the young Phrygian in his talons, and flew back to Olympus, where he made Ganymede his cupbearer. From *Jove*'s point of view, the abduction of Ganymede very obviously reflects the way in which Orpheus is drawn to young teenage boys.

But any myth about the relation between a human and a god invites considera-tion from the point of view of the *human*. Ganymede has been carried away from his 'social' reality and now lives as an eternal boy/young teenager whose sole func-tion is to serve a powerful *idea* (a world of fantasy). Ovid has adapted the myth to suggest that the same is true of Orpheus, who has also abandoned *his* social world and who also (in Virgil's version) serves a powerful idea: an unhealthy obsession with his lost Eurydice.

The next song, one of several stories in the *Metamorphoses* about the unhappy loves of Apollo, carries a warning.

Hyacinth and Apollo: Psychological Inflation

One day, Apollo and his favourite are testing their skill with a discus. Apollo throws first. As Hyacinth runs forward, the discus bounces off a rock and smashes into his face. Apollo's art proves useless. He promises Hyacinth: 'Whenever I strike my lyre, it will be of you that I sing. In its markings, this flower will imitate my groans, and in years to come, a hero will be linked with it'. Whereupon the boy's blood is transformed into a purple hyacinth, and on its petals are the letters AI AI (suggestive of 'alas, alas').

The irony is self-evident. Apollo can throw his discus further than any human, and yet not far enough to outpace his young favourite. The god of *healers* is unable to heal the wound which he has unwittingly inflicted. Like Orpheus (who is his son), Apollo loses someone dear to him. The story can be read from his point of view. The most aloof of the gods is so smitten by the boy that he 'abandons both his lyre and his duties at Delphi': that is, he loses his footing in *his* 'reality'.

But Ovid's version primarily reflects Hyacinth's perspective—and to compete with a god, even in play, suggests psychological inflation. The reference to a later 'hero' is probably to the episode in the *Iliad* when Ajax (Greek = *AI-as*) hurls a large stone (cf. discus) at Hektor, striking him in the neck and almost killing him.[5] The myth thus contrasts heroic conflict with an inappropriate friendship and contest. Just as Hyacinth is cruelly punished for his inflation, so Orpheus is being cruelly punished for his morbid self-engrossment.

The *subject* of the first three embedded stories (Cypress, Ganymede, and Hya-cinth) is homosexual love. But a myth is never about its subject. Ovid is neither advocating nor repudiating homosexuality *per se*.[6] The overarching theme of all three stories is the *inappropriate* attitude of a young man. And their fates suggest that if Orpheus continues to nourish his introverted fantasies, he too might lose his footing in his social world.

The Greek Orpheus was associated with the mystery religions, with initiation; that is, with *development*. Ovid's Orpheus remains obtuse to the implications of the songs he sings. If his (unconscious) imagination is to help him develop, it needs to change its tactic. His next song is the first of five myths about hetero-sexual love.

The Horned Beasts and the Forward Ones: The Need to Honour Venus

Ovid had a gift for adapting myths to suit his purpose, but he probably devised the story of the Horned Beasts (*Cerastae*) and the Women of Amathus (the *Propoetides* = Forward Ones). Ironically, it is the least successful section of the song of Orpheus. Its purpose, however, is clear: it is a warning not to disrespect Venus.

The story is set in Amathus, a small town on the southern coast of Cyprus (near modern Limassol), famous for its mines and for a temple dedicated to Aphrodite/Venus (sometimes known as Amathusia).

Outside the city gates is an altar sacred to Jove, the protector of strangers. As soon as Venus realises that the women of Amathus have been sacrificing strangers (the Horned Beasts) on these altars, she transforms them into savage bulls and, because they have forgotten all shame (and so are already unnaturally 'hardened'), she changes the women into flint.

The myth is loosely based on a tradition of 'sacred prostitution' which may have existed in ancient Cyprus.[7] It is not clear why Venus takes up her cudgel for Jove (the protector of strangers). What is clear is that neither the strangers (the Horned Beasts) nor the women of Amathus show any regard for Venus. And this reflects the behaviour of Orpheus. He teaches Thracian men the charms of pederasty but continues to reject the advances of women. That is, he is both behaving like a 'horned beast' *and* offending Venus. The purpose of the myth is to suggest that he needs to discover a desire to *honour* Venus.

The first four myths embedded into the story of Orpheus end in tragedy—and yet they have made no impression on Orpheus. If he is to make a connection between the myths about which he sings and his own situation, a story is needed which will shake him out of his psychological block by clearly indicating that he must put an end to his self-imposed isolation.

Pygmalion: The Need to Enter into a New Relationship

Orpheus has lived alone for many years. As a result, he has become obsessed by an impossible and maudlin longing. The story of Pygmalion reflects this. It is based on an old tale about a king of Cyprus who falls in love with a beautiful statue. Ovid was probably the first to introduce the motif of the statue *coming to life*. It was an inspired modification.

Sickened by the behaviour of the women of Amathus, Pygmalion has lived alone for several years. He spends his time carving ivory into a figure of a young woman about to take a step forward, and yet held back by timidity. Such is his craftsmanship that one can hardly believe that the figure is only a work of art.

Pygmalion gradually begins to burn with desire for the body he has shaped. One day, he seems to feel the firm material yielding to his fingers. On the feast-day of Venus, he takes a gift to her altar and prays: 'O Gods, let me marry someone like my ivory girl'. Venus grants his wish. On returning home, Pygmalion goes directly to his statue and can hardly believe his senses. His statue has come to life. He pours out his thanks to Venus—and before nine full moons have passed a girl is born. She is called Paphos.

The myth suggests that art is not about trying to represent the outer world. It is about striving to express an inner image which corresponds to either a desire or a concern. A work of art is determined by the concern uppermost in the artist's mind at the time of its creation. We have seen how this applies to Virgil and his epyllion. Ovid's 'song of Orpheus' suggests the same.

Pygmalion's *activity* may harbour a theory, but his *desire* represents an impossible and maudlin fantasy. One might have expected him to be punished for this. But Pygmalion's obsession with his statue is a metaphor for Orpheus' sickly obsession with his memory of Eurydice (in Virgil's version). The challenge facing Orpheus is to 'interpret' the myth: that is, not to imagine that Eurydice will come back to life, but to rediscover a need to engage in a new relationship.

Orpheus, however, is a slow learner, and Ovid underlines this. The next two stories, as well as the embedded myth they include, form a tightly knit sequence. And they foreground the terrible consequences of harbouring illicit or ill-considered desires.

When Paphos is sixteen, she gives birth to a boy called Cinyras. The following story is set sixteen years later. It is about Cinyras and his teenage daughter, who develops an incestuous infatuation with him stirred 'not by Cupid, but by one of the Furies'.

Cinyras and Myrrha: Unconscious Desire

Myrrha is a young woman from a good family in Arabia Felix (modern Yemen), which was famous for its perfumes. One day, several young men come to propose to her—to no avail, for she is consumed by her longing for her father. That night, however, revolted by her own turbulent thoughts, she tries to hang herself. Her nurse catches her just in time, and then, reluctantly, agrees to help her.

Soon after, while Myrrha's mother is at the Cerealia (an annual festival held in honour of Ceres, the goddess of grain and agriculture), Cinyras is sleeping alone. When the nurse tells him of a girl 'about the same age as Myrrha' who is in love with him, he promptly tells her to bring her to him. That night Myrrha conceives. On the third night, curious to see what his young bedfellow looks like, Cinyras lights a lamp. Speechless with horror, he reaches for a sword which hangs beside the bed.

But Myrrha has fled. By the time she arrives in Saba, she is exhausted. She prays to be transformed and her prayer is answered. Her tears begin to roll down her bark. And everywhere, the myrrh that oozes from her trunk is honoured.

This is the longest story in the sequence (205 lines): longer than Ovid's version of the myth of Orpheus and Eurydice (169 lines). Ovid has an uncanny ability to project himself into the turbulent thoughts of young women, and his depiction of Myrrha's confused longing is shockingly vivid. But a myth is never about its subject—and the story of Myrrha can also be read as a story about a *man*'s unconscious repression.

There are several indications that Cinyras harbours an 'unconscious' love for his daughter. Indeed, Ovid underlines this: 'If only he had been childless, he might have been a happy man'. When Myrrha is asked to choose a husband, the focus switches from Myrrha's confusion to Cinyras. He is flattered when she tells him that she would like to marry a man 'like' him. Although she is a young woman of marriageable age, he treats her as if she were still a child, kissing her on the lips. And when told there is a young woman of 'the same age' as his daughter who is willing to sleep with him, he immediately summons her.

His daughter's name is derived from the resin of *Commiphora myrrha*, a short, bushy tree covered with sharp thorns which flourishes in the southern Arabian Peninsula. In antiquity, it was already well known for its perfume. It is mentioned frequently in the Old Testament.[8] In the Song of Songs, both the Bride and the Groom liken the effect the other has on them to that of myrrh: 'My beloved is to me a sachet of myrrh resting between my breasts' (the Bride, 1.13); 'I'll go to the mountain of myrrh and to the hill of frankincense' (the Bridegroom, 4.6). The Sethians, a Gnostic sect, likened their notion of a light-pneuma to the scent of myrrh.[9] That is, the scent of myrrh was associated not only with an erogenous sensation, but also with the source of life. Ovid is unlikely to have read the Song of Songs, but he would certainly have been aware of similar associations. Theophrastus, a follower of Aristotle, identifies myrrh as a perfume particularly suited for women.[10] That is, as holding a strong attraction for *men*.

Ovid likens the effect of a strong perfume to a powerful desire. In terms of its *subject*, the myth of Cinyras and Myrrha explores the unthinkable passion of a young woman for her father. But in terms of its *theme*, it explores what can happen in the unconscious imagination of a man who allows the natural erotic desire he has for his wife (a *living* Eurydice) to move 'unnaturally' onto his daughter (a Eurydice in his *imagination*).

When read from the point of view of Cinyras, the myth suggests that he needs to kill not his daughter (as he seems to intend), but his own unconscious sexual fascination with her. When read from the point of view of Orpheus, the myth suggests that he needs to free himself of his unhealthy obsession with an *image* of Eurydice and return to society.

Orpheus, however, remains as obtuse as ever. The following story underlines his problem.

Adonis and Venus: A Failure to Transition from Adolescence to Maturity

When it is time for Myrrha to give birth, Lucina (goddess of childbirth) eases the delivery of the child from the tree that encloses him. 'Time is fleeting' and Adonis, the child of his sister and his grandfather, soon becomes synonymous with youthful male beauty.

The Sumerian myth of Innana and Dumuzi can be traced to about 3000 BCE; the Babylonian story of Ishtar and Tammuz, to about 2000 BCE; the Anatolian story of Cybele and Attis, to about 1200 BCE; and the Greeks told a comparable story about Aphrodite and Adonis. Ovid's account of the myth of Adonis *parodies* these age-old myths about a mother goddess and her divine lover.

One day, while Cupid is playfully kissing Venus, one of his arrows happens to pierce her breast. As she pushes him away, her eyes fall on a young man and she becomes so entranced by his beauty that she abandons Cyprus, and even her home amongst the gods. Instead, she accompanies Adonis when he hunts and, dressed like Diana, she cheers on the hounds, and helps him to chase those animals which it is safe to hunt.

She warns Adonis to be afraid of dangerous animals. When he asks her why, she replies: 'I shall tell you why, and you will marvel at the terrible outcome of an ancient crime. But my unaccustomed exercise has tired me. Let us lie down together on this grassy bank'. And with these words, she draws him down beside her and lays her head on his chest.

Ovid adjusts the story to his purpose. He describes Cupid as a mischievous boy and Adonis as a typical male adolescent, whose favourite pastime is hunting, which symbolises both his *quest* for his adult identity and his *difficulty* in recognising it.[11]

But his most important modifications are to the character of Venus. In Greek antiquity, Aphrodite was regarded as the personification of powerful sexual desire. From the time of the sculptor Praxiteles (fourth century BCE), she was usually depicted naked. Ovid introduces her dressed like Diana (Artemis), a virgin goddess who presides over female adolescence (virgin = unattached, independent, unmarried). She governs that phase in a young woman's life between puberty, when she gradually becomes aware of her adult identity, and attachment, which is governed jointly by Venus (desire, sexuality) and by Juno (marriage, relationship). The image of Venus, goddess of sexual love, dressing and behaving like *Diana* is laugh-out-loud absurd.

So too is the portrayal of Venus as an anxious and over-protective mother, so determined to shield Adonis from harm that she will not let him test his mettle. Like a tired lover, she rests her head against Adonis. Then, like a good mother, she tells him a story. Its relevance to Orpheus needs no underlining.

Hippomenes and Atalanta: The Need to Honour Venus

The goddess of sexual love tells Adonis a story about the importance of recognising what *she* personifies. The first part is about her role in stirring desire. The second part carries a warning about what might happen to a man who forgets to thank her for her help. Ovid's version of the myth of Hippomenes and Atalanta is the second longest in the sequence, and it illustrates the consequences of denying Venus her due.

Atalanta was admired for her beauty, and she could run like the wind. An oracle warns her that if she marries, while still alive, she will die, and so she sleeps alone. When suitors call, she tells them: 'If you insist, let us race. If you win, a wife will be your prize. But if you lose, you must accept instant death'. Despite these terms, many come to test their speed—and they perish.

Hippomenes is the great-grandson of Neptune, God of the Ocean, and 'Tamer of Horses'. Although humans have learned to navigate the ocean and to tame horses, both the ocean and horses retain an unpredictable nature. Although Hippomenes appears to be level-headed, he is prey to sudden and ungovernable impulses. He scoffs at those prepared to risk their life for a young woman. But as soon as he sees Atalanta running naked, he burns with desire for her. He decides to try his luck—and for the first time, Atalanta feels worried for her suitor. She advises him to desist. She has fallen in love but does not know it. Meanwhile, her father demands that the usual race be held.

Venus continues. 'Hippomenes begged me to smile upon the love which Atalanta had aroused in him. I was moved by his plea. I had just left the garden of my temple in Tamassus (central Cyprus), and I had three of its golden apples with me. Revealing myself only to him, I explained how he could put them to use'.

The joke is that Venus is *not* associated with athletic prowess. The apples recall a late Hellenistic story about the Judgement of Paris, in which all the gods are invited to the marriage of Peleus and Thetis, except Eris (Strife), who arrives with an apple for 'the fairest'. Asked to decide who is the fairest between Hera, Athena, and Aphrodite, Paris chooses Aphrodite, a choice quickly followed by *strife*—in the form of the Trojan War.

During the race, Hippomenes throws an apple in Atalanta's path, hoping to distract her. In true folk-tale fashion, on the third attempt the bait diverts her sufficiently for him to win. But he forgets to thank Venus for her help—and she feels slighted. She resolves to make an example of the couple so that others will pay her greater respect. As the young lovers are walking near a holy temple to Cybele, she fires Hippomenes with irresistible desire. He and Atalanta enter the temple and defile it. Outraged by their behaviour, Cybele transforms them into lions, and she uses them to pull her carriage.

Cybele (the Great Mother goddess of Anatolia, Syria, and Phrygia) was identified with Rhea, and is thus the mother of Zeus and the Olympian gods. She is often represented standing, pregnant, in a chariot drawn by two lions. Ovid is the first to suggest these lions are Hippomenes and Atalanta.

The first part of the myth represents the challenge facing Hippomenes (to acknowledge the help given to him by Venus, which would suggest that he is ready for adult sexuality). The second part illustrates the consequences of his failure to thank Venus for her help. Hippomenes and Atalanta are cruelly punished for their ungovernable desire: they have their desire tamed for ever—and they now serve the Great Mother.

Venus ends her story with a warning: 'So, Adonis, avoid all dangerous animals, lest your boldness bring sorrow to us both'. Whereupon she mounts her swan-drawn chariot and disappears. But Adonis is a teenager: he promptly forgets her advice and goes hunting.

The Death of Adonis: The Failure to Transition to Adulthood

The traditional myth about the death of Adonis hinges on Persephone deliberately stirring Ares to anger by suggesting that Aphrodite prefers Adonis to him. Ares promptly takes the form of a wild boar, finds the pair together, and gores Adonis to his death.[12] Ovid adapts this material to suit his purpose and, as always, his version of the story is both comic *and* poignant.

Orpheus continues his song. Adonis' hounds soon pick up a scent, which they follow until they rouse a wild boar from its lair. But the 'grandson of Cinyras' is unprepared; he throws his spear ineptly. The boar shakes itself free, and then charges at him, sinking its tusks deep into his groin. Adonis collapses on the ground.

Venus is on her way to Cyprus when she hears his dying groans. Promptly retracing her course, she hurries to his side, tears at her hair, and beats her breasts in despair: 'My grief will be remembered. Every year, women will weep for your death'. And she transforms the 'child of Cinyras' into a delicate anemone (windflower).

Cinyras represses his desire for his daughter. His grandson, Adonis, is punished for his reluctance to assume responsibility for his adult sexuality—and this punishment is vividly illustrated by the boar driving straight for Adonis' groin. Ovid, however, passes quickly over the accident.

He focusses on the suffering of Venus. The image of Venus pounding at her breasts is both comic and deeply moving, for it is based on a centuries-old Middle Eastern tradition. The *Adonia* was held in early spring when married women planted delicate flowers in a shallow container with little soil.[13] When the flowers died, they mourned the premature death of a beautiful young man who has yet to discover the world of adult sexuality—and who never will.

And this, of course, anticipates the fate of Orpheus in the frame-story. Ovid depicts Orpheus as emotionally stuck not because of an obsession with his dead wife (as in Virgil), but because he is tied to Cybele, to the Great Mother; that is, despite the cumulative 'warnings' provided by the eight embedded myths which he chooses to sing, he *remains* deeply unconscious of his adult sexual needs.

Orpheus has understood nothing. Like Aristaeus, he has had the experience but missed its meaning. It is time for him to face the consequences.

The Death of Orpheus: The Failure to Enter into a New Relationship

Orpheus' song is interrupted by the appearance of frenzied Ciconian women. They charge toward him, but their spears and stones are so moved by his voice that they fall at his feet as if to beg forgiveness. This rouses the women to insane fury. Little by little, their screams drown out his song and they kill him. Ovid recounts the brutal death of Orpheus with the same laconic distance that characterises the first part of the myth.

There is a wicked, tongue-in-cheek coda. As Orpheus's head and lyre drift down the Hebrus and find their way to Lesbos, his shade speeds to the underworld. Once again, Orpheus passes through its halls, then searches the Elysian Fields until he finds his Eurydice. They fall into each other's arms. Sometimes they walk side by side; sometimes she leads the way; and sometimes he does. But now, he can turn and look at her without worry.

The reader is tempted to assume that the reunion of Orpheus and Eurydice is a reward for their great love. But Ovid's Orpheus never expresses *any* desire for Eurydice: it is not even clear whether he *ever* loved her. His emotions are dormant, and they might always have been. He sings of eight myths about love, but he clearly does not understand their relevance to himself. Ovid's ending should remind the reader that the *only* happiness that the couple enjoys is as 'shades' in the underworld. Not until the early Renaissance does a version of the myth foreground love *and* give the myth an almost persuasive 'happy ending'.

Most anthology accounts of the myth of Orpheus and Eurydice end with their reunion in death. But Ovid *continues* the story with a short passage in which a furious Dionysus appears, intent on punishing the Maenads for *their* crime.

The Revenge of Dionysus: The Failure to Honour Orpheus

The purpose of this further coda is unexpected, but crucial. Ovid is reminding the reader that Orpheus was widely regarded as a central figure in the most famous mystery rites of antiquity: those practiced at Eleusis.

Lyaeus (Dionysus) would not allow this crime against the poet of his sacred rites to go unpunished. The Thracian women are stopped in their tracks and pulled into the ground. Their struggles to escape only tighten the hold of the pliant roots. Their shapely legs are quickly covered with bark, their arms become branches. They are transformed into oak trees. Lyaeus means *loosener* or *deliverer*, but, with wry irony, Ovid here portrays Dionysus as a *binder*. He punishes the Maenads by transforming them into trees. That is, he concedes that they are a symbol of growth, but he deprives them of both their human sexuality and their violence.

Hippomenes, Adonis, and Orpheus are not punished for any material or physical crime. They are punished for a mistaken *attitude*: for failing to thank Venus for her help (Hippomenes), for emotional unreadiness (Adonis), and for an inability to move on in his life (Orpheus). In a similar fashion, the Maenads are punished for *not remembering* that Orpheus is associated with ancient rites pertinent to individual development.

The joke, of course, is that although the *figure* of Orpheus was associated with individual development, Ovid's Orpheus shows no emotional bond with Eurydice, and no interest (despite the eight myths about which he sings) in entering a new relationship. He remains unaware that he has any need to develop.

Conclusions

Virgil turned to the myth of Orpheus and Eurydice to comment on the challenge facing Aristaeus. In his account of the song of Orpheus, Ovid harnesses eight separate myths to comment on the challenge facing Orpheus. Each of these myths specifies an aspect of the challenge facing him. Each indicates why he is unable to meet this challenge. And each represents a 'stage' in a cumulative argument.

- The myth of Cypress suggests that Orpheus suffers from arrested emotional development.
- That of Ganymede implies that he is in thrall to an overwhelming and irresistible image (viz. Orpheus' obsession with Eurydice).
- That of Hyacinth suggests that his obsession will rebound on him and destroy him.
- The story of the Women of Amathus and the Horned Beasts indicates that his most pressing need is to honour Venus (i.e. to acknowledge his own adult sexuality).
- That of Pygmalion illustrates Orpheus' need to transform his desire from a maudlin and inappropriate obsession with a lifeless image (of his dead wife) to love for a living person.
- The story of Cinyras and Myrrha shows how a man who has a weak interest in his wife might develop an inappropriate desire for a daughter-figure (i.e. a fantasy yearning for an ideal *image* of a younger woman).
- Both the myths of Adonis and Venus and of Hippomenes and Atalanta suggest that Orpheus is finding it difficult to transition from a stage of psychological growth identified with 'adolescent independence' (associated with Diana) to 'adulthood' (represented by sexuality, associated with Venus; and attachment, associated with Hera, goddess of marriage).
- The death of Adonis underlines the possible consequences of Orpheus' failure to change his way.
- The death of Orpheus illustrates the consequence of an inability to learn from the products of his own unconscious (The Song of Orpheus).
- The Revenge of Dionysus reminds the reader that what has been at issue throughout is *individual development*.

The eight embedded myths that make up the song of Orpheus have been re-imagined with the purpose of *prompting* Orpheus to do what Virgil's hero could not: to embark on a new relationship. And in psychological terms, this is probably good advice.

If Ovid's account of the first part of the myth of Orpheus and Eurydice is little more than an amusing parody of Virgil, the song he attributes to Orpheus is a literary and psychological *tour de force*. Whereas Virgil's Orpheus yearns only for 'Eurydice lost', Ovid suggests that he should be yearning for a 'Eurydice still to be found'. Even more clearly than Virgil's epyllion, the song of Orpheus suggests that the instinctive promptings of the unconscious have a purposive and a *life-affirming* function (even if not recognised as such).

Ovid may be the first poet to exploit the fact that a myth can be read from the point of view of different characters. It is not until the early seventeenth century that two playwrights respond to and exploit this insight by giving Eurydice greater importance in the myth.

Both Virgil and Ovid turn to the myth to explore an aspect of human nature. In other words, both show an interest in what today we would describe as *personal psychology*. But this interest in personal psychology did not last long. Augustan Rome soon over-reached itself. In the following chapter, we explore versions of the myth produced between late antiquity and the end of the Middle Ages; that is, during a period when an emergent interest in *personal psychology* was buried once again by an age of collective and *religious allegory*.

Notes

1 B. Otis, *Ovid as an Epic Poet* (1966), Cambridge: Cambridge University Press, 1970, p. 83.
2 Ovid, Metamorphoses (10: 1-707 and 11: 1-84), tr. Frank Justus Miller (1916), 2 vols. Cambridge, MA: Harvard University Press, 1984, vol. 2, pp. 64–127 (preceded by stories of Byblis and Iphis, followed by story of Midas).
3 For example, H. Fränkel, *Ovid: A Poet between Two Worlds*, Berkeley: University of California Press, 1945, and B. Otis, *Ovid as an Epic Poet* (1966), Cambridge: Cambridge University Press, 1970. Those who have praised it for its artistry include S. Mack, *Ovid*, New Haven, CT: Yale University Press, 1988; C. Segal, *Orpheus: The Myth of the Poet*, Baltimore, MD: Johns Hopkins University Press, 1989.
4 See, for example, C.G. Jung, 'The Practical Use of Dream-Analysis', *The Practice of Psychotherapy*, *CW* 16, 1931/1934, p. 150 and 'The Tavistock Lectures', *The Symbolic Life*, *CW* 18, 1935, p. 78.
5 Homer, *Iliad* (14: 406-417), tr. A.T. Murray, 2 vols. (bk. 24, *ll*. 77-99). Loeb Classical Library. Cambridge MA: Harvard University Press, 1999, vol. 2, pp. 96–97.
6 According to W.S. Anderson, 'unlike his contemporaries, Ovid shows no personal interest in pederasty': see 'The Orpheus of Virgil and Ovid: *flebile nescio quid*', in J. Warden (ed.), *Orpheus: The Metamorphoses of a Myth*, Toronto: University of Toronto Press, p. 45.
7 Herodotus, *Histories* (1: 199.5), in *The Landmark Herodotus*, tr. A.L. Purvis, ed. R.B. Strassler. New York: Pantheon, 2007, p. 107; also M. Stol, "Temple Prostitution", in *Women in the Ancient Near East*. Berlin: de Gruyter, 2016, pp. 419–435.
8 For example, Genesis 37.25, Exodus 30.23.
9 T. Aquinas (attrib.), *Aurora Consurgens*, ed. M-L. von Franz, tr. R.F.C. Hull and A.S.B. Glover, London: Routledge & Kegan Paul, 1966, pp. 379–80.
10 Theophrastus, *On Odours* (10: 42), in Theophrastus, *Enquiry into Plants*, tr. A. Hort. Loeb Classical Library. Cambridge MA: Harvard University Press, 1926, pp. 364–365.
11 Cf. Ovid's account of the story of Narcissus and Echo, Metamorphoses (3: 339-510), tr. Frank Justus Miller (1916), 2 vols. Loeb Classical Library. Cambridge, MA: Harvard University Press, 1984, vol. 1, pp. 148–161.
12 R. Graves, 'Aphrodite's Nature and Deeds' (18.h-j), *Greek Myths*, London: Cassell, 1958, pp. 69–70.
13 M. Detienne, *Les Jardins d'Adonis*, Paris: Gallimard, 1972; also, M. P. Dillon, '"Woe for Adonis": But in Spring Not Summer', *Hermes* 131 (Jahrg., H.i), 2003, pp. 1–16.

Chapter 3

The Myth of Orpheus and Eurydice, Classical Philosophy, and Christian Allegory

Late Antiquity and the Middle Ages

The long Middle Ages lasted 1,000 years: they span the fall of the Western Roman Empire, the division of Europe into East and West, the rapid collapse of Western Europe, its gradual recovery, the Roman church's long stranglehold on thought and education, and, finally, the beginnings of a renewed desire to celebrate secular values and a humanist culture. They also represent an intriguing chapter in the history of the myth of Orpheus and Eurydice.

This chapter explains how an unlikely *classical* myth came to be harnessed to the expression of *Christian* values. In late antiquity, shaken by the turbulent times, writers abandoned their nascent interest in the psychology of individual human types and turned to allegory to testify to their *collective* convictions. In late antiquity, writers allegorised moral philosophy. During the Middle Ages, scholar-monks interpreted the myth of Orpheus and Eurydice in the light of their religious beliefs and their ideas about Christian virtues.

The first part looks briefly at the first version of the myth to foreground the importance of music. It then focuses on a short poem by Boethius, whose works became a cornerstone of the long Middle Ages. The second part outlines how the gradual revival of interest in classical texts produced a sustained interest in Boethius' version of the myth. The third briefly illustrates one of the ways in which the myth was harnessed to explore supposedly Christian values. It then turns to explore four works written in the early fourteenth century, all of which illustrate the transition from an age of religious allegory to a new age of sophisticated secular literature.

Late Antiquity

An *allegory* differs from metaphor in two respects. It refers not to a single image or issue, but to a broad system of thought; and whereas a metaphor is open to wide-ranging interpretation, allegory seeks either to win or to bolster adherence to a *specific* way of seeing and understanding the world.

The early Christian apologists were quick to adopt allegory to win others to their views. Their defining image of Christ—Christ as Good Shepherd—was allegorical: cf. 'The Lord in my shepherd' (Psalm 23) and 'Jesus said "I am the good shepherd"' (John 10:11).

DOI: 10.4324/9781003519584-5

In the Eastern Mediterranean, Orpheus very quickly became assimilated into this image. Both Orpheus and Christ are men of peace; they both reject a life of sensual pleasure; they both descend into 'Hell'; and crucially, both are victims of violence. More specifically, like Adam in the Garden of Eden, Orpheus gathers wild animals around him. Like David, he is a musician. Just as Isaiah describes what will ensue upon the coming of the Messiah—'the sheep will live with the wolf, and the kid will sleep alongside the leopard' (Isaiah 11:6)—so the oldest images of Orpheus are of a musician who can calm all nature with his music. Until the time of Constantine, Christians needed to disguise their adherence to the new faith. As a result, many early representations of *Christ* as Good Shepherd are invested with the attributes of *Orpheus*—that is, playing a lyre to a gathering of wild animals and birds. Examples include the fresco in the Catacombs of Domitilla in Rome (cubiculum IV; late fourth century) and the famous Orpheus mosaic from a burial chamber in Jerusalem (early sixth century; now in the Archaeological Museum, Istanbul).

Christianity quickly spread from the Eastern Roman Empire to the Western Empire. But two different languages (Greek, Latin), and two very different views about the priorities and government of the church (tradition, papal authority), meant that the Orthodox and Roman churches could never agree. These differences became a dividing line between Eastern and Western Europe.

In 330, at the entrance to the Bosporus, the emperor Constantine built himself a new capital: a 'New Rome'. As Constantinople, it became the capital of the entire Roman Empire, but more immediately, of the Eastern Empire, which prospered and gradually evolved into the Byzantine Empire.

Meanwhile, the Western Empire became embroiled in incessant border wars. Away from the borders, the wealthy continued to build and modernise their astonishingly comfortable villas. But the eastern borders of the empire stretched for over 2,000 miles—and they were difficult to defend. Gradually, various tribal groups (Franks, Huns, Goths) found weak spots and held them. In 395, the Western Roman Empire collapsed. After a brief revival of its fortunes, in 476, it collapsed again.

Following the death of Ovid, the next two significant responses to the myth of Orpheus and Eurydice were written in the early sixth century—that is, over a hundred years *after* the Sack of Rome by the Visigoths (410). Both were influenced by Virgil, and both represent different facets of a late *classical* moral philosophy. But in contrast with Virgil's epyllion, both are allegories; both explore the relation between philosophy and music; and both were to exercise a lasting influence on subsequent thinkers and writers. And they could not be more different.

Fulgentius: Orpheus, Music, and Profound Truth

Fabius Planciades Fulgentius is the first writer to argue that Eurydice represents something for which *everyone ought to strive*. He was probably a North African of Berber origin and a teacher of rhetoric. He wrote an idiosyncratic study of mythology in which he offers allegorical interpretations of some fifty myths, often based on somewhat fanciful etymologies.[1] Although an admirer of Virgil, Fulgentius radically changes the implications of Virgil's account of the myth.[2] In his view, Orpheus (music) *helps* human beings to civilise themselves through a sustained quest to discover Eurydice (profound and harmonious truth). That is, Fulgentius turns to the myth to illustrate the *opposite* of Virgil—and by doing so, although presumably unwittingly, he also demonstrates how easy it is for a man to *justify* his pursuit of whatever he earnestly desires.

The second response to the myth was by Boethius, whose version of the myth is closer to Virgil: it illustrates how easy it is for a man to be *mistaken* in his desires.

Boethius: Orpheus and the Source of Moral Good

Anicius Boethius came from a privileged Roman family. He was twenty-five when he was made a Senator by Theodoric the Great, the Ostrogoth leader whom he served for the rest of his life.[3] He wrote works on education, translations of Aristotle, and commentaries on several philosophical texts. He also argued that only by studying mathematics and music could one graduate to the proper study of philosophy.[4] In his late forties, he was accused of being part of a Senate conspiracy. Scholars continue to doubt whether he was culpable. Whatever the case, he was thrown into prison where, while awaiting execution, he wrote the work for which he is most famous.

On the Consolation of Philosophy (524) consists of an *imaginary conversation* between the author and a female personification of Philosophy and her handmaid, Music.[5] It is composed of five 'books' (parts), divided into sections, most of which end with a short, didactic poem which serves to illustrate and round off its argument.

Book three is about true happiness. Like Epicurus, Boethius distinguishes between two kinds of happiness. Happiness which depends on circumstances which are subject to change. And happiness which cannot be shaken—but which he argues can only be found by seeking the 'source of good/goodness' (*fons boni*). As human beings are *naturally* inclined toward this, their *deepest* wish is to be governed by this 'divine helmsman', whom he also calls 'god'. Their task, therefore, is to keep their minds fixed on 'god'. To forget god (moral good) is to err.

The section ends with a short and overtly didactic poem on the story of Orpheus and his 'wife'. For Boethius, as for Virgil, Orpheus personifies a typical human error. His backward glance at his wife confirms that his passions have drawn him toward moral darkness (*orphne* = darkness). He has forgotten that the true *fons boni* is God. The poem ends with the moral that anyone who turns away from the 'light' that flows from God will inevitably lose this light for ever and end in eternal 'darkness'. That is, the poem illustrates the importance of always keeping one's attention fixed on the source of one's own *moral integrity*.

Boethius was a moral philosopher steeped in classical learning. And yet, sometime after his death, a group of Christians learned of his last work and, presumably because they misread his claims about 'god' and individual moral integrity, they assumed that he *must* have converted to Christianity. They found his (ostensible) remains and had them buried in a Christian church.[6] And despite there being no evidence for it, their almost certainly mistaken supposition survived until late in the *twentieth* century. People believe what they want to believe.

Throughout Western Europe, the *Consolation* gradually became a bestseller, and for the next 700 years, its *classical* allegory was interpreted by scholar-monks in terms of supposedly *Christian* virtues. It was repeatedly translated into all the modern European languages. For example, in the late ninth century, it was translated into Old English, supposedly by 'Alfred the Great'.[7] In the fourteenth century, it was translated into Middle English by Chaucer.[8] And most poignantly, in 1593, as she approached her sixtieth year, it was translated into early modern English by Queen Elizabeth I.[9]

The Early Middle Ages

During the Middle Ages, Eastern and Western Europe enjoyed almost opposite trajectories. In Eastern Europe, Constantinople quickly became a vibrant trading centre, a reputation it retained throughout its long and slow decline. In the seventh century, its southern and eastern borders were clipped by the rapid expansion of the Islamic Rashidun Caliphate; in 1204, it was sacked by the disgraceful Fourth Crusade; and in 1453, the city fell to the Ottoman army.

In contrast, the collapse of the Western Roman Empire was followed by a period of persistent migrations-cum-invasions.[10] For over 300 years, skills at which the Romans had excelled were ignored. By the eighth century, there was an acute need to rediscover some of their forgotten skills, most obviously, in education, administration, and building. There are three distinct moments when the recovery of various aspects of *classical* learning—initially in Latin—helped to promote significant progress.

The first of these medieval 'renaissances' was the *Carolingian Renaissance*, a term used to describe the beginnings of the educational programmes and administrative skills instigated by Charlemagne and his son during the eighth and ninth centuries.[11] This led to the first major stone buildings since the fall of the Roman Empire (notably, Charlemagne's Palatine Chapel in Aachen/Aix-la-Chapelle, 792–805), and to the first versions of the myth of Orpheus and Eurydice influenced by Boethius, and yet suggesting or illustrating *Christian* convictions.[12]

The second was the *Ottonian Renaissance*, a term used to describe a fresh revival of interest in classical and educational works instigated by Otto I of Saxony during the tenth century.[13] Over the next 200 years, Boethius' ideas about the importance of the *trivium* (grammar, logic, and rhetoric) and what he called the *quadrivium* (arithmetic, geometry, music, and astronomy) gradually evolved into the 'seven liberal arts' of medieval education—and they remained the cornerstones of education until well into the Renaissance.

The importance of Boethius rests on his educational writings. Even so, it would be difficult to exaggerate the influence of *The Consolation of Philosophy*. Because it was widely believed that its author had written as a Christian, the short poem about Orpheus and his wife was assumed to be about the need to keep one's attention fixed on a Christian God. And at least three eleventh-century poems based on the myth of Orpheus and Eurydice end with the happy return of Eurydice to life.[14]

Meanwhile, a new century ushered in the third, and the most consequential, of the medieval renaissances: the Renaissance of the twelfth century.[15]

The Late Middle Ages

Ever since the collapse of the Roman Empire, Western Europe had resisted cultural interactions with its Mediterranean and other neighbours. Even the Carolingian and Ottonian Renaissances did little to change this. The politics of the Roman church were insular and dogmatic. They led to the blinkered zeal and brutality of the Crusades (1095–1291), as well as to an increasing discrepancy between the church's advocations and its practices. Some protested its theology (the Cathars), others, its inappropriate worldliness (Francis of Assisi)—and in the fourteenth century, also its insistence on the use of Latin (John Wycliffe, Jan Hus).

The Twelfth Century Renaissance is often linked with the School of Chartres, a phrase which refers to small group of scholar-monks who worked independently and who were amongst the first to show a sustained interest in the achievements of non-Latin cultures.[16] Bernard of Chartres and John of Salisbury pursued an interest in Greek philosophy. William of Conches studied Islamic philosophy, science, and medicine.[17] That is, they sought to understand the most persuasive ideas advanced (and sometimes tested) in different cultures. This new interest quickly led to advances in a range of fields including medicine, philosophy, science, architecture, and social and political thinking. The first European universities date from this time (Bologna, 1088; Oxford, 1096).

For our purposes, however, the most significant development was the revival of interest in *individual* secular experience. From the beginning of the twelfth century, and at least partly influenced by Islamic poetry, new forms of song and poetry arose (Troubadour poetry).[18] Today, Petrarch is best known for his collection of poems, now known as *The Songbook* (*Il Canzoniere*), which explores the turbulent emotions triggered in him by his love for Laura. But its original title was *Rerum vulgarium fragmenta* (= lit. *Fragments of Common Things*; i.e. 'Fragments of Ordinary Experience written in Italian). The poems were written between 1327 and 1368 and published posthumously in 1374—and they influenced Western European poetry for the next 250 years.

Petrarch refers to their subject in his essay-letter, 'Ascent of Mont Ventoux' (in the South of France), often referred to as the first work which shows an appreciation of nature for its own sake.[19] But its primary interest is *not* the poet's wonder at the view. It is his self-conscious awareness of his own feelings, including the silliness of his love for Laura. It is his realisation that his perceptions are dictated less by what he sees (whether Laura or the view from Mont Ventoux) than by his own *subjective tendencies*. This insight represents a watershed in the modern understanding of *personal* experience—for it is, of course, a precondition for self-awareness.

Even devout Catholic monks began to reflect on their personal experience—although not always with any evidence of self-awareness.

Scholar-Monks: A Distrust of Female Desire

Virgil, Ovid, and Boethius had all implied that Orpheus was mistaken in trying to recover Eurydice from the underworld. During the Middle Ages, scholar-monks sought to identify the source of this error. Unsurprisingly (cf. the story of Adam and Eve), they found it not in Orpheus, but in Eurydice.

For example, in his comments on Boethius' poem, William of Conches fuses the traditions of Virgil, Fulgentius, and Boethius. While fleeing from Aristaeus (Virtue), Eurydice (Concupiscence) finds herself in a meadow representing pleasure, where she is bitten by a snake. Orpheus (Eloquence) aspires to learn 'the knowledge of earthly things', but *despite himself*, he is tempted by ardent sexual desire.[20] That is, just as Eve was held responsible for the Fall, so Eurydice was held responsible for stirring a morally disruptive sexual desire in Orpheus.

A 150 years later, Nicholas Trivet, an English Dominican priest, reworks this interpretation. He identifies Orpheus as intellect and Eurydice as affect, and he sees human beings as constantly torn between these two impulses. Although their intellect (Orpheus) naturally draws them 'upward' to the *fons boni*, their passions (Eurydice) drag them down to Hell, whose monsters symbolise the dangers that beset rational beings.[21] And Trivet's commentary continued to be read until well into the *seventeenth* century.

Both clerics identify Orpheus with positive qualities and Eurydice with a kind of sexual desire which will destroy a *man*. Both had wide-ranging intellectual interests, and yet, neither could free himself of the deep-rooted distrust of women and an abhorrence of female sexuality which haunted Western European Christian teaching.

Nevertheless, by the early fourteenth century, a welcome 'wind of change' was blowing—and, once again, writers turned to the myth of Orpheus and Eurydice to express an interest in secular human nature. Four versions of the myth, written almost simultaneously, illustrate this unusually clearly. The first two discussed here illustrate the emergence of a humanism rooted in Catholic teaching. The next two illustrate the re-emergence of a secular humanism; that is, a renewed interest in *human* nature and *human* love.

We begin with a version of the myth which gives it an unexpected 'happy ending'.

Giovanni del Virgilio: Orpheus Becomes a Monk

Giovanni del Virgilio, who was born in Bologna about 1300, based his interpretation of the myth on both Virgil and Boethius. It begins with Orpheus married to Eurydice (= profound judgement). She wanders through a field (= delights in worldly things)—and she is watched by Aristaeus (*aristos* = best + *theos* = God), who represents the divine mind. Because Eurydice strays from the good path, the serpent bites and kills her. Upon losing her, Orpheus humbly *praises* God. As a result, Eurydice is returned to him, but on condition that he does not look back at her. On losing her a second time, he finally renounces temptation (the delights of the world, which are the path to Hell). He becomes a monk and by devoting his soul to God and his body to the pursuit of service to his fellow human beings, he demonstrates *profound judgement* (which is Eurydice). The ending thus fuses the implications of the versions by Fulgentius and Boethius. Orpheus recovers from his 'waywardness' and takes his place in a new (social/spiritual) reality.[22]

Giovanni del Virgilio was a friend of Dante, whose most famous work might appear to have nothing to do with the myth of Orpheus and Eurydice. And yet, as has long been recognised, it cleverly reorders the myth's narrative structure and explores its same motifs and concerns (loss, longing, descent, entitlement, determination, and self-awareness) for its own purpose.

The Divine Comedy: *An Allegory about Human Choice*

For 600 years, the myth of Orpheus and Eurydice had been associated with religious allegory. But ironically, the greatest religious allegory of the Middle Ages represents an early indication that both literature and the myth were about to be reclaimed for the exploration of *secular* concerns.

The Divine Comedy (1310–1320) is about the poet's spiritual journey toward God. Famously, it is in three parts. Virgil guides Dante 'down' through the nine circles of Hell, and then 'up' through the seven terraces or circles of Purgatory. At the top, Virgil (who died before Christ came into the world) can go no further. Beatrice now leads Dante through the planetary spheres that compose Paradise until he comes to 'the Love that moves the sun and the other stars'. The possible significance of the work lies far beyond the scope of this study. Here, we shall comment on only two moments.

The first is Dante's meeting with Orpheus, which occurs soon after he begins his journey. He finds Orpheus in Limbo (the first circle of *Hell*), amongst classical philosophers including Socrates, Plato, and Aristotle, and directly next to Cicero and 'Seneca the moralist'.[23] In other words, Dante regards Orpheus as a *philosopher* who has helped human beings to improve themselves, and, by doing so, has contributed to the advance of civilisation.

The second is Dante's meeting with Boethius, which occurs toward the end of his journey, in *Paradise*, in the fourth Heaven (the sphere of the Sun and the Wise), where it becomes impossible for anyone to bathe in the light of the Sun/God and to hear the celestial music and *not* to yearn to do so for ever. Here Dante meets Thomas Aquinas, who introduces him to some of the wisest men of all time, including Solomon and Boethius. And Dante underlines his debt to Boethius, whom he describes as

the blessed soul who with eloquence reveals
the world's deceits to those who listen well.[24]

By 'deceits', he means the world of false appearances. That is, human beings are tempted to pursue *material* riches, which causes them to turn away from the *real* world, which is the love of God. And yet, as Erich Auerbach was perhaps the first to emphasise, Dante has a claim to being the first writer to configure the 'living historical reality' of human nature. For the focus of Dante's argument is not on the 'promise' of eternal salvation: it is on human choice or, rather, human determination.[25] That is, Dante has reformulated Virgil's epyllion about the need for an Epicurean moral integrity as a wide-ranging epic about the human need to choose the Christian faith.

A related concern features at the heart of a work first published within a few years of Dante's masterpiece, and which has a section on the myth of Orpheus and Eurydice.

L'Ovide moralisé: *Christian Belief and Human Nature*

The *Ovide moralisé* (*Ovid Moralised*, 1317–1328) is an anonymous free translation of Ovid's *Metamorphoses* into French. Each tale is followed by an emphatically moralising Christian commentary.[26] As a result, the work runs to a staggering 72,000 octosyllabic lines. In the section on the myth of Orpheus and Eurydice, Orpheus is identified with Christ, and just as Christ is hung from a cross and descends alive into Hell, so Orpheus descends into the underworld to 'deliver the soul' of all good Christians.

About 1340, the *Ovide moralisé* was translated into Latin, the *lingua franca* of Europe at the time.[27] And in one respect, it is more intriguing than the original. In the Latin translation, Orpheus (Christ) becomes responsible for liberating not the soul, but 'human nature'. This change illustrates the beginnings of a renewed interest in the complexity of what it means to be *human*.[28]

Nevertheless, the clearest example of this renewed interest is an entertaining verse romance written about the same time.

Sir Orfeo: *Love, Identity, and Socio-Political Responsibility*

The earliest lays (narrative poems with lines of eight syllables) were probably written in Brittany (N-W France); that is, they have a Celtic origin, and they were very likely sung by minstrels moving from one great house to another. The earliest surviving lays are the 'Breton lays' of Marie de France, the first woman we know of who wrote in a modern European language. Her lays are of very different length (from 118 to 1,184 lines), they subscribe to the conventions of 'courtly love', and they are told with an innocent comic seriousness which gives them considerable charm.[29] They circulated widely and were enormously influential.

Sir Orfeo is an anonymous Breton lay written in Middle English. The oldest surviving manuscript is from about 1330.[30] Sir Orfeo is a 'generous and courteous knight' who lives in Traciens (suggestive of Thrace, in northern Greece), which, the poet promptly tells us, is the ancient name for Winchester (in southern England). There are other oddities. Sir Orfeo's father is descended from Pluto (the god of the underworld), and his mother, from Juno (the goddess of marriage).

Sir Orfeo is married to Lady Heurodis, who likes to take a daily nap under a grafted tree in their orchard. One day, she has a dream in which the king of Fairyland tells her that tomorrow he will come for her. To avert this, the following day, Sir Orfeo has a thousand knights guard her as she sleeps. Despite his precaution, Heurodis is spirited away, no one sees how.

Sir Orfeo asks his High Steward to look after his kingdom and sets off to find her. For ten years, he lives in a wilderness. He eats berries and roots and becomes prematurely withered. But when he plays his harp, wild animals gather around him. Sometimes, he catches sight of the King of Fairyland, who is always accompanied by a thousand well-dressed knights.

One day, he sees Heurodis amongst a group of ladies, all on horseback, practising falconry. Their eyes meet, but before they can speak, the ladies ride away. Sir Orfeo follows them through a 'rock'. Three miles inside, he finds himself on a plain with a magnificent castle. He presents himself at the door as a minstrel. In the great hall, a pile of dead bodies lies next to the living. But he also sees Heurodis, and he asks permission to play for the king. When he is finished, the king offers to give him whatever he asks.

Sir Orfeo asks for Heurodis, who has gone to lie beneath a tree. Shocked by the impudence of this apparently elderly minstrel, the king angrily rejects the request. But when reminded of his promise, he relents and gives the pair his blessing. They return to Traciens, where Sir Orfeo learns that his Steward has indeed been true, and he and his Queen resume control of their kingdom.

The lay is rooted in Celtic folklore. The *grafted tree* (beneath which Heurodis lies) and the *rock* are gateways between the 'real' world and the 'fairy' world. The latter is not an 'underworld', nor does it carry any infernal connotations. It is a *parallel* realm of imaginal beings.[31] Sir Orfeo has a thousand knights; so too does the Fairy King. The fairy-tale castle, richly decorated with gold, is typical of the fairy realm of Irish folklore. Despite the pile of dead bodies, Sir Orfeo considers it a 'Paradise'. And returning to the real world is a motif familiar to Celtic shamanism.[32]

As in the Augustan myth, the emphasis falls on the experience of Sir Orfeo. When he loses Heurodis, he feels he can no longer be king. He learns how to survive in the forest, even in winter. He becomes prematurely aged, and yet, at-one with nature. He is given occasional glimpses of the fairy world (hunting, without killing an animal; knights in armour, without any war to win). It is an ideal world in which knights and ladies go through the motions of life, but without any evidence that they *feel* it. The fairy world reflects the tension between Sir Orfeo's ideals and his conventional feelings.

The poem distinguishes between the 'outer' and the 'inner' individual. Only after recognising that he is, to borrow from *King Lear*, a 'poor bare, forked animal' is Sir Orfeo ready to recover both Heurodis and his crown. But there is one more test—and it is a motif new to this version of the myth: the test of his Steward. Just as Sir Orfeo has shown the constancy of his love for Heurodis, so the Steward has been constant in his loyalty to Sir Orfeo. The suggestion is that if a person is so overwhelmed that they cannot cope with their social reality, they need someone dependable (partner, friend, or analyst) to look after their concerns until they feel able to resume control of their responsibilities. To ensure the successful outcome, the Steward *must* be loyal, and he is.

Sir Orfeo is the first version of the myth to emphasise a concern with human *identity* (as opposed to an aspect of human *behaviour*); the first to give the reader the impression that the poet is describing a *human* love.[33] And the first to explore a *socio-political* responsibility. Sir Orfeo learns that the heart of kingship is not power (his thousand knights), but love and loyalty (which are, of course, also central to Shakespeare's *King Lear*).

Perhaps unexpectedly, *Sir Orfeo* is also an important influence on the last major adaptation of the myth from the age of allegory. It is something of an anomaly, but nonetheless intriguing. It is the first version of the myth since Fulgentius to *emphasise* the importance of music.

Robert Henryson: Orpheus, Musical Theory, and Self-Awareness

Little is known about the Scottish poet Robert Henryson, except that he may have had a connection with Dunfermline Abbey (Fife), and that his works date from the late fifteenth century. He is best known for *The Moral Fables of Aesop the Phrygian* and *The Testament of Cresseid*.

His *Orpheus and Euridices*, which is written in a marked Scottish dialect, was published posthumously about 1505. It is in two parts. The first consists of an idiosyncratic account of the myth, ostensibly based on Boethius. The second offers a *moralitas*: an allegorical and moral interpretation based on Nicholas Trivet's commentary on Boethius (Orpheus represents 'intellect'; Euridices, 'desire').

Henryson's Orpheus derives his talent for music not from his father Apollo, but from 'the sweet liquor' of his mother's milk. Euridices, 'the mighty Queen of Trace', declares her love for him and they marry. Then comes a moralising warning: their love has grown like a flower which has bloomed too early, and thus is fated to wither.

As soon as Euridices dies, Orpheus sets out to recover her. He hurries along 'Watling Street' (which here means the Milky Way) until he comes to Saturn.[34] He then goes on to the other major planets. He learns nothing, except that the music of the spheres ('the soul of this world', according to Plato) represents a musical theory. In two seven-line stanzas, reference is made to the intervals of a fourth, a fifth, an octave, a twelfth (octave + fifth), and a double octave.[35] The descent into Hell has another oddity. In the house where Rhadamanthus (Pluto) and Proserpine live, he sees several figures from history, each responsible for a wrong (Ahab and Jezebel; Herod and Pontius Pilate; and, somewhat oddly, Priam and Hector).

He finally comes across Euridices: she is thin and deathly pale. But when Orpheus turns, Pluto reclaims her, Orpheus faints, and it is some time before he can find his way home—alone.

Henryson then interprets his account of the myth in the *moralitas*, which focuses on the moral implications of the mythological figures that Orpheus encounters in Hell. They contribute little or nothing of interest. The *moralitas* does not expound on the significance of the two most unexpected features of this version of the myth: the celestial 'passage' through the spheres and the lesson in musical theory.

As the text survives, Henryson's poem is not entirely persuasive. It may be incomplete. But it might also harbour an intriguing ending. At the outset, Orpheus is a skilful *performer*. By the end, he has learned musical *theory*. He discovers that it cannot bring back the dead. But his new-found understanding of musical theory may have been intended as a metaphor for self-therapy: that is, to help him process his grief.

Conclusion

From late antiquity to the end of the Middle Ages, writers interpreted the myth of Orpheus and Eurydice through *allegory*—that is, by exploring it in the light of a dominant collective ideology, initially classical (Boethius, moral philosophy), but from the eighth to the early sixteenth century, Christian (a religious morality).

Throughout the Middle Ages, the stranglehold on thought and writing exercised by the Roman church inevitably affected versions of the myth. By the twelfth century, however, even devout scholar-monks and other writers were beginning to show an interest in what other traditions had to offer. The great Gothic cathedrals, the new universities, and the Arthurian epics embody new aspirations and a new dynamism. And in the early fourteenth century, after more than 800 years, versions of the myth were once again beginning to express the importance of secular values and of individual choice and responsibility.

Soon after, a further *renaissance* arose, almost simultaneously, in Italy and in Northern Europe. For our purpose here, its most important aspect is that it brought an end to the age of allegory and introduced a new age—an age of *pastoral*, a genre particularly well suited to explore the complications of *human* love.

Notes

1 See L.G. Whitbread (tr.), *Fulgentius the Mythographer*, Columbus: Ohio State University Press, 1971.

2 See J.B. Friedman, *Orpheus in the Middle Ages*, Cambridge, MA: Harvard University Press, 1970, p. 89; also, P. Vicari, '*Sparagmos*: Orpheus amongst the Christians', in J. Warden (ed.), *Orpheus: The Metamorphoses of a Myth*, Toronto: University of Toronto Press, 1982, p. 67.

3 J. Marenbon, *Boethius*, New York: Oxford University Press, 2003.

4 See L. Schrade, 'Music in the Philosophy of Boethius', *The Musical Quarterly* 33 (2), 1947, pp. 188–200.

5 Boethius, *The Theological Tractates [...] The Consolation of Philosophy*, tr. S.J. Tester, Cambridge, MA: Harvard University Press, 1973, pp. 306–311; also, *The Consolation of Philosophy*, tr. P. Walsh. Oxford: Oxford University Press, 2008.
6 San Pietro in Ciel d'Oro, in Pavia, Italy (which also, and equally improbably, houses the ostensible remains of Saint Augustine of Hippo).
7 S. Irvine and M. Godden (ed. and tr.), *The Old English Boethius with Verse Prologues and Epilogues Associated with King Alfred*, Cambridge, MA: Harvard University Press, 2012.
8 *Chaucer's Translation of Boethius's 'De Consolatione Philosophiæ'*, ed. R. Morris (1868), Oxford: Oxford University Press, 1969 (reprint); see also, T.W. Machan, *Techniques of Translation: Chaucer's Boece*, Norman, OK: Pilgrim Books, 1985.
9 Elizabeth I's translation of Boethius' *The Consolation of Philosophy* is in the National Archives, Kew, UK (SP 12/289 f.48).
10 See G. Halsall, 'The Barbarian Invasions', P. Fouracre (ed.), *The New Cambridge Medieval History, Vol. 1: c. 500–c.700*, Cambridge: Cambridge University Press, 2005, pp. 35–55.
11 See E. Patzelt, *Die Karolingische Renaissance: Beiträge zur Geschichte der Kultur des Frühen Mittelalters*, Wien: Österreichischer Schulbücherverlag, 1924; also, J.J. Contreni, 'The Carolingian Renaissance', in W.T. Treadgold (ed.), *Renaissances before the Renaissance: Cultural Revivals of Late Antiquity and the Middle Ages*, Stanford: Stanford University Press, 1984, pp. 59–74.
12 See E.A. Newby, *A Portrait of the Artist: The Legends of Orpheus and Their Use in Medieval and Renaissance Aesthetics*, New York: Garland, 1987.
13 H. Naumann, *Karolingische und Ottonische Renaissance*, Frankfurt-am-Main: Englert und Schlosser, 1926; and P.R. et J. Verger, *Des nains sur des épaules de géants: Maîtres et élèves au Moyen Âge*, Paris: Tallandier, 2006, p. 59ff.
14 P. Dronke, 'The Return of Eurydice', *Classica et Mediaevalia* 23, pp. 198–215 (p. 198).
15 C.H. Haskins, *The Renaissance of the Twelfth Century*, Cambridge, MA: Harvard University Press, 1927.
16 See E. Jeauneau, *Rethinking the School of Chartres*, tr. Claude P. Desmarais, Toronto: University of Toronto Press, 2009.
17 See W. Montgomery Watt, *The Influence of Islam on Medieval Europe (*1972*)*, Edinburgh: Edinburgh University Press, 1994.
18 See D. de Rougemont, *Love in the Western World* (1939/1972), tr. Montgomery Belgion, Princeton, NJ: Princeton University Press, 1983.
19 Petrarch climbed the mountain in 1336; the essay-letter describing his experience was written in 1350. Petrarch, *Familiar Letters*, book 4.1; see M. Bishop, *Petrarch and His World*, Bloomington: Indiana University Press, 1993.
20 P. Vicari, '*Sparagmos*: Orpheus amongst the Christians', in J. Warden (ed.), *Orpheus: The Metamorphoses of a Myth*, Toronto: University of Toronto Press, 1982, p. 67.
21 J.B. Friedman, *Orpheus in the Middle Ages*, Cambridge, MA: Harvard University Press, 1970, pp. 109–114.
22 J.B. Friedman, *Orpheus in the Middle Ages*, Cambridge, MA: Harvard University Press, 1970, pp. 122–124.
23 Dante, *Inferno* 4, 139–144, in *The Divine Comedy*, tr. A. Mandelbaum. Everyman's Library. New York: Knopf, 1995, p. 76.
24 Dante, *Paradiso* 10, 125–126 (my translation): cf. *The Divine Comedy*, tr. A. Mandelbaum. Everyman's Library. New York: Knopf, 1995, p. 426.
25 E. Auerbach, *Dante: Poet of the Secular World* (1929), tr. Ralph Manheim, Chicago, IL: University of Chicago Press, 1961, pp. 174 and 132.
26 C. De Boer et al. (eds), *Ovide moralisé* (1915–1938), Wiesbaden: Sändig, 1966.

27 See F.W. Sternfeld, 'Orpheus, Ovid and Opera', *Journal of the Royal Musical Association* 113 (2), 1988, pp. 172–202.

28 F.W. Sternfeld, 'Orpheus, Ovid and Opera', *Journal of the Royal Musical Association* 113 (2), 1988, p. 183.

29 J. Rychner (ed.), *Les Lais de Marie de France (1966)*, Paris: Champion, 1983.

30 'Sir Orfeo' (The Auchinleck Manuscript), in *Old and Middle English c.890–c.1450: An Anthology*, 3rd Edition, ed. E. Treharne, Oxford: Wiley-Blackwell, 2009, pp. 550–563; also, 'Sir Orfeo', in *Medieval English Verse*, tr. B. Stone, Harmondsworth: Penguin, 1971, pp. 213–229.

31 J. Carey, 'Otherworld', in J. T. Koch (ed.), *Celtic Culture: A Historical Encyclopedia*, 5 vols., Santa Barbara, CA: ABC-CLIO, 2006, vol. 4, pp. 1403–1406.

32 See, for example, G. Herm, *The Celts*, London: Weidenfeld & Nicolson, 1976, p. 153.

33 See K.R.R. Gros Louis, 'The Significance of Sir Orfeo's Self-Exile', *The Review of English Studies* 18 (71), 1967, pp. 245–252.

34 Watling Street is an ancient British road, developed by the Romans, which went from Dover, through London, and then northwest to Wroxeter, in Shropshire (a major town under the Romans).

35 See stanzas 31 and 32. Henryson probably derived his understanding of music from Macrobius, *Commentary on the Dream of Scipio*, and perhaps also from Boethius, *De institutione musica* (The Fundamentals of Music).

Chapter 4

The Myth of Orpheus and Eurydice and the Exploration of Love

The Renaissance and Early Baroque

Politics rarely represent the best of an age. For a thousand years, Western Europe had been turned *inward*, claiming authority over a religion born under other skies—and in which authority has no place. With the Renaissance, this changed. Western Europe now turned *outward*. It exploded onto the world stage—often to the detriment of other cultures.

The Renaissance is characterised by an attitude of mad entitlement and fanatical intolerance, by aggressive competitiveness and constant wars, both civil and international.[1] It spans the final stages of the brutal 'reconquest' of Spain by Christian forces, the 'discovery' of the New World and the beginnings of the careless genocide of its native peoples, the growth of bitter divisions within Western Christianity (The Reformation and Counter-Reformation), and wars of a brutality that defies belief (the Dutch War of Independence, 1568–1648; about one million dead; the Thirty Years' War, 1618–1648; over four million dead).[2]

And yet, these same years also witness a sea-change for the better in European culture. The Renaissance and early baroque introduce the beginnings of a dynamic and individualistic *secular* culture which re-lays the foundations of Western values. Western Europe reinvents itself. And the myth of Orpheus and Eurydice plays a surprisingly important part in this revolution of concerns not only in the arts, but also in society.

This chapter looks at versions of the myth of Orpheus and Eurydice produced between 1460 and 1640—and they are characterised by increasing literary and psychological sophistication. The first part outlines the importance of the myth to the evolution of modern drama and opera. The second explores the association of Orpheus with the widespread cult of melancholy and lament. And the third considers two masterpieces from the Golden Age of Spanish drama.

Pastoral and the Exploration of Love

Pastoral was the heart of the Renaissance—and it served as the perfect genre for the exploration of human nature and, especially, for the analysis of all the many forms of love. Like myth, pastoral *invites* discussion—and readers were ready for this. Pastoral romances were the first 'bestsellers': from *Arcadia* (by Sannazaro, 1504)

DOI: 10.4324/9781003519584-6

to *Arcadia* (by Philip Sidney, 1581/1590). Pastoral dramas, such as Tasso's *Aminta* (1573), Guarini's *Il Pastor fido* (*The Faithful Shepherd*, 1585), and Shakespeare's *As You Like It* (1599) enjoyed extraordinary popularity—as did pastoral operas well into the eighteenth century (Handel, *Il Pastor fido*, 1712; Mozart, *Il Re pastore*, 1775). For 300 years, the privileged classes discussed the strengths and weaknesses of each character: their delights and disappointments, their intrigues and jealousies, and their betrayals and revenges.

And yet, ironically, this renewed interest in pastoral began with an unexpected, unwelcome, and improbable commission.

Poliziano's Favola: The First Play in a Modern European Language

While at the court of Lorenzo de' Medici in Florence, Poliziano (Agnolo Ambrogini) established his reputation as a classical scholar, and a poet of classical verse.[3] In 1480, he was asked by Cardinal Francesco Gonzaga, who was from Mantua, to write the libretto for a musical drama to celebrate a double family engagement. He was not flattered by the commission. He later claimed that he wrote it in only two days, surrounded by constant uproar. Be this as it may, the work he produced represents a turning point in European cultural history.

La Favola di Orfeo (*The Tale of Orpheus*, 1480; published 1494) is the first *pastoral* of the Renaissance; the first *play* written on an emphatically *secular* subject in a *modern* European language (Italian); and the first version of the myth to treat the love between Orpheus and Eurydice as if it were between ordinary human beings. It blends and adapts the stories told by Virgil and Ovid.[4] Although none of the original music has survived, its dominant form was that of a *strambotto* (a sophisticated 'rustic song' in which most of the dialogue was probably sung).[5]

Aristaeus, a young shepherd, tells Mopsus and Tirsus about his passion for Eurydice. Mopsus advises him to forget his infatuation. Eurydice enters, sees Aristaeus, and turns to exit. Aristaeus runs after her, begging her to believe in his love.

Orpheus enters, singing (in Latin) a tribute to Cardinal Francesco Gonzaga. When a shepherd rushes in to tell him that his 'most beautiful nymph is dead', he switches to Italian to express his loss.

There is a scene change. In the underworld, Orpheus begins a dirge for Eurydice. He then pleads with Pluto, Minos, and Proserpine to give her back to him. Proserpine forecasts the triumph of pity.

Orpheus is leading Eurydice out of Hades, so overjoyed that he reverts to Latin for verses borrowed from Ovid. He turns and is horrified to see Eurydice being drawn back into the underworld. She sings six lines based on those given to her by Virgil (they are all she gets in this early musical). Orpheus determines never to fall in love with another woman, for women are 'lighter than a leaf in the wind'.[6] Instead, he will find solace in the love of adolescent girls and boys. Angered by his words, Bacchantes chases Orpheus offstage and then return to announce he is dead.

But as the play was devised for a festive occasion, they quickly begin to celebrate with a comic drinking song to Bacchus.

Despite a few clever lines, the work is no masterpiece, and yet, it made a strong impression. For like myth, pastoral represents an 'other world', but with this crucial difference: the feelings expressed in pastoral are more strongly rooted in a social reality. They represent typical human feelings with which the audience can easily identify.

Poliziano's *Favola* represents the beginning of modern Western drama. A revival of about 1506, mounted to entertain the French ambassador to Milan, had designs by Leonardo da Vinci: it was the first time that a scene change was made in view of the audience.[7] Soon, purpose-built theatres began to be constructed throughout Italy (Ferrara, 1513; Rome, 1545), and then in cities elsewhere (Paris, 1548; Shoreditch/London, 1576).

Poliziano was a friend of Marsilio Ficino, a scholar who sought to align Catholic tradition with the 'eternal truth' contained in the writings of Orpheus, Pythagoras, Plato, and other 'ancient sages'.[8] His great achievement was to translate Plato's works into Latin (1484), thereby making many of his works available to Western European scholars for the first time. He was also a skilled performer on the lyre. Poliziano once complimented him for his contribution to the revival of classical (esp. Greek) learning with an audacious analogy:

> [Ficino's lyre], far more successful than the lyre of Thracian Orpheus, has brought back from the underworld what is, if I am not mistaken, the true Eurydice, that is, Platonic wisdom with its 'wide-ruling judgment'.[9]

That is, Poliziano likened the recovery of Greek philosophy from the neglect it had suffered during the Middle Ages to the myth of Orpheus and Eurydice, but with this difference. Orpheus failed in his undertaking. Ficino was successful in his.

Just over a century later, the myth of Orpheus and Eurydice became the subject of another new kind of musical drama: it soon became known as opera.

Peri's Euridice: The Earliest Surviving Opera

Opera arose in response to three specific needs: the need to explore the complexity of love (for which *pastoral* provided the perfect genre); the need to explore conflicting emotions (for which *drama* provided the perfect vehicle); and the desire to convey the intensity of these emotions (for which *music* provided the perfect medium). It began when the development of the overarching plot was mirrored by an equivalent development in the music.

The first opera was *Dafne* (1598). Its libretto was by Ottavio Rinuccini; its music by Jacopo Peri—but only fragments of it survive. Two years later, Ferdinando I Gonzaga invited the same team to produce a new work to mark the signing of the marriage contract between Maria de' Medici and Henry IV of France.

Euridice (1600) was first performed in a large room in the Palazzo Pitti, in Florence.[10] Its most striking innovation was clever, but awkward: Rinuccini has Venus (Love) lead Orpheus into the underworld. Key events are told by minor characters. Eurydice's death is *described* in a haunting half-aria by a friend (which begs comparison with Gertrude's report of how Ophelia drowns in *Hamlet*). Orpheus' grief, and his vision of Venus descending in her chariot to cheer him, is *described* by Arcetro. There is an over-dependence on recitative and half-arias, which means that the choruses provide the most interesting singing. As a result, the work is rarely performed today.

Nevertheless, Peri's *Euridice* is the earliest surviving opera. It successfully conveys the *dolci affeti* (sweet affections) of the protagonists. It is the first version of the myth to place the power of unshakeable human love at the heart of the myth. At the end, and far more convincingly than in Poliziano's *Favola*, Orfeo and Euridice emerge from the underworld alive. And this improbable *lieto fine* (= joyous ending) was to prove enormously influential.

Rivalry is endemic to opera, as it is to life. The success of *Euridice* prompted Francesco (the son of Vincenzo I Gonzaga, Duke of Mantua) to commission a new opera for a private performance in the family palace. It was to be on the *same* myth. But what a difference seven years can make! Whereas Peri's *Euridice* belongs to the Renaissance, Monteverdi's *Orfeo* belongs to the early baroque, which emphasises surprise, contrast, movement, and attention-grabbing detail.

Monteverdi's Orfeo: Words Enhanced by Music

Monteverdi's *Orfeo* is the earliest opera still regularly performed by all the great opera companies of the world. It is also the first version of the myth to illustrate the emotional development of Orpheus and of his turbulent feelings.

Claudio Monteverdi was born and grew up in Cremona, a town with a lively musical culture soon to become famous for its luthiers (violinmakers), including Nicolò Amati and Antonio Stradivari ('Stradivarius'). When only fifteen, he published his first motets (for three voices). In his early twenties, he entered the service of Vincenzo Gonzaga, who employed an ensemble of talented musicians. In his late twenties, he became their leader (*maestro di cappella*).

L'Orfeo was commissioned in 1606.[11] Its libretto is by Alessandro Striggio the Younger, and the opera was first performed at the family palace in Mantua during Carnival 1607, most probably in the Galleria dei Fiumi (Hall of the Rivers)—that is, for a small and highly privileged audience.

The libretto blends material from Poliziano's rendering with material from Rinuccini, but it has a far more coherent dramatic thrust than either. Like Shakespeare's *Antony and Cleopatra* (with which it is almost exactly contemporary), it foregrounds the intensity and development of the protagonist's feelings—and these feelings are heightened by *music*. The differences between *L'Orfeo* and earlier versions of the myth may appear small, but they represent a giant leap forward not only for opera, but also for the gradual evolution of the myth of Orpheus and Eurydice.

- In the Prologue, a personification of *Music* bids all be still while she tells the story of Orpheus. This foregrounds the importance of music to the work.
- Act 1 begins with shepherds and shepherdesses rejoicing at the coming wedding of Orpheus and Eurydice, and it has Orpheus sing of his happiness (*Rosa del ciel*). This gives the protagonists a stronger 'social' reality than any earlier version of the myth.
- The emphasis on Orpheus' happiness heightens the tragic moment when, in Act 2, he learns of Eurydice's death.
- In Act 3, Orpheus is guided toward the underworld by Hope (which underlines *human* motivation), but when they arrive at the gates of the underworld—on which are written the famous lines from Dante's *Inferno*, 'Abandon all hope you who enter' (*Lasciate ogni speranza voi ch'entrate*)—Hope must abandon him.[12] In a delicately orchestrated virtuoso aria, Orpheus persuades a reluctant Charon to carry him over the Styx (*Possente spirto* = O Mighty Spirit). This is immediately followed by his moving plea to the gods of the underworld (*Rendetemi il mio ben* = Give me back my darling).
- Act 4 follows the traditional story of the condition.
- Act 5 begins with a motif popular at the time: Orpheus is alone, singing of his despair, and his words are answered by Echo. When he vows to be true to Eurydice, Apollo appears from above (*deus ex machina*) and invites Orpheus to rise with him to Heaven where he can meet his Eurydice again. In the finale, shepherds and shepherdesses rejoice on his behalf.

In 1607, the opera ended in tragedy. The scene with Apollo was added in the revised score of 1609, resulting in an effect not unlike that produced by Shakespeare's so-called 'problem comedies' (*All's Well That Ends Well*, *Measure for Measure*). The events appear to be moving toward tragedy—until the introduction of the *deus ex machina*.

Monteverdi's Orfeo travels through a far broader spectrum of human emotions than any earlier rendering. They are all psychologically convincing human emotions, and each is brilliantly evoked in music. In the first act, he is blissfully happy. In the second, he is shattered by the news of Eurydice's death. In the third, his plea to the gods of the underworld is deeply moving. In the fourth, he sings a hymn to his lyre (i.e., to *music*), and his echo-aria in the fifth act is a masterpiece in the use of this device to convey deeply felt emotions. *L'Orfeo* represents one of the most memorable versions of the myth.[13]

A year after its success, Duke Vincenzo commissioned Monteverdi to write two works to celebrate the marriage of his son, Francesco Gonzaga, to Margaret of Savoy. Both had a libretto by Rinuccini, and one of these was *L'Arianna* (1608), an opera on the myth of Ariadne. All that survives of Monteverdi's music is the searing *Lament* sung by Ariadne after Theseus has abandoned her. It reflected the cult of *melancholy* with which Orpheus had already become associated.

Orpheus, Melancholy, and Lament

According to Huizinga, during the late Middle Ages, 'a sombre melancholy' weighed on people's souls, which he contrasts with the 'optimism' of the Renaissance.[14] But for all its vitality, the Renaissance produced a new fashion for sombre melancholy, as illustrated by Dürer's engraving, *Melencholia I* (1514).[15] Melancholy became a popular subject for poems, accompanied songs, and unaccompanied madrigals—and it was most often associated with disappointment in love. By the 1590s, in England, young men were commissioning miniature portraits of themselves in self-conscious melancholic poses: for example, Nicholas Hilliard's *Young Man Leaning against a Tree amongst Roses* (c.1590) or Isaac Oliver's *Young Man Seated under a Tree* (c.1592).[16]

Several of Shakespeare's best-loved songs are melancholic: for example, the haunting 'Come away, come away, death' (in *Twelfth Night*, 1601), or Desdemona's poignant 'Willow Song' (in *Othello*, 1604). And Orpheus is the subject of one of his best-loved songs.

Shakespeare: 'Orpheus with his Lute'

Shakespeare usually pokes fun at his male melancholics, such as Jacques (in *As You Like It*), and yet he almost always sympathises with his female melancholics: for example, Olivia (in *Twelfth Night*), the Queen (in *Henry the Eighth*), and with the Gaoler's daughter (in *The Two Noble Kinsmen*, written with John Fletcher).

King Henry the Eighth (1613), also written with John Fletcher, is Shakespeare's penultimate play. At the beginning of Act 3, the Queen (Katharine of Aragon) has failed to provide her husband with a male heir, and she is soon to be divorced. She asks one of her waiting women to console her with a song. Its subject is Orpheus and his ability to charm all nature with his music—the demi-god's oldest attribute. And yet, the context tells us that this is not Orpheus of ancient Greece; it is Orpheus who has emerged from the underworld without Eurydice and is mourning her death on a mountaintop.

The song is beguilingly simple, and yet deeply moving.

> Orpheus with his lute made trees,
> And the mountain tops that freeze
> Bow themselves when he did sing.
> To his music, plants and flowers
> Ever sprung, as sun and showers
> There had made a lasting spring.
>
> Everything that heard him play,
> E'en the billows of the sea,
> Hung their heads and then lay by.
> In sweet music is such art,

> Killing care of grief and heart—
> Fall asleep, or hearing, die.[17]

Shakespeare clearly empathises with the Queen: he wants the audience to feel her sadness for themselves, and to reflect on its cause. Several later English composers set the words to music, including Matthew Locke (1677), Ralph Vaughan Williams (1901), and the American composer William Schuman (1945).

Three years after Shakespeare's death, a version of the myth was published in Venice. It associates Orpheus with the related cult of the musical *lament*—and it is truly surreal.

Stefano Landi: Orpheus and the Importance of Music

Like most mannerist or early baroque art, Stefano Landi's *La Morte d'Orfeo* (*The Death of Orpheus*, 1619) is deliberately unsettling.[18] It is also both very amusing and deeply moving. It consists of a collage of scenes, *all* of which involve a lament.

The early acts describe *premonitions* that Orpheus is about to be killed. The first act contrasts the laments of Thetis and of three 'personifications' of nature (river, dawn, breezes).

In the second, while the gods celebrate Orpheus' birthday, Apollo worries about his son's fate.

In the third, the Maenads engage in a haunting echo-chorus: it begins with them regretting that they will no longer be charmed by Orpheus, and yet it ends with them urging his death. Whereupon shepherds lament the grief of all nature.

In the fourth act, Calliope laments the death of her son. In the last act, Orpheus arrives in the underworld, but on realising that Eurydice has forgotten him, he drinks from the river of oblivion.

In the finale, while shepherds (at stage level) rejoice that Orpheus *as god of music* still lives, the gods (from the balcony) welcome Orpheus to 'heaven', give him a cloak of stars, and pay homage to his function as demi-god of music.

The opera explores and celebrates the universal need for music—but with a poignant reminder that, all–too-often, we turn to music to express our deep-rooted sense of loss and longing.

A close contemporary of Landi was Sigismondo d'India (1582–1629). Although he wrote no large-scale works, he was a master of both the accompanied song and the unaccompanied madrigal. His fourth book of music for one and two voices includes the 'Lament of Orpheus' (1621), for which he wrote his own libretto.[19] It consists of a highly charged and dramatic recitative typical of the early baroque. Usually accompanied by a double harp, it is one of his finest works.[20] And its distinguishing characteristic is that Orfeo is *aware* that his hope is unlikely to be granted, which makes it strangely moving.

The final section of this chapter looks at adaptations of the myth by the two greatest dramatists of Spain's Golden Age. Both are conceptually breathtaking—and yet they could hardly be more different.

Orpheus in the Golden Age of Spain

In the sixteenth century, empowered by gold stolen from the 'New World', Spain briefly became the greatest European power. Following the secession of the Netherlands (1581), it went into a slow but steady decline, not because of its military or naval defeats, but because of its aristocratic contempt for the hustling, ruthless determination which was fuelling business enterprise in cities such as London and Amsterdam.

And yet, this very contempt for commerce may have helped its literary, artistic, and musical culture to reach new heights. For this was the age of Cervantes, Quevedo, and Saint John of the Cross; of El Greco and Velazquez; and of Tomás Luis Victoria, possibly the greatest composer of the Counter-Reformation. Most of the stolen gold was wasted; the cultural legacy continues to enrich the world.

In early seventeenth-century Spain, theatre had a distinctive social function.[21] Many of the most necessary social institutions (such as hospitals, homes for the elderly, and schools) were dependent on the support they received from theatre companies. This ensured a much greater civic involvement in theatre than anywhere else in Europe.

These years produced two extraordinary versions of the myth of Orpheus and Eurydice. Both give Aristaeus almost more importance than Orpheus, and both harbour unexpected and surprisingly 'modern' implications. The earlier is by an almost exact contemporary of Shakespeare.

Lope de Vega: From Infatuation to Constant Love

Lope de Vega (Lope Félix de Vega y Carpio) was a larger-than-life individual, and the range and extent of his literary achievement is jaw-dropping. He wrote epic poems (*La Dragontea*, 1598), pastoral romances (*Arcadia*, 1598), chivalric romances (*The Beauty of Angelica*, 1602, which is a three-volume sequel to Ariosto's *Orlando Furioso*), a narrative-fiction—*not* a play—related *entirely* in dialogue (Dorothy, 1632), and over 2,000 sonnets. Today, however, he is best known as the author of some 400 plays, of which between thirty and eighty are widely regarded as masterpieces (including *The Fraudulent Truth*, 1608; *The Nobleman from Olmedo*, 1621; and *Love in Love*, 1630).[22]

In *The Most Constant Husband* (*El marido más firme*, 1621), Lope de Vega turns to the myth of Orpheus and Eurydice to explore how an excessive infatuation with an idealised *image* of a contra-sexual other might cause the individual to lose their hold on reality.[23] Careful to allay the fears of the authorities, in his preface, he insists that his play has a Christian moral. Today, the reader is more likely to be intrigued by its psychological implications.

There are three acts, all of which unfold in rapid, witty, and pithy dialogue. Each is concerned with a different stage in a vividly imagined process. The first offers an intriguing analysis of infatuation. The second suggests that jealousy stems not from rivalry with a social other of the *same* sex, but from a person's misplaced infatuation with an *image of the opposite sex*. The third shows how emotional hurt (tragedy) can be averted by compromise.

As in Virgil's epyllion, the play hinges on the tension between a credible *social* reality and an emphatically *imaginal* reality. And the relation between them is complex.

Aristeo, the young king of Thrace, belongs to a social reality, but he has wandered into Arcadia, an imaginal reality. His ostensible purpose is to hunt; that is, to 'return into [himself]' (*volver en mi*) in the hope that he will learn something important about himself. By chance, he comes upon Eurídice and he immediately becomes infatuated with her. When Camilo chides him for his madness, telling him that he risks losing his crown (= his hold on his habitual social reality), he promptly sends his confidant back to Thrace to look after his kingdom, disguises himself as a farmhand (*labrador*), and seeks work with Claridano, an elderly shepherd with two children: Fílida and Albante. His objective is to win Eurídice for himself.

Fílida and Eurídice are friends, but they belong to different realities, and (to the spectator) *visibly* so. Fílida is a farmworker (*labradora*) who belongs to the 'social' reality of Arcadia (pastoral). In contrast, Eurídice is a nymph (*ninfa*), and dressed as such. She wears (reader, try not to laugh) 'a short sleeveless dress, a headscarf with feathers, and knee-length ancient Greek sandals with ribbons attached around her calves'—which signals that she belongs to the deeper reality of myth. Even *within* Arcadia, there are two 'levels' of reality.

Eurídice, a devotee of Diana, is upset because Venus has told her that her marriage will be 'short, enjoyable, and ill-fated (*breve, gustoso, perdido*)'. When Aristeo declares that he loves her, she promptly sends him packing. Her friend Fílida suggests that she consult Orfeo, a local musician and seer, and ask him to interpret Venus' warning. She fails to add that *she* is infatuated with Orfeo.

That is, both characters from a (quasi-credible) *social* reality (Aristeo, Fílida) are infatuated with characters who belong to an *imaginal* reality (Orfeo, Eurídice)—and their infatuation is immediately reflected in this reality. For, although Orfeo scorns the 'blind love' (*amor vendado* = infatuation/sexual desire) aroused by Venus, as soon as he and Eurídice see each other for the first time, they both *instantly* become infatuated with the other. She suggests that he 'call on her father' (= to arrange their marriage). That the happiness of Orpheus and Eurydice is fated to be short-lived suggests that Aristeo and Fílida need to rethink their misplaced infatuations.

The wedding ceremony of Orfeo and Eurídice explains their error. A wall bearing a large portrait (= *image*) of the actress playing the part of Eurídice collapses. Aristeo and Fílida ponder the implications. Both realise that they have been relating only to an *image* in their own imagination—and yet, neither can control their desire. As they join forces to achieve their separate aims, Aristeo realises that his infatuation has made him 'a stranger to himself, a hunter lost in a forest'.[24] That is, to be infatuated is not to be 'in love'; it is to lose one's better self. Both Aristeo and Fílida become aware of their jealousy.

The second act explores the destructive nature of jealousy—not in relation to love, but in relation to *infatuation*. Eurídice admits that she has no idea what jealousy is, whereupon Fílida sets out to teach her by telling her that Orpheus is infatuated with *her*. She then tells Eurídice where she can meet Orfeo. It is a trap. Aristeo appears. Eurídice promptly turns to leave and is bitten by an asp. Orfeo arrives just in time to hear her say she has been killed by 'jealousy'. As Orfeo lifts her to take her to a sage, in the hope he can do something, he notes 'I am carrying her, and yet it feels as if *she* is carrying me in her arms'.[25] This represents how Aristeo's infatuation with Eurídice has caused him to lose his grip on reality.

The third act explains how Aristeo and Fílida are persuaded to recover their finer qualities and to recognise that *they* are suited to each other. It begins with Orfeo (who personifies Aristeo's mistaken attitudes) delivering a long, painful lament. He has clearly gone mad. He determines to recover his 'soul'. Fílida realises that her love for Orpheus is hopeless, and yet, she still encourages Aristeo to wait to see whether Orfeo returns from the underworld with Eurídice—all the while, hoping that he will emerge alone.

This further 'madness' is reflected by the return of Albante (Fílida's brother) to Arcadia. He is determined to kill Aristeo, whom he believes has 'compromised' his sister by not proposing to her. Fabio promptly reappears from the underworld, followed by Orfeo. Whereupon Aristeo and Albante enter, fighting. Despite his madness, Orfeo devises the way to stop the fighting. He suggests that Aristeo marry Fílida—and the play ends with him promising the audience 'the second part' of the play.

Like Virgil, Lope de Vega relates the myth to Aristeo; and like Ovid, he explores the role that manipulation plays in seeking what we desire. *The Most Constant Husband* is the first version of the myth to *analyse* distinct aspects of desire. It also harbours two intriguing theories. The first is about the nature of jealousy. The play suggests that jealousy is stirred not by a possible rivalry with a *social* other, but by an inappropriate infatuation with an idealised *image* of the contra-sexual other. The second is about what defines a lasting relationship. For the play illustrates the *process* by which Aristeo gradually comes to realise that what he felt for Eurídice was only infatuation, and to recognise that he loves (or might come to love) Fílida. The plot unfolds in fours distinct stages:

1 Aristeo and Fílida fall in love with mythic images (Eurídice and Orfeo).
2 The two mythic images (Orfeo and Eurídice) represent an *unshakeable* bond.
3 As soon as they realise this, Aristeo and Fílida renounce their misplaced infatuations.
4 Aristeo and Fílida agree to marry.

The play implies that a lasting 'marriage' cannot be built on infatuation, compatible or otherwise. Jung would later develop this point. He argues that an intimate relationship between two individuals must be complemented by the compatibility of the deeply rooted *images/notions* that they have about the other.[26]

Sadly, we do not know why Lope de Vega never wrote 'the second part'. Was it because he lost interest in the characters of Aristeo and Fílida? Or because he could not imagine how to relate the next stage in their relationship to the myth of Orpheus and Eurydice? Or because he could not imagine how to bring about a reunion of Orfeo and Eurídice?

Thirteen years later, a younger contemporary, already making a name for himself as a poet, achieved his first major success as a dramatist with an equally unexpected and breathtaking version of the myth of Orpheus and Eurydice.

Calderón: Eurídice and the Creation, Fall, and Redemption of Humankind

Calderón de la Barca was almost forty years younger than Lope de Vega. Between 1625 and 1642, he served in the Spanish army, including in Italy and Flanders. During these years, he wrote about seventy plays, including *Life is a Dream* (1635), widely regarded as one of the finest plays of the century.[27]

He also became famous for his *autos sacramentales*, short plays written to be performed during Corpus Christi (a Catholic festival, held to celebrate the real presence of Christ in the Eucharist). They were 'street theatre', usually performed on a temporary stage in a public square. Calderón's *The Great Theatre of the World* (1630s) is one of the best-known examples of the genre.

Another is *The Divine Orpheus* (*El Divino Orfeo*, 1634), a pastoral drama which recasts the myth of Orpheus and Eurydice as an allegory of nothing less than the Creation, the Fall, and the Redemption of humankind. It has one act, composed of three scenes and an epilogue.[28]

The first scene re-imagines the Creation. Orfeo (a fusion of God *and* Christ) begins to create the world through *song*. After each stage of the creation, Aristeo (Satan as courtly devil) provides an ironic comment. On the sixth day—instead of God creating 'man' and then fashioning 'woman' from one of man's ribs—Orfeo sings:

> Let human nature
> Be formed in my own image!
> Come, my spouse, to my cottage
> Where everyone will serve you.[29]

That is, Orfeo creates Eurídice (who represents not only *all* of humankind, but also human nature) and identifies her as his 'spouse' (which reworks the tradition that the church, as community of believers, is the 'bride' of Christ). He invites her into his *cabaña*, a word which, in Spanish, can mean both 'cabin' (cottage) *and* a large flock (for example, of sheep). That is, Orfeo as divine shepherd is inviting human beings both into his home *and* to join his flock.

Eurídice is dressed as a farmhand (*labradora*). She is accompanied by two shepherdesses, Love and Grace, who are followed by Albedrío, a rustic who personifies Freewill. The heart of the scene is a lengthy discussion between Love, Grace, and Albedrío about *free will*. Orfeo will neither dictate nor even advise what Eurídice should do. She must choose for herself. In other words, human beings *must be free to choose*.

The second scene is set in the Garden of Eden. Aristeo tells Albedrío that he is a shepherd who has been sent into exile. Although Albedrío distrusts both him and his story, he agrees to introduce Aristeo to Eurídice. Almost a quarter of the play consists of the story that Aristeo devises to try to seduce Eurídice. But as soon as he speaks ill of Orfeo, Eurídice refuses to listen further and exits.

While Aristeo hides in a tree (= becomes a serpent), Grace and Albedrío quarrel. Grace thinks that Eurídice should reject the fruit; Albedrío (Freewill) thinks she should accept it. Eurídice returns and is promptly bitten by the 'serpent', which she now realises is Aristeo. Orfeo enters and mourns his loss, whereupon Love tells him to rescue her using a harp, shaped like a cross, made from the wood of the tree which brought about her death.

The third scene is set in the underworld, and it rests on the notion that Christ so loved the world that he came into it to save sinners (1 Timothy 1: 15; cf. John 3: 16.). Aristeo enters and explains that in the underworld he is called Plutón (Pluto). Aqueronte (Charon) finally allows Orfeo to pass. The descent of Orfeo into the underworld is equated with the descent of Christ into Hell. Orfeo now appears on a cross, high above the stage, and asks Plutón to return Eurídice. When Plutón refuses, Orfeo has no difficulty freeing her with his song. The suggestion is that the spiritual beauty of the Christian message (the song of Orpheus) is so great that Eurídice doesn't hesitate before choosing it. When Plutón warns her that she must not look back, Orfeo reassures her. He will *always* be there for her—and for all human beings—contained in the host and the chalice, to guide her into eternal light.

There is a brief coda in which Aristeo is swallowed by a serpent and sinks into Hell, which implies that Satan has lost his hold on human nature.

The Divine Orpheus is an extraordinary reworking of classical myth into Christian polemic.[30] It is arguably the most audacious version of the myth to date, for by emphasising that humans must be *free* to accept Christ's love, he produced one of the most striking and *progressive* works of the Counter-Reformation. For even more emphatically than Dante, it underlines the need for human beings to be *free* to *choose* whether to accept God or not. And in marked contrast with medieval versions of the myth, Calderón invests this responsibility in Eurídice—a *female* character.

Conclusion

After almost a thousand years of philosophical and religious allegory, Western Europe rediscovered a taste for a sophisticated *secular* culture. Pastoral played a key part in this development. So too did the myth of Orpheus and Eurydice, which provided the subject for the first pastoral, the first play written in a modern European language, and for two of the first three operas. It also provided a structure of metaphors for writers and musicians to explore melancholy, a form of depression which was often associated with the pain of loss and longing that stemmed from disappointment in love. And it provided other astonishing metaphors—whether for the intellectual endeavour of the Renaissance, or for the re-imagining of the Creation, Fall, and Redemption of humankind. In a similar fashion, it also provided the perfect genre for the exploration of human love: for desire and deception, for instinct and manipulation, and for longing and loss. And these quickly grew in sophistication: from Peri to Monteverdi, and from Landi to Lope de Vega.

By 1634, however, the early baroque was evolving into a new age—an age characterised by radically new tendencies.

Notes

1 The term *renaissance* is surprisingly recent. It was first adopted by Jules Michelet in *Histoire de France:* vol. 7: *Renaissance*, Paris: Chamerot, 1855 and, soon after, by Jacob Burckhardt in *Die Cultur der Renaissance*. Basel: Schweighauser, 1860. The notion of a 'northern renaissance' was not widely accepted until after an exhibition of 'The Early Flemish Primitives' in Bruges (1902).

2 M. Clodfelter, *Warfare and Armed Conflicts: A Statistical Encyclopedia of Casualty and Other Figures , 1492–2015*, 4th ed. Jefferson, NC: McFarland & Co, 2017, p. 17; P. H. Wilson, *Europe's Tragedy: A History of the Thirty Years War*, London: Allen Lane, 2009, pp. 787 and 791.

3 See A. Poliziano, *Greek and Latin Poetry*, tr. Peter E. Konx. Cambridge, MA: Harvard University Press, 2018.

4 For text: Angelo Politian & Torquato Tasso, *'Orpheus' and 'Aminta'*, tr. Louis E. Lord, London: Oxford University Press, 1931; CD recording: *La Favola di Orfeo* (with music by Serafino d'all Aquilano, Bartolomeo Tromboncino, Marco Cara, and Michele Pesenti), Huelgas Ensemble, cond. Paul van Nevel, New York: RCA Victor, 1982.

5 See N. Pirrotta and E. Povoledo, *Music and Theatre from Poliziano to Monteverdi*, tr. K. Eales. Cambridge: Cambridge University Press, 1982.

6 Francesco Maria Piave famously reworked this phrase in Verdi's *Rigoletto*: 'La donna è mobile/Qual piuma al vento' (Woman is more changeable than a feather in the wind).

7 See, Leonardo da Vinci, Codex Arundel 263, folios 321*v* and 224*r*, British Library, London.

8 M. Ficino, *Platonic Theology*. Theologia platonica, 1482: see J. Hankins, *Plato in the Italian Renaissance*, 2 vols., Leiden: Brill, 1989, pp. 300–318.

9 Quoted by J. Warden, 'Orpheus and Ficino', in J. Warden (ed.), *Orpheus: The Metamorphoses of a Myth*, Toronto: University of Toronto Press, 1982, p. 86.

10 Recording (CD): Jacopo Peri. *Euridice*, Ensemble Arpeggio, cond. Roberto de Caro. Arts Music GMBH, 1992/1995. For the first performance, see T. Carter and F. Fantappiè, *Staging 'Euridice': Theatre, Sets, and Music in Late Renaissance Florence*, Cambridge: Cambridge University Press, 2021.

11 See J. Whenham, ed. *Claudio Monteverdi: 'Orfeo'*, Cambridge: Cambridge University Press, 1986; recordings: (on DVD) Monteverdi, *L'Orfeo*, dir. J-P. Ponnelle, with Monteverdi Ensemble of the Zurich Opera House, cond. N. Harnoncourt, Unitel/Deutsche Grammophon, 1978/2006; (on CD) cond. C. Cavina, with La Venexiana (Glossa (Belgium), 2007.

12 Dante, *Inferno*, Canto 3.

13 And yet, *L'Orfeo* fell victim to the rapidly changing taste of the seventeenth century. It was not until 1834 that scholars began to rediscover Monteverdi, and not until 1911 that his operas once again began to be performed.

14 J. Huizinga, *The Waning of the Middle Ages*, London: Pelican Books, 1922, p. 31.

15 Dürer produced two states, numbered *I* and *II*. Numerous copies of the engraving exist, for example in the British Museum (London) and the Albertina (Vienna). The most influential reading of the work is still *Erwin Panofsky, The Life and Art of Albrecht Dürer* (1943), 4th ed., Princeton: Princeton University Press, 1955, pp.156–171.

16 The Hilliard is in the Victoria and Albert Museum, London; the Oliver is in the (British) Royal Collection.

17 Shakespeare, *King Henry VIII*, Act 3, scene 2'.

18 Recording (CD): Stefano Landi, *La Morte d'Orfeo*, Tragicomedia and Currende, dir. Stephen Stubbs, on Accent (ACC 8746/47 D), 1987.

19 *Le Musiche del Cavalier Sigismondo D'India a 1 et 2 voci, libro quarto* (1621); recording: Sigismondo d'India, *Lamento d'Orfeo*. Nigel Rogers, tenor. London: Virgin Classics, 1992.

20 A harp with two parallel rows of strings: the first, playing a diatonic scale; the second, the pentatonic scale, thereby enabling a full chromatic sound.

21 J. Thacker, *A Companion to Golden Age Theatre*, Woodbridge, Suffolk: Tamesis, 2007; also, E.A. Cowling, T. de Miguel Magro, et al. (eds.), *Social Justice in Spanish Golden Age Theatre*, Toronto: University of Toronto Press, 2020.

22 A.W. Samson and J.W. Thacker (eds.), *A Companion to Lope de Vega*, Woodbridge, Suffolk: Tamesis, 2008.

23 F. Lope de Vega y Carpio, *El marido más firme*, Barcelona: Linkgua ediciones, 2014; also, S.C. Ausín, *Edición de 'El marido más firme' de Lope de Vega para alumnos de Educación Secundaria Obligatoria*, tesis doctoral, Logroño, Spain: Universidad de la Rioja, 2014.

24 S. Camarero Ausín, *Edición de El Marido más firme para alumnos de Educación Secundaria Obligatoria*, Logroño: Universidad de la Rioja, 2014, p. 238, my translation.

25 S. Camarero Ausín, *Edición de El Marido más firme para alumnos de Educación Secundaria Obligatoria*, Logroño: Universidad de la Rioja, 2014, p. 316, my translation.

26 Jung called this the 'marriage quaternio', see C.G. Jung, 'The Psychology of the Transference' (1946), *CW* vol. 16, pp. 163–323.

27 R. Norton and J.W. Thacker (eds.), *A Companion to Calderón de la Barca*, Woodbridge, Suffolk: Tamesis, 2021.

28 See P. León, 'Orpheus and the Devil in Calderón's *El divino Orfeo* c.1634', in J. Warden (ed.), *Orpheus: The Metamorphoses of a Myth*, Toronto: University of Toronto Press, 1982, pp. 183–206.

29 Calderón de la Barca, *El divino Orfeo: Versión de 1634*, ed. J. Enrique Duarte, Pamplona: Universidad de Navarra, 1999, p. 5, my translation.

30 Calderón thoroughly revised his play in 1663, in which version it was, until recently, better known.

Chapter 5

The Myth of Orpheus and Eurydice and Social, Personal, and Political Concerns

The Late Baroque and the Age of Sensibility

In Europe, the years 1640–1800 witnessed a series of dramatic shifts in the balance of power. The Treaty of Westphalia (1648) sealed the decline of Spain, broke the power of the Holy Roman Empire, gave greater autonomy to the German states, independence to the Netherlands, control of the Baltic to Sweden, and it paved the way for the rise of three new maritime powers: Holland, France, and Great Britain.

The founding of the Dutch East India Company (1602), and of stock exchanges in London (1669) and Paris (1724), promoted opportunism and exploitation. Merchants and others laid claim to lands on which they had never set sight. Overseas plantations made increasing use of slaves: a practice made possible by ruthless sellers (the African slave trade), even if fuelled by buyers (the European slave trade). Entrepreneurs and shareholders enriched themselves beyond their wildest dreams. It was the coming-of-age of *homo economicus* (economic man); that is, of a person whose desire for financial gain brushes aside all moral considerations. Their shenanigans were approved by political theorists, who argued that, however dubious an enterprise might be, successful self-interest contributes to the public good (increase of trade, expansion of markets, greater prosperity for all).[1] It was not long before the new mercantile powers sought to monopolise the markets they had opened. This led to the first 'world war': the Seven Years' War (1756–1763), which was fought not only in Europe, but also in the Americas, Africa, India, and South-East Asia.

These developments provide the background to the age of reason and the enlightenment, a time when the foundations of the modern world were re-laid. For the booming economy and increased prosperity promoted new ideas and concerns. They triggered a rapid advance in science, the beginnings of the agricultural revolution, and, toward the end of these years, the beginnings of the industrial revolution. They also triggered a huge expansion of literacy, the emergence of a new middle class, and, in government, the beginnings of (two-party) political debate.

This chapter looks at versions of the myth of Orpheus and Eurydice produced during a time which witnessed not only the first literary works to show a sustained interest in social and political concerns, but also the first works to explore the complexity of individual feelings. It is in two parts. The first part looks at a selection of versions of the myth produced during the late baroque (the age of reason),

DOI: 10.4324/9781003519584-7

with a focus on two new developments: the first version of the myth to foreground a social concern, and the first version to use the myth as a foil to explore powerful female desire. The second part explores versions of the myth produced during the age of sensibility (the enlightenment), with a focus on two developments: the new importance given to Eurydice in Gluck's immensely influential opera, and the first version of the myth to harbour a political concern.

The Late Baroque (the Age of Reason)

The late baroque lacked all modesty. It was an age of land-grab and indecent social disparity. The wealthy lived in 'splendid isolation' from the realities of their nations, while those whom they dispossessed either became their servants and lacqueys, or else drifted toward a neighbouring city, where they often fared even worse.

Wealth, however, did trickle down. And it was from the new middle classes that came the landmark thinkers of the age of reason (1640–1740). They established some of the foundational principles of the modern world: the importance of empirical argument (Descartes), the laws of motion and gravity (Newton), and the need for 'declared and received laws' to protect individuals against absolutism and to guarantee religious toleration (John Locke). These years also see the first well-argued and sustained demands for greater political equality.

Meanwhile, the myth of Orpheus and Eurydice remained firmly associated with pastoral. Even so, artists and writers now turned to the myth to express new concerns, both personal and social. One of the earliest to do so was a French painter who turned to landscape to express a *personal* feeling.

Nicolas Poussin: Orpheus and Intimations of Mortality

To a modern sensibility, early visual illustrations of Orpheus can be disappointing. During the late Middle Ages, Orpheus began to feature in woodcuts and illuminated manuscripts. During the Renaissance, he became the subject of oil paintings. In the 1630s, there was a vogue for scenes of him playing to animals, of him pleading with Proserpine and Hades, and of his death.[2] Few of these early representations of Orpheus 'speak' to us today.

In contrast, Nicolas Poussin's *Orpheus and Eurydice* remains strangely haunting, not because it illustrates a forgotten scene from Virgil's account of the myth (which it does not), but because it represents a curious combination of melancholy and contented nostalgia, of loss and longing—in other words, of a complex *mood* which the painter associated with the myth.[3]

Poussin was from Normandy (northern France). As a young man, he went to Paris where he worked in several studios. In 1624, on his third attempt, he finally succeeded in getting to Rome, where he settled. He painted brightly lit and lively mythological and religious works which he sold to wealthy aristocrats while they were on their Grand Tour. In his late forties, he turned to landscape painting. He painted these in a studio, composed from sketches made earlier, usually outdoors.

In the foreground, at either left or right, or both, there is usually a part of a tree or a building which serves to direct the viewer's gaze into the centre of the composition (a technique called *repoussoir*). And in the middle distance, there is almost always a group of figures which he associates with a myth.

It is uncertain when exactly he painted *Orpheus and Eurydice*. A probable date is about 1648; that is, when the artist was approaching his mid-fifties. The painting uses the framing device of a late-afternoon sky and lengthening shadows to draw the eye into a sun-lit meadow on which Orpheus is playing his lyre to a group of four figures. Their upper bodies are bathed in light, but their feet are already wrapped in evening shadow. Behind a standing man, Eurydice has just noticed a snake—too late to escape it. And beneath the tree on the right are two garlands, suggesting the tragedy occurs on her wedding day. Eugène Delacroix later wrote that the painting 'brilliantly and movingly captures the eternal opposites of joy and sorrow'.[4]

More to the point, it revisits a theme that Poussin had already explored in two earlier works, both called *Et in Arcadia Ego* (*Even in Arcadia am I*): that is, even in an idealised pastoral world, human beings are subject to Death. *Orpheus and Eurydice* is another *memento mori* (*A Reminder of Death*), but with an important difference.[5] The wistful melancholy conveyed by the impending death of Eurydice cannot efface the sun-lit moment. It suggests that the painter was aware that his life was now slowly drawing to its close (= loss), but also that he feels able to withstand any sudden tragedy which might befall him, perhaps because he is hopeful (long-ing?), or even confident, that his *art* will survive.

Meanwhile, an opera performed in Paris the previous year was the first version of the myth to include a sustained attack on *abusive social behaviour*.

Buti and Rossi: Calling Out Abusive Social Behaviour

When Louis XIII died, aged only 41, he left instructions to ensure that his wife, the Spanish-born Anne of Austria, would *not* become regent. She quickly ensured that she did, and she appointed the Italian-born Cardinal Mazarin as her first minister. He promptly commissioned the first major Italian opera to be performed in Paris.[6] Francesco Buti supplied the libretto, and Luigi Rossi, the music.

Orfeo was designed to impress. It requires an unusually large orchestra and a large cast of soloists. It was first performed in March 1647, in the original theatre of the Palais-Royal.[7] Sung in Italian, it lasts about three and a half hours. With inter-missions, the premiere lasted *six* hours and it was attended by the entire court—including the nine-year old Louis XIV, for whom the subject could not have been more inappropriate.

Like Virgil's epyllion, *Orfeo* rests on the relation between an almost credible *social* reality and an *imaginal* reality. But now, for the first time, the *social real-ity* is represented by the three protagonists of the Augustan myth (Aristeo, Orfeo, Euridice, also her father and her nurse) and the reality of *myth* is represented by other mythic figures (Venus, Cupid, Jove, Juno, Apollo, etc.).

Aristeo is determined to seduce Euridice, but she has no interest in him. As a result, he is sulking. When he asks Venus for her help, she insists that he stop moaning and *look the part* of a lover. When he blames Cupid for having wounded him with his arrows, Cupid retorts that the only person that he has ever wounded is *himself*.[8] The implication is clear: desire is not instilled by a mischievous God, nor is it irresistible. It is a *human* emotion which everyone must learn to deal with in a responsible fashion.

The machinations of Aristeo and Venus are contrasted with the starry-eyed love of Orfeo and Euridice, both of whom see the *other* as the soul of their *own* soul. The contrast is amplified by two rivalries in the mythic world. The first is traditional. Juno, guardian of fidelity and marriage (but also a friend of Momus, an unsavoury backbiter) is determined to save Orfeo and Euridice. Venus, who personifies sexual desire (and is a friend of the lecherous and sardonic satyr) is equally determined to help Aristeo. The second rivalry is unexpected, for the opera sets Venus (as goddess of sexual desire) against her son, *Amore* (= love; Cupid's name in Italian). Rather than betray the 'true love' (*un vero affetto*) between Orfeo and Euridice, Cupid chooses to defend them—in other words, to take arms *against* his mother.

In the second act, Aristeo and Venus, who is disguised as an old bawd, are planning how to seduce Euridice. When Euridice once again rejects Aristeo and leaves to go to a temple, Venus sings a rollicking bawdy aria in which she explains that the only way to avoid the upsets of love is to change your lover daily (*Amanti, se bramate*). Meanwhile, Euridice sings that for as long as she has Cupid on her side, she is unafraid of Venus. This bravado, or insolence, is immediately punished: she is bitten by a snake. She rejects the help of Aristeo, and her last thoughts are of Orfeo.

In Act 3, Orfeo asks the Three Fates (the dreaded *Moirai/Parcae*) to re-tie the thread of Euridice's life. They cannot. Instead, they offer to lead him to the underworld. Meanwhile, Euridice's Shade (= ghost) appears to Aristeo and roundly expresses her loathing of his conduct (*Empio, e pur vivi?*). He goes mad.

Meanwhile, Venus and Juno carry their tiff to the underworld. Orfeo sings of his loss (*Amor m'è scorta*) and everyone is subdued. There is a ballet, during which the audience is allowed to assume that he and Eurydice have escaped the underworld. Then Charon announces that, at the last moment, Orfeo turned and forfeited her. Meanwhile, Venus tells Bacchus that his son, Aristeo, has committed suicide. In revenge, Bacchus instructs his 'nymphs' to kill Orfeo, who now enters, hoping to die (*Lasciate Averno*). A chorus sings the depressing moral: 'In this ever-changing world where every good is ephemeral, true love and good faith can hope for no reward'. Whereupon Jove intercedes, raises Orfeo's lyre to eternal glory, and changes Orfeo and Euridice into stars.

Rossi's *Orfeo* was commissioned for a political purpose: to awe the nobles and to cement Mazarin's position. Nevertheless, the libretto harbours some important new concerns. It foregrounds ribaldry, illicit longing, jealousy, suspicion, and vindictive revenge. It is the first version of the myth to tackle a social problem. It suggests that the predatory behaviour of privileged young men is both socially unacceptable and psychologically harmful not only to the deceived woman, but also, if he has any conscience, to the seducer (Aristeo goes mad and commits suicide). It suggests that, without the devious stratagems devised by Venus (= compulsive erotic desire), there might be 'Paradise on Earth'.

The next major version of the myth of Orpheus and Eurydice also uses it as a foil to explore predatory desire, but with an unexpected gender reversal. The predatory desire belongs to Queen Orasia, an older woman, and the object of her desire is Orpheus, a young musician whom she employs at her court.

Du Boullay and Telemann: Orpheus as Foil to an Unrestrained Passion

During his life, Georg Philipp Telemann enjoyed far greater success than his contemporary, Johann Sebastian Bach. In 1721, aged forty, he moved to Hamburg, a bustling multilingual commercial centre. The following year, he became music director of the Hamburg Opera, for which he composed numerous works.[9]

They include *Orpheus: or the Wonderful Constancy of Love* (1726).[10] Its *plot* is derived from an earlier French opera with a libretto by Michel du Boullay.[11] But the words of its arias are borrowed from *other* works—and they are left in the original languages of the operas from which they are borrowed, whether German, Italian, or French. All the music, however, is by Telemann, who delights in veering between the different musical traditions that each aria suggests.[12]

The plot borrows from Racine's *Phèdre* (1677). Orasia, Queen of Thrace (viz. Phaedra), is smouldering with desire for Orpheus (viz. Hippolytus), a recently married singer at her court. She has Eurydice killed, assuming that she can now have her way with Orpheus. Horrified, he flees to the countryside. Meanwhile, his friend Eurimedes proposes to Cephisa, who rejects him. He then advises Orpheus to see if he can reclaim Eurydice from the underworld.

While Orpheus persuades Pluto to free Eurydice, Ascalax (Pluto's confidant) tells Eurydice that Orasia was responsible for her death. He also tells her the condition. But as Orpheus and Eurydice are about to leave the underworld, he turns. He emerges from the underworld alone to find Orasia waiting for him. When he angrily repulses her, she orders her Bacchantes to tear him apart. No sooner have they done so, however, than distraught, she determines to commit suicide.

The opera's implications are intriguing. A *male* author (du Boullay) imagines the burning passion, hypocritical wheedling, uncertainty, and anger of one *female* character (Orasia) as detrimental to another, whom she has killed (Eurydice); that is, as responsible for the latter's confinement to an underworld. Not until the twentieth century is a comparable experience explored by a *woman* (pp. 101–102).

Although the opera is based on a *renaissance* commonplace (the court = devious stratagems; the country = innocence) and foregrounds *baroque* emotions, it also anticipates values more often associated with the *enlightenment*. For example, when Eurimedes (a friend of Orpheus) proposes to Cephisa, she rejects him *not* because she is 'a follower of Diana', but because, to marriage, she prefers her independence (her 'freedom', German *Freiheit*; although when her attendants celebrate her decision, they sing in French, *N'aimons que la liberté*). In similar fashion, in the underworld, although Pluto is afraid that Orpheus might be leading a political insurrection against him, he is so moved by Orpheus' humble plea (*Trà speranza, e trà timore*) that he allows Eurydice to join him. And yet, as soon as Eurydice joins Orpheus, she *chides* him for wishing to exact revenge on Orasia. That is, the opera anticipates concerns which became associated with the age of sensibility.

The Age of Sensibility (the Enlightenment)

The age of sensibility and enlightenment spans the years 1740–1800—and it can be characterised by two developments.

The first was the beginning of a sustained concern with the abuse of privilege, with social and gender inequality, and above all, with the importance of education. Francis Hutcheson wrote about 'unalienable' rights (1725).[13] Montesquieu argued for a separation of government powers (*The Spirit of the Laws*, 1748). And in a bestselling work of 1760, targeted at 'young ladies', Madame Le Prince de Beaumont challenged the male stranglehold on education: 'Yes, you tyrant men, my aim is to rescue women from the crass ignorance to which you have condemned them … I want to teach them to think, to think correctly, in order to help them to live better'.[14]

In short, writers were beginning to challenge outdated social and political assumptions, and the increasing number of newspapers helped to spread their views. A new interest in the dignity of *all* human beings led to the American Declaration of Independence (1776), to the challenge to absolutist government which culminated in the French Revolution (1789–1799), and to the birth of political radicalism in the British Parliament (Whig politics of the 1790s; Thomas Paine, *Rights of Man*, 1791).

The second development of the time was a rapid expansion of interest in the nature, value, and complexity of subjective experience—whether in a person's private thoughts and feelings (Hume, *An Enquiry Concerning Human Understanding*, 1748; Rousseau, *Julie, or The New Heloise*, 1761), in the education of a child's individual personality (Rousseau's *Emile*, 1762), in the power of the imagination (Baumgarten, Goethe, early romanticism), or in individual 'sensibility' (Mackenzie, Jane Austen).

For the privileged, the enlightenment was an age of leisure—and their leisure promoted the development of three new art forms, all of which stirred new kinds of inwardness. All three were designed both to *relax* and to *stimulate* the senses: that is, to foster reflection and critical discussion. The new middle class soon clamoured to enjoy all three.

The first was the English *landscaped garden*, which promoted a taste for 'nature'—albeit a nature produced by considerable (low-paid) human labour: for example, at Stowe, by William Kent (1730s), at Chatsworth, by Capability Brown (1760s), and at Woburn Abbey, by Humphrey Repton (1770s). The fashion for such 'parks' soon spread through much of Europe, and some soon opened to the public (Janko Kráľ Park in Bratislava, Slovakia, 1776; Parc Monceau in Paris, 1778).[15]

The second was the cult of complex and refined *music*, which led to a new emphasis on originality and technical perfection (C.P.E. Bach), and which found its apogee in the piano sonatas, string quartets, and symphonies of Haydn, Mozart, and Beethoven. Works commissioned for performance in the elegant reception rooms of the privileged soon began to be performed in theatres and concert halls open to the public, such as the Burgtheater in Vienna (from 1741), and the Rotunda in Ranelagh Gardens (from 1742), both of which quickly became fashionable.

The third was the *literature of sensibility*, including the poetry of Edward Young, Thomas Gray, and James Macpherson, and the modern novel, which (in contrast with Renaissance pastorals) were usually set in a contemporary social world. Its two predominant concerns were the relation between *sensibility* and *character* (Prévost, *Manon Lescaut*, 1731; Rousseau, *Julie, or The New Heloise*, 1761; and Goethe, *The Sorrows of Young Werther*, 1774/1787) and the desire to challenge misguided *social* and *political* attitudes (Lessing, Emilia Galotti, 1772; Godwin, *Things as They Are: The Adventures of Caleb Williams*, 1794).

All three of these new aesthetic forms helped to trigger new kinds of private pleasure and to increase the valorisation of inwardness. And how individuals responded to them soon became an important aspect of their personality.

These pages explore the influence of the values of sensibility and the enlightenment on versions of the myth of Orpheus and Eurydice. The first section takes a close look at Gluck's hugely influential opera; the second explores a selection of works influenced by this opera; and the third considers an unexpected concern in an unfinished opera by Haydn.

Calzabigi and Gluck: Orpheus and Music to Pierce the Heart

In the mid-1740s, Christoph Willibald Gluck visited London, where he admired the acting of David Garrick. The English actor-manager was already famous for adopting a more natural and psychologically persuasive performance style: he wanted acting to 'pierce the heart and humanise the mind'.[16] His views were soon taken up by all the dramatic arts. Gluck, meanwhile, continued composing full-length operas, none of which develops the influence of Garrick, and almost all of which have passed into history. Admiration alone is never enough.

Ranieri de' Calzabigi was an unscrupulous chancer with a gift for responding to the moment. Soon after arriving in Vienna, at a time when Rousseau's *Julie* was a runaway bestseller, he met Gluck and produced a libretto for a new opera which invited performers to act as if they sought to 'pierce the heart' of their audience.

Orfeo ed Euridice was first performed in 1762, in Italian, at the Burgtheater in Vienna—and it is of course a pastoral.[17] It has a single, straightforward plot focussed on Orfeo. The only other characters are Euridice (soprano), who has one major aria, and *Amore* (Love/Cupid, sung by a high 'soubrette' soprano), who has two shorter ones. Although often described as the first of Gluck's 'reform operas', neither Calzabigi nor Gluck used this phrase until several years *after* the event.[18]

The first act opens with a chorus of nymphs, around a prominent funerary urn, mourning Euridice's death. Orfeo, who stands apart, interrupts their lament three times with a piercing and plaintive cry: 'Euridice! Euridice!' Following his first lament, '*Chiamo il mio ben così*' (Thus I call upon my love), Cupid takes pity on him and tells him how he can reclaim his wife.

Act 2, set in the underworld, begins with the dance of the Furies. Orfeo arrives, and accompanied by a harp and pizzicato strings, pleads to be allowed past. The Furies loudly refuse him admittance. Finally, he explains that he resembles *them*:

> Angry shades! Like you, I suffer a thousand pains.
> My hell is within me (*Ho con me l'inferno mio*). I feel it in my inmost heart
> [...]
> O, you would not be unkind if you could experience,
> even for an instant, what it is to die/languish for love (*languir d'amor*).[19]

That is, the Furies are appeased not by Orfeo's music (his playing and/or singing), but by his *tears* and *grief* and by his readiness to *die for love*—that is, by his 'sensibility'. To a tremendous chord from the orchestra, they allow the 'victor' (*vincitor*) through the Gates of Hell. Virgil considered weeping and feeling sorry for oneself to be unmanly. In the age of sensibility, they made one a hero.

Orfeo finds himself in the Elysian Fields, where the 'fortunate shades' (Blessed Spirits) are dancing to a serene melody on the flutes. He expresses his amazement in '*Che puro ciel*' (How pure a sky!).[20] Euridice is summoned, and the act ends with him leading her away without looking at her.

The third act is set in a rocky gorge. This is the first version of the myth to expand on the reasons why Orfeo turns, and the first in which Eurydice is given more than a cursory personality. It is a masterpiece of dramatic irony, and it hinges on the tension between two attitudes. Orfeo personifies *outdated* assumptions about male authority. Euridice embodies attitudes associated with an *enlightened sensibility*. They love each other, and yet, their incompatible *attitudes* make the tragedy inevitable.

The scene begins with an extended recitative duet of unusual intensity. Orfeo is struggling to stop himself even glancing at Euridice. Confused by his behaviour, she wonders why he does not embrace her. She begs him for 'but one glance' (*Ma un sguardo solo*). Struggling not to look at her, he tells her: 'Follow me and *be quiet*' (*Ma vieni e taci*). The abruptness is shocking. 'No!' she replies, 'death is dearer to me than to live with you!' She will not submit to arbitrary and tyrannical orders. She cannot bear such unexpected pain. She prefers her peace and independence. Unable to bear her reproaches any longer, Orfeo turns—only to watch her sink lifeless to the ground.

He is shattered. He sings 'What will I do without Euridice?' (*Che farò senza Euridice?*), a plangent and haunting lament in which he gives way to a yearning to join her in death. But Cupid intervenes, restores Euridice to him, and leads them both to the Temple of the God of Love. A three-part ballet precedes the final chorus of shepherds and shepherdesses ('May Love triumph', *Trionfi Amore*).

The joy of the 1762 production is its structural simplicity. In 1774, Gluck was invited to expand the work for performance in Paris, as *Orphée et Eurydice*, at the Théâtre du Palais-Royal, a much larger venue than the Burgtheater and with a larger and more modern orchestra (for example, the cornets were replaced by clarinets).[21] The revised work has some wonderful additional music, but it suffers from precisely the kinds of fault (added ballets, new arias) from which Gluck *claimed* that he wanted to free opera by his 'reforms'.

The claim about 'reform' should be taken with a pinch of salt. The opera looks back shamelessly to earlier traditions: for example, the jaunty (and embarrassingly inappropriate) all-purpose baroque overture, the character of Cupid, and the insistent renaissance laments. But it also represents the age of enlightenment and sensibility. Orfeo's tears are a reminder that the opera was first performed when Rousseau's *Julie* was all the rage. Similarly, by refusing to submit to Orfeo's high-handedness, Eurydice reflects the increasing resistance to patriarchal assumptions. She is portrayed not simply as a vehicle of male desire, but as a spirited, independent woman with a mind of her own. That is, she illustrates the values of the enlightenment. And lastly, the ending is brought about not by the 'gods', but by *Amore* (Love).

The opera was a huge success. For it not only pierces the *heart*; it also helps to humanise the *mind*. It expects the audience to feel the sufferings of Orpheus and Eurydice as their own. Both when Orfeo tells Euridice to 'be quiet' *and* when Eurydice misunderstands him, the audience gasp with recognition: how easy it is to cling to one's own views and to destroy a relationship? When Orfeo asks, 'What would I do without Euridice?' members of the audience cannot help but wonder what *they* would do if they lost what they valued most. *Orfeo ed Euridice* illustrates how the difficulties of individual relationships often stem from deeply ingrained but mistaken *social* attitudes.

As we shall see, the opera inspired countless works—and one of the first was in an unexpected medium.

Responses to Gluck: Felicitous and Infelicitous

Antonio Canova was born in 1757, into a family of stonecutters in Possagno (thirty-seven miles northwest of Venice). He was eighteen when he was commissioned to produce a pair of figures in soft stone to be placed on top of the pillars either side of the entrance gate to the Villa Falier in Asolo. His first mature works are the separate figures of Orpheus and Eurydice (1775–1776).[22] They depict the tragic moment. Orpheus is turning and raising his right hand to his head in horror as he realises his mistake. He is looking toward a shocked Eurydice, who is falling backward into the underworld. The figures blend late baroque drama with a rococo sensibility. Whispers of their technical mastery quickly circulated.

For the next forty years, Canova was the most celebrated sculptor of his age, sometimes almost neoclassical, but often with a lingering delight in rococo titillation, as in *Cupid and Psyche* (1787–1793, in the Louvre) or in the callipygian *Three Graces* (1814–1817, in the V&A, London).

Meanwhile, an equally telling, but more worrying tendency of the age of sensibility had been gathering momentum. About 1740, just as enlightenment thinkers were urging women to take control of their lives, there arose a simultaneous fashion for depicting women as weak-kneed, wilting creatures, always ready to burst into tears or to swoon: for example, the heroine in Richardson's *Pamela* (1740), or the trio of collapsible women in David's painting, *The Oath of the Horatii* (1784).

An example of how this trend affected the myth of Orpheus and Eurydice is provided by the first of four decorative panels painted in the early 1770s by André Corneille Lens for a small *château* near Anvers (France). It shows Eurydice walking toward the viewer, supported by six tearful *putti* who are escorting her to the underworld. She has the upwardly turned eyes with which, for over a hundred years, painters had been investing both the Madonna *and* Mary Magdalene.[23] In other words, the painting tries to update the stylised intensity of the Counter-Reformation for the age of sensibility. Instead, it produces a sickly rococo sentimentality.

Gluck's opera has many virtues, but it is sadly deficient in comedy. Toward the end of the century, there arose a vogue for 'rescue operas'—and one of these brought welcome humour back into the myth. For Mozart's *Abduction from the Seraglio* (1782) is a thinly disguised version of the myth of Orpheus and Eurydice. It opens with the discovery that the heroine, Konstanze (viz. Eurydice) has been abducted by pirates and sold to Pasha Selim (viz. Pluto). Her fiancé, Belmonte (viz. Orpheus), promptly sets off to rescue her from the despotic clutches of Selim's servant, the crotchety, sadistic, but nonetheless comic Osmin. In the end, owing to the generosity of Pasha Selim—a Muslim more 'enlightened' and generous than Belmonte's Christian father—he wins her back and they return to their own country. The myth has been given a new and 'exotic' setting, some boisterous humour, a happy ending, and an 'enlightenment' moral—as well as Mozart's wonderfully varied and irresistible music.[24]

A few years after writing it, Mozart briefly met up with his one-time teacher and good friend. Joseph Haydn was on his way to London, where the highlight of his visit was to be another rescue opera, also based on the myth of Orpheus and Eurydice.

Badini and Haydn: Orpheus and a Despotic Father/King

Ever since his late twenties, Haydn had worked for the Esterházys, an old Austrian-Hungarian family: mostly at Eszterháza (1763–1784), their enormous and recently built palace complex (now in western Hungary). There, several times a week, he directed either operas or concerts, and these often included his own compositions. His patrons were good to him. No wonder that all his life Mozart yearned for such patronage. And no wonder that Beethoven, who enjoyed the patronage, refused the livery. For the winds of change were blowing. Eszterháza was no sooner completed than the French Revolution erupted. And soon after, Nikolaus I, Haydn's extravagant but generous and musical patron died. His heirs, however, were quick to give Haydn permission to accept an invitation to go to London.

Haydn arrived in London in early January 1791, soon after the publication of Edmund Burke's *Reflections on the Revolution in France*, which was critical of the Revolution. In March, Thomas Paine published the first part of his blistering 'answer'. *Rights of Man* quickly aroused such vociferous support that Pitt's government (which, generally speaking, was by no means illiberal) instituted a 'reign of terror' on anyone even suspected of holding radical views—and this was two years *before* Robespierre instituted an even greater 'reign of terror' in France (1793–1794).[25]

Today, Haydn's stay in London is most often remembered for the first series of his 'London Symphonies' (1791–1792) and the six Opus 64 'Tost Quartets'.[26] But the highlight of his visit was to have been a new opera commissioned to inaugurate the rebuilt King's Theatre in the Haymarket. In the event, George III refused to re-license the theatre, and Haydn never completed the work. The libretto, by Carlo Francesco Badini, has not survived. We know the text only from Haydn's abandoned manuscript score, which is for about two hours of music.

L'Anima del Filosofo (*The Philosopher's Soul*) is in four acts. The first two hinge on Creonte insisting that his daughter, Eurydice, marry Arideo (Aristaeus). She, however, is in love with Orfeo. Rather than be bullied by a tyrannical father into a marriage with a man she does not love, she runs away from home and is captured by wild shepherds, from whom she is rescued by Orfeo and his music. The 'allegory' is transparent. The wild shepherds represent the 'monstrous' aspect of Creonte, who is prepared to sacrifice his daughter's happiness to his whim. But on learning that Orfeo has saved Euridice, Creonte reflects, 'Whoever loses his beloved, loses himself'. And just before he gives Orfeo and Euridice his blessing, he admits that his 'feelings' were acting like 'tyrants' over him—but still he cannot control them.

Hence, in the following act, Arideo contrives to take Eurydice captive, whereupon she is bitten by a snake and dies. Orfeo laments her death. Meanwhile, on learning the news, Creonte determines to punish Arideo. In Act 3, Orfeo seeks the help of Genio, the Cumaean Sibyl (who, in antiquity, delivered the prophecies of Apollo at Cumae, near Naples), and asks her where he can find his 'soul'. She promises that he will see her again—but only if he can *control his passions*. In the last act, they descend into the underworld. Although he is warned not to look at her, Eurydice unwittingly moves to where he cannot help but see her, which leads to Orpheus' death at the hands of the Bacchantes, by poison. The opera probably ended with Creonte recognising that despotic behaviour has no place in an enlightened world.

Had Haydn completed the work, which would surely have included further reference to Creonte, some of its problems might have been ironed out. Nevertheless, even in its present state, *L'Anima del Filosofo* has a place in our story. In Virgil's epyllion, the myth of Orpheus and Eurydice reflects a challenge facing Aristaeus; in Haydn's opera, it represents a challenge facing Creonte. Just as every lover must learn to control their passions, so every father and king must learn to control their despotic and 'tyrannical' tendencies. It is the first version of the myth of Orpheus and Eurydice to include an attack on the arbitrary and oppressive exercise of power—that is, to harbour an emphatically *political* message.

Conclusion

Today, many assume that opera only follows in the footsteps of drama or prose fiction (novels). The operas we have looked at in these pages suggest otherwise. In France, Buti-Rossi's *Orfeo* is the first version of the myth of Orpheus and Eurydice to expose a social vice—and it antedates, by about eighteen years, the best-known French play on the same subject: Molière's *Dom Juan* (1665), which was first performed in the same theatre.[27] And if Badini-Haydn's *L'Anima del Filosofo* had been performed when intended, it would have been highly topical. It would have mirrored the views of Thomas Paine and his supporters.

In similar fashion, Poussin's painting of the myth is the first to show a keen awareness of the relation between the artist's *personal* circumstances and their art. Calzabigi-Gluck's *Orfeo ed Euridice* is the first to re-imagine the feelings of *both* protagonists in relation to concerns pertinent to the age of sensibility and enlightenment. That is, from the late eighteenth century, writers and other artists were beginning to foreground not only social and political concerns, but also the tension between social expectations and individuality.

These changes reflect a watershed in Western culture. From this time forward, the predominant concerns of writers and other artists were a sustained interest in *social* and *political* concerns, and a new interest in the complexity of *private feelings*. More than 200 years later, they are still wrestling with these twin concerns, both of which are often found in the same work. And they usher in a new cultural age: romanticism.

Notes

1 B. Mandeville, *The Fable of the Bees: Or, Private Vices, Public Benefits* (1705/1714), ed. P. Harth. London: Penguin, 1989.

2 For example, Jan Brueghel and assistants, *Orfeo* (Madrid, Museo del Prado, on loan to Museo Municipal de Bellas Artes de Santa Cruz de Tenerife); Sinibaldo Scorza, *Orfeo che ammansisce gli animali*, Genoa: Zerbone Collection; Frans II Francken the younger, *Orphée aux Enfers*, Nîmes: Musée des Beaux-Arts; Nicolaes Knüpfer's *De dood van Orpheus*/The Death of Orpheus, Utrecht: Centraal Museum.

3 Poussin, *Orphée et Eurydice*, Paris: Louvre, 1648.

4 E. Delacroix, 'Poussin', *Moniteur universel*, 26, 29, and 30 June 1853, in *Œuvres littéraires*, tome II, *Essais sur les artistes célèbres*, Paris: Crès, p. 91.

5 Poussin, *Et in Arcadia Ego*, Derbyshire: Chatsworth House, 1627; *Les Bergers d'Arcadie*, 1638 (also called *Et in Arcadia Ego*, Louvre, Paris).

6 At the time, Francesco Sacrati's *La finta pazza* (The Feigned Madwoman, 1645) was the only Italian opera to have been performed in France.

7 There is an excellent recording on CD: Luigi Rossi, *Orfeo*, Les Arts Florissants, cond. William Christie, Arles: Harmonia Mundi, France, 1991; also, an edited modern staging on DVD with Pygmalion and Raphaël Pichon (2017).

8 The reference is to the story of Cupid and Psyche, in which Cupid scratches himself with one of his arrows, and the next thing he sees is Psyche, of whom his mother (Venus) is fiercely jealous: in Apuleius, *The Metamorphoses* (or *Golden Ass*).

9 Sadly, many of his manuscript scores of this time were lost to the Allied bombing of Hamburg during the Second World War.

10 There is an excellent recording: Telemann, *Orpheus, oder Die wunderbare Beständigkeit der Liebe*, Akademie für Alte Musik Berlin, cond. R. Jacobs, Arles: Harmonia Mundi, 1998.

11 *Orphée, tragédie mise en musique par M. de Lully l'aîné* (Paris: Ballard, 1690), with music by [mainly] Louis and Jean Louis Lully (sons of the great Jean-Baptiste Lully).

12 See R.A. Rue, "Mixed Taste', Cosmopolitanism, and Intertextuality in Georg Philipp Telemann's Opera *Orpheus*', Master of Music (MM), Bowling Green State University, Ohio, 2017, p. 41.

13 F. Hutcheson, *An Inquiry Concerning Beauty, Order, Harmony, and Design*, ed. P. Kivy. The Hague: Martinus Nijhoff, 1973; and *A System of Moral Philosophy, in Two Books* (1755), ed. D. Carey. New York: Continuum, 2005.

14 Mme Le Prince de Beaumont was a French governess, working in London, who wrote a series of educational works for children, including *The Young Misses Magazine* (1756), targeted at girls between five and thirteen; the quotation is from the preface to *The Young Ladies Magazine* (1760), targeted at the same girls, now four years older.

15 See M. Symes, *The English Landscape Garden in Europe*, Swindon: Historic England, 2016.

16 D. Garrick, in the 'Occasional Prologue for the Opening of Drury Lane Theatre, 8 Sept 1750.'

17 For a 'period' production on DVD, filmed in the Český Krumlov Baroque Theatre (Czechia), see C.W. Gluck, *Orfeo ed Euridice*, Collegium 1704 and Collegium Vocale 1704, conducted by Václav Luks; film directed by Ondřej Havelka (Classart-Unitel-ORF, 2013).

18 Despite his ostensibly 'reformist' intentions, Gluck continued to include 'gods' in his operas: Apollo in *Alceste* (1767); Cupid and Pallas Athene, in *Paride ed Elena* (1770; both in Vienna) and Diana in both *Iphigénie en Aulide* (1774) and *Iphigénie en Tauride* (1779; both in Paris).

19 From libretto to Gluck, *Orfeo ed Euridice*, Orchestra and Chorus of the Royal Opera House, cond. Sir Georg Solti, 1970 (CD 1989), pp. 14–15, my translation.

20 An aria cleverly adapted from a melody used in an earlier work (Ezio, 1750), but now with a haunting accompaniment by solo oboe, flute, and bassoon.

21 The earlier theatre, in which Rossi's *Orfeo* was performed, burned down in 1763. Gluck's opera was performed in the new theatre, slightly to the east, which opened in 1770 and could hold about 2,000 spectators.

22 A. Canova, *Orfeo* and *Euridice*, Venice: Museo Correr.

23 Classic examples of the mannerism include Murillo's *The Immaculate Conception of Los Venerables* (1660–1665; Prado), and Greuze, *The Souvenir* (1788, Wallace Collection).

24 One might easily argue that (albeit more loosely) the same holds for Mozart's *The Magic Flute* (1791); or that Beethoven's *Leonore, or the Triumph of Marital Love* (1805/06), revised as *Fidelio* (1814), represents a powerful gender-reversed variation of the same genre and myth.

25 See E. Vallance, *A Radical History of Britain*, London: Little, Brown, 2009, esp. Part 4: The Age of Paine, pp. 203–282.

26 The Hanover Square Rooms, on the south-east corner of the square, were a major venue for concerts from 1775 until the late nineteenth century. In 1900, the building was demolished, and replaced.

27 *Dom Juan* is not typical of Molière's work: most of his plays attack pretensions rather than vices.

Chapter 6

Romantic Identification with Orpheus

The Nineteenth Century

It has often been suggested that the French Revolution and the Napoleonic Empire shaped the nineteenth century. In one sense, they did. Following the defeat of Napoleon, conservative forces in the great European nations did everything possible to argue that both had been ghastly mistakes.[1] When further revolutions broke out, in 1830 and 1848, similar forces were quick to stifle them—as they did, throughout the century, to any and every expression of radical political thought (Comte, Fourier, Proudhon, Marx).

And yet, it became increasingly clear that governments were out of touch with the cruel economic divide that continued to characterise their nations. Rapidly changing economic conditions could make life a struggle even for owners of businesses; but, as many writers attested, it could be wretched beyond words for their workers.[2] For the canny few, however, financial services offered obscene rewards. They allowed Ferdinand de Rothschild to build Waddesdon Manor (1889). The exterior of this 'weekend home' is modelled on seventeenth-century French *châteaux*, while its interiors are a fusion of extravagant eighteenth-century French and sumptuous English Victorian taste. By 1900, despite a rapidly growing middle class, the gap between the extremely rich and the poor was still as stark and unforgiving as it had been in medieval times.

The other great challenge facing writers in the nineteenth century was to better understand the part that *subjectivity* plays in human experience.[3] Wordsworth identifies the main subject of both *The Prelude* and *The Recluse* as 'the mind of man'.[4] He argues that the test of great art is whether it enlarges our response either to the outer world or to the workings of the human imagination.[5] Philosophers explore the nature of subjectivity more keenly than ever before (Schelling, Hegel, Nietzsche). Toward the end of the century, psychology emerges as a distinct discipline. And throughout the century, there is a marked increase of interest in ancient Greece and in its myths.

Creative writers and other artists begin to respond to the Greek myths in a new way: as if they represent a 'deeper' aspect of human experience or reflect a 'deeper' aspect of their own personality. As a result, many turn to the myth of Orpheus and Eurydice because they *identify* with Orpheus. All-too-often, their self-indulgent

DOI: 10.4324/9781003519584-8

posturing results in works of embarrassingly poor taste. Sometimes, however, it produces works with unexpected and intriguing implications.

This chapter is in three parts. The first looks at a selection of versions of the myth produced during the romantic period (1790–1855). They include French paintings, a long short story by a young German poet, a sociological study, and the first work to harness the myth to explore a mental breakdown. The second part looks at a selection of versions produced during the French Second Empire (1852–1870), including Offenbach's witty operetta (the only work considered in this chapter which does not reflect the author's identification with Orpheus). The third part considers the most important versions from the late nineteenth century.

Orpheus in the Romantic Period

Traditionally, artists had usually worked to a commission from the privileged. During the late eighteenth century, this changed. Artists increasingly sought to market works that reflected their own way of seeing. And with the advent of romanticism, they often had inflated ideas about the value of their way of seeing.

Throughout the romantic period, the dominant style of French academic painting continued to be neoclassicism. It was a style well-suited to produce resonant images pertinent to a collective socio-political culture (e.g. Jacques-Louis David, *The Oath of the Horatii*). But it was singularly ill-suited to represent an emergent individual sensibility. When painters of the romantic period project themselves into the feelings they associate with Orpheus, all too often it results in an embarrassing narcissism.

Jacques Réattu was from Arles, in the south of France. In 1792, he painted *Orpheus in Hell Pleading with Pluto and Proserpine*.[6] Seated beneath an arch are the well-fed residents of the underworld, Pluto and Proserpine, dressed in Roman Imperial regalia. They are listening to Orpheus while he hides his modesty with his lyre. In 1866, Arles celebrated the opening of the Musée Réattu: a mere twenty years later, van Gogh described its holdings as 'a joke'.[7]

Meanwhile, the opening scene of Gluck's *Orphée et Eurydice* became a popular subject for French painters. Charles Landon's *The Grief of Orpheus* (1796) is a small work.[8] Sitting against Eurydice's tomb is a nude Orpheus, buried in his self-conscious grief. In Pierre Narcisse Guérin's version, exhibited at the *Salon* in 1802, a young nude Orpheus stands leaning disconsolately over Eurydice's tomb.[9] And in 1814, the young Ary Scheffer, a German artist working in Paris, invested *The Death of Eurydice* with an unexpected association.[10] Against the warm golden glow of a late summer evening, Orpheus, his nudity covered by a bright red cloak, holds the dead Eurydice in his arms in a way that recalls paintings of the deposition of Christ, but with the genders reversed. The association is in questionable taste.

All these works are marred by the artist's self-conscious identification with the figure of Orpheus. In contrast, during these same years, a young German writer who identified with Orpheus produced two altogether more interesting responses to the myth.

Novalis: Orpheus and the Reconciliation of Opposites

In the mid-eighteenth century, writers and public figures within the separate German-speaking states began to call for a unified German nation. And long before this was achieved (in 1871), this emergent nationalism produced one of the most remarkable explosions of critical and creative talent in European history: Kant, Hegel, and Schopenhauer; Goethe, Schiller, and Hoffmann; Haydn, Mozart, Beethoven, and Schubert; as well as Friedrich, Runge, and Koch.

Georg Friedrich Philipp von Hardenberg (1772–1801), better known as Novalis, played a short but significant part in this cultural ferment.[11] In his mid-twenties, he began the *Hymns to the Night* (*Hymnen an die Nacht*), six prose-poems written in the first person, with occasional sections in verse. Intense and questioning, they rework the metaphors central to the myth of Orpheus and Eurydice.[12]

He then began *Henry von Ofterdingen* (*Heinrich von Ofterdingen*), which explores the same metaphors (loss, longing, descent, and the calming effect of music). It illustrates German romantic fascination with the Middle Ages.[13] It fuses religious/spiritual, intellectual, and emotional concerns into a new kind of philosophical-cum-psychological tale that is both a *Bildungsroman* (a novel about the 'education' of the main character) and a *Kunstmärchen* (a work whose hero is an artist, or which explores an aesthetic theory).

At the outset of Part one (The Expectation), Henry has a dream in which he sees a blue flower (*eine blaue Blume*) and, at its centre, the face of a young woman with a tender expression. He and his mother join a group of merchants on a journey; their ostensible purpose is to visit his grandfather. The narrative consists of stories told by the different characters during the journey, some of which involve embedded stories. When they arrive in Augsburg, Henry's grandfather introduces him to Klingsohr and his daughter, Mathilda. It was her face which Henry saw in his dream, at the heart of the blue flower.

Part two (The Fulfilment) continues the story of the hero's wanderings. Henry is lamenting the death of his beloved Mathilda when he comes across a girl with whom he has a dream-like conversation. When he asks her where they are going, she replies, 'Always toward home' (*Immer nach Hause*).[14] For Henry, 'home' is where he will be reunited with Mathilde. According to Ludwig Tieck, the poet's journey was to have taken him to ancient Greece and to the Orient, and to culminate in a mystical realm where 'the Christian religion is reconciled with the pagan, and in which the legends of Orpheus and Psyche will be sung'.[15] But Novalis had barely begun Part two, when he died, aged only twenty-nine, from either tuberculosis or cystic fibrosis.

Most of the stories told in *Henry von Ofterdingen* seek to reconcile opposite tendencies. For example, one evening, although enthralled by the tales of an elderly crusader, Henry suddenly feels a need for a lute (an instrument which he cannot play). He goes outside, where he meets a young girl from the Holy Land. The tale contrasts the crusader's love of war and desire for possession with the love of peace and poetry preferred by the girl's people. In similar fashion, Klingsohr's story (sometimes published as a separate *Märchen*/fairy tale) illustrates how a country which has lost its way can flourish again only if its king (Arcturus) integrates those qualities which he lacks.

The *Novelle* was widely admired. Throughout much of Europe, the phrase *blue flower* came to represent romantic yearning, especially for an idealised young woman.[16] And yet, the defining characteristic of the work is its *critical* spirit: its determination to engage with 'opposites' and, most intriguingly, its insistence that true poetry comes *not* from inspiration, but from a careful *analysis* of one's inner experiences—in both of which, it anticipates later claims by Jung.

Meanwhile, in Paris, a historian of ideas became the first to harness the myth of Orpheus and Eurydice to a sociological argument—and he identified so strongly with Orpheus that he made it his 'personal myth'.

Ballanche and Delacroix: Orpheus as Symbol of Redemption and Civilisation

As a young man, Pierre-Simon Ballanche was shaken by the violence of the revolutionary forces which besieged and then ransacked Lyon in 1793. Following the final defeat of Napoleon, he found his way to Paris, where he attended the *salon* (reception parties) hosted by the still irresistibly beautiful Juliette Récamier.[17] She was not, however, just a pretty face: her close friends included some of the greatest writers of the time, including Chateaubriand, Germaine de Staël, and Benjamin Constant. Ballanche soon became infatuated with her. Both were from Lyon, both were in their mid-thirties, and both were deeply melancholic.[18]

Ballanche had a mystical streak. In *An Essay on Social Institutions* (1818), he argues that societies can only evolve by coming to terms with the symbols thrown up by their age, for 'everything is a veil which must be lifted, everything is a symbol which must be glimpsed, everything contains truths which must be discerned'.[19]

Essays in Social Palingenesis (1827–1829; palingenesis = rebirth) argues that *societies* must evolve before individuals can do the same, and this is achieved by 'a succession of painful initiations into mystery'.[20] He summarises this in a gnomic phrase: 'Ordeals, atonements, freedom' (Épreuves, expiations, liberté).[21] That is, every age needs to suffer and come to terms with a *crisis* before a new age can begin. France must come to terms with all the implications of the French Revolution—even the most difficult to accept—before it will be able to progress.

The second part of this study is devoted to the figure of Orpheus as a psychological *principle* responsible for taking the achievements of Prometheus further. Orpheus 'arranges, unites, and joins'.[22] He is almost as necessary as Christ, for the desire to see an outdated state replaced by another is a precondition for redemption. Ballanche was projecting onto Orpheus his own determination to arrange, unite, and join—and he dedicated his *Essays* to 'she whom he regarded as a personification of [Dante's] Beatrix'.

For thirty-five years, he and Juliette Récamier enjoyed a close, but (apparently) chaste relationship. When he died in 1847, he was buried in the same grave as her parents and her husband. Two years later, Juliette joined them.[23] It is the first example of Orpheus dying *before* Eurydice, confident that he will be with her for all eternity.

Ballanche's ideas about the nature and importance of symbols were hugely influential. Baudelaire would describe the course of human life as a progress through a 'forest of symbols'.[24] Late nineteenth-century symbolism is rooted in his claims. And his sociological argument anticipates Jung's claims about psychological individuation.

Amongst those whom he influenced was the painter Eugène Delacroix, whose ceiling paintings in the Library of the Palais Bourbon, in Paris (1843) do not immediately appear to have any connection with literary culture. At one end of the gallery is Attila, sweeping all before him, thus causing suffering. At the other, is Orpheus, playing before attentive rustics. The inscription reads: 'Orpheus comes to civilise (*policer*, from Greek *pólis*) those Greeks who are still savages and to teach them the arts of peace'. That is, Orpheus is a symbol urging humankind to overcome its sufferings and to find redemption in the new urban modernity.

Over a decade later, he was asked for a series of four paintings illustrating the seasons. The subject he chose for Spring is bizarre: the moment when Eurydice, bitten by a snake, collapses and dies, still half supported by a shocked Orpheus.[25] But if considered in the light of Ballanche's claims, the *death* of Eurydice is an 'ordeal', which is likened to Spring because, if one *engages* with the ordeal, it will lead to 'atonement' and, through atonement, to 'freedom' and redemption.

By associating the myth with a theory, Ballanche and Delacroix kept it at arm's length. In contrast, one of their younger contemporaries became so fascinated by inner experiences which he associated with the myth that he lost his grip on his social reality. It is the first response to the myth to associate it with a schizophrenic breakdown.

Nerval and Aurélia: An Over-Identification with Orpheus

Gérard de Nerval was still in his teens when he translated Goethe's *Faust* (part one) into French prose (1828).[26] It was a huge success, and because French was the *lingua franca* of the time, it introduced Goethe's masterpiece to Europe and the world. In the following years, Nerval wrote travel-writing, short stories, essays, and poems. Although well-respected by his contemporary writers, they were all commercial failures.

In 1854, he published 'El Desdichado', a sonnet whose first-person narrator describes himself as an inconsolable 'widower' whose only 'star' is dead, and whose lute transcribes 'the black sun of melancholy'.[27] That is, he imagines himself as Orpheus grieving for Eurydice. In the last three lines, the association is underlined. He identifies his depression with the descent of Orpheus into the underworld, but with a difference. He distinguishes between the *two* 'Eurydices' that haunt him. One moment, he experiences her as the embodiment of idealised purity; the next, he perceives her as a terrifying fantasy-image whose 'shrieks' represent a chilling warning to step back from his obsession with the myth before it is too late.

His last work was *Aurélia: Dream and Life* (*Aurélia, ou le Rêve et la Vie*), a fascinating but harrowing short story that has evident parallels with the myth of Orpheus and Eurydice: the death of a beloved young woman, a (middle-aged) man's unbearable sense of loss, his descent into an underworld (of dream and vision), her second death, and his despair.[28] The first part was published in the *Revue de Paris* on 1 January 1855.[29]

Nerval's purpose is to describe 'a long illness which he suffered *solely* in the mysteries of [his] mind'—and he assures the reader that, while he was experiencing his extraordinary visions, he had never felt better. He dates his illness from the moment that Aurélia exiled him from her heart. As the narrator struggles to come to terms with his feeling of debilitating loss, he experiences a series of visions which blend images suggestive of persons known to him with images suggestive of universal mythology. They include several of the most characteristic motifs of romanticism: the idealised feminine, the 'other', the city, a fascination with the Orient, and the mine. Toward the end of part one, Aurélia dies, and the narrator is overcome by a feeling that he has been dispossessed by his own double—an alter-ego who, in the 'world of spirits', has contrived to 'marry' Aurélia.

The second part of *Aurélia* was published posthumously. Its epitaph is the plaintive cry from Virgil's epyllion: 'Eurydice! Eurydice!' It begins with the realisation: 'I have lost her—a second time!' He knows that it is now his turn to die. The thought of God triggers a process of tortuous self-reproach. He does not feel he is worthy even to visit Aurélia's tomb. His mental health deteriorates. He is confined in different clinics and asylums. The narrative culminates in a vision of the goddess Isis telling him that she is all the different women he has ever loved. The final pages recall the ending to part two of Goethe's *Faust*. The narrator has a final dream of Aurélia forgiving him and interceding for him with an almighty deity who is at once Christian *and* pagan.

It is a text one cannot read without a shiver of horror, for it recounts—to use the final phrase of the work—a 'descent into hell'. The second part is unrevised. Had Nerval lived, he might well have further revised the whole. The author was sick and homeless, and it was winter. He was still in his forties when, one night, in a Paris alleyway, he hanged himself from a grid. There were some pages from *Aurélia* in his pocket. The second part of *Aurélia* was published just over a fortnight later.

From a psychological perspective, its most striking claim is that the author 'cannot doubt the truth of what he has *seen* so vividly' in his dreams and reveries. He wanted to discover how those *images* and *notions* which filled him with 'infinite delights' related to the reality of his life. He wanted to contribute to a better understanding of powerful inner experiences.[30] The parallel with Jung's work is clear. Nerval's miserable death illustrates two of Jung's later claims: the danger of identifying over-strongly with a mythic character and narrative; and the danger of surrendering oneself to the imaginal world of dreams and fantasies without an understanding of their compensatory or corrective function.[31]

Western Europe was changing fast and, like Baudelaire, Nerval felt alienated by the *new* Paris rising around him: the Paris of the Second Empire.[32]

Orpheus in the Second Empire

In 1848, Louis-Napoléon (a nephew of Napoleon I) became the first elected President of France, and by a wide margin. Four years later, in a *coup d'état*, he became Napoléon III, founder of the Second Empire. Victor Hugo berated him mercilessly as *Napoléon le petit* (Napoleon the Little) and the epithet stuck.[33] More recently, Philippe Séguin has argued he should be called *le Grand* (the Great), and for good reason.[34] He was a social and educational reformer, he modernised the administration, and he extended the French railway system. In Paris, he promoted the rebuilding of the water supply and the sewers, as well as the radical urban replanning of Hausmann's *grands boulevards*. The Second Empire witnessed an economic boom, which led to the first department stores (Bon Marché, 1852; Au Printemps, 1865).

We begin with a work which has become synonymous with the period. And it parodies Second Empire *society*.

Offenbach and Operetta: Orpheus and Social and Political Satire

Jacques Offenbach was of German Jewish descent. When young, he moved to Paris, where he soon established himself as an energetic impresario and a prolific composer of sparkling one-act operettas with only two or three main characters. In 1855, he rented a small theatre in the Passage Choiseul (between the Palais-Royal and the Paris Opera), renamed it the Bouffes-Parisiens, and asked Ludovic Halévy to produce the libretto for a full-blown operetta based on a Greek myth. The result was first performed in 1858, in two acts divided into four scenes. In 1874, Offenbach asked Hector Crémieux to expand the libretto into four acts, the version most often heard today.[35]

Orpheus in the Underworld (Orphée aux enfers) laughs at the pomposity of individuals, their duplicities, and their hypocritical double standards in marriage. It pokes fun at the police, at legal shenanigans, and at the government of Napoleon III—in other words, at most of Second Empire society. And it does so with an effervescent irreverence.

Like Virgil and Ovid before him, Offenbach parodied the myth he inherited. In the first act, Orpheus and Eurydice are married, but they cannot stand the sight of each other. Orpheus considers his music irresistible; Eurydice cannot bear it. She is in love with Aristaeus. Orpheus accidentally causes her death, whereupon Aristaeus reveals that he is Pluto. But as soon as Orpheus tells the audience that he is delighted to be rid of Eurydice, prim-and-proper Public Opinion appears and *insists* that he reclaim his wife.

The second act is set on Mount Olympus. The gods think only of their amorous adventures. Jupiter chides them for not behaving like models of propriety. But when he berates Pluto for having kidnapped Eurydice, the blatant hypocrisy stirs the gods to rebellion. Revolution is prevented only by the timely arrival of Public

Opinion and Orpheus—and once again she *insists* that he ask Jupiter to return Eurydice to him. The gods, bored with Olympus, hurry to the underworld to ensure that the order is carried out—and to have some fun.

Act 3 is tongue-in-cheek farce. Eurydice is bored. When Jupiter puts Pluto on trial, Cerberus bites him. The lights go out. When they come back on, Cupid (the role is sung by a woman) offers to help his 'daddy'. Jupiter summons a Chorus of Policemen to no avail. He transforms himself into a fly so that he can get into Pluto's boudoir, where Eurydice is being kept hidden. She is delighted to have even a fly to play with. Meanwhile, Pluto announces a party, during which Jupiter plans to slip away with Eurydice to Olympus.

In the last act, Eurydice is dressed as a Bacchante (here, party-girl). The gods sing a Hymn to Bacchus. The music quickly warms into the famous *galop infernal* (in English, can-can). Pluto sees Jupiter sneaking away with Eurydice and reminds him that Public Opinion is about to arrive with Orpheus. Jupiter is at a loss what to say; Cupid suggests the condition; and Orpheus turns. When Pluto claims Eurydice for himself, Jupiter transforms her into a priestess of Bacchus—to the delight of all, except an indignant Public Opinion.

The public loved it, both for its Gallic humour and its catchy and sometimes deliberately silly tunes. But predictably, some critics sided with Public Opinion (e.g. Jules Janin, in *Le Journal des débats*), berating the operetta for treating the myth in such a cavalier fashion and for poking fun at the emperor. Undeterred, in April 1860, Napoleon III attended a performance; the following year, he made Offenbach a member of the Légion d'Honneur. It was the latter's first full-length operetta with a large cast, and there were many more to come. They prompted the evolution not only of Viennese operetta (Strauss the Younger), but also of the operettas of Gilbert and Sullivan.

The success of *Orpheus in the Underworld* coincided with a renewed appetite for Gluck's more earnest version of the myth—stirred by an unexpected re-orchestration of its score.

Romanticism and Gluck: An Obsession with Orpheus

Gluck has indeed been fortunate (German *Gluck* = lucky), for as soon as he appears to be going out of fashion, someone revitalises interest in his work.

E.T.A. Hoffmann was born in Prussia (north Germany). He was a lawyer, a conductor, a composer (*Undine*, 1816), and a music critic of genius.[36] Today, however, he is best known as the author of some of the finest examples of the German *Novelle* (a lengthy short story, often based on a tension between a social and imaginal reality, and which explores an *uneasiness* or *disquiet* with the experience it describes (e.g. 'The Sandman', 1816).

One of Hoffmann's early experiments with the genre is 'Ritter Gluck', which is set in the present (1809). A narrator describes two meetings he has had with a tall, enigmatic character, wearing eighteenth-century clothes, carrying a sword, and who is scornful of the current Berlin music scene, which he compares unfavourably with the works of Gluck. The narrator finally asks him, 'Who are you?', to which the stranger replies, 'I am Ritter Gluck' (*Ritter* = knight: a title conferred on Gluck by Pope Benedict XIV in 1756). The point of the story is *not* to decide whether the character is a lunatic, a joker, or an apparition, but to reflect on the author's own 'uneasy' admiration of Gluck.

In 1854, when Franz Liszt mounted a production of *Orfeo ed Euridice* in Weimar, he replaced Gluck's overture with his own prelude.[37] Although *equally* inappropriate (it does not anticipate any of the events of Gluck's opera), it makes an evocative symphonic poem—and it strongly suggests the influence of Ballanche. Introduced by two harps which represent Orpheus' lyre, it takes the form of a gentle crescendo, which then slowly dies away. It foregrounds the poignancy of Orpheus' unbearable loss and suffering and his search for redemption.

Gluck's greatest champion, however, was Hector Berlioz, who held Gluck in high regard. In his widely admired treatise on orchestration (1843), he cites Gluck more often than he cites Beethoven (whom he also famously championed), and in his posthumous *Memoirs* (1870), he refers to Gluck as 'the Jupiter of our Olympus'. And he had a lifelong interest in the myth of Orpheus and Eurydice. In 1827, he wrote a cantata, *La Mort d'Orphée* (The Death of Orpheus).

In April 1858, no sooner had he completed his masterpiece—the four-hour opera *Les Troyens* (The Trojans)—than he turned his attention to re-orchestrating Gluck's *Orphée et Eurydice*. The following year, in Paris, the re-orchestrated opera ran for 138 performances, which ensured the opera's continued success throughout the remainder of the nineteenth century.

In 1860, Frederic Leighton attended a performance at the recently restored Royal Italian Opera (now the Royal Opera House, London). Soon after, he began a painting in which he depicts the moment when Orpheus pushes Eurydice away from him, clearly struggling with *his* longing to look at her and the knowledge that if he does, he will lose her for ever.[38]

He showed the painting to his friend, the poet Robert Browning, who immediately wrote a prose-poem based on it, which he subsequently set as verse.[39] And Browning fixes his attention not on Orpheus, but on *Eurydice*'s desire for more than just a glance:

> But give them me, the mouth, the eyes, the brow!
> Let them once more absorb me! One look now
> Will lap me round for ever [...]
> Hold me but safe again within the bond
> Of one immortal look! [...]
> Look at me![40]

Browning had a gift for projecting himself into imaginary characters. For example, into the unsavoury narrator of 'My Last Duchess' (1842) or, most intriguingly, into the spectrum of different characters in *The Ring and the Book* (1868–1869). But 'Eurydice to Orpheus' is unusually ambivalent. On the one hand, Eurydice's plea (*Look at me!*) has continued to resonate for women: Anita Brookner, a gifted art critic, borrowed it as the title of a best-selling novel (1981); so too did Jennifer Egan (2001).[41] And yet, the poem gives Eurydice no individuality apart from her desire to be 'absorbed' by Orpheus and to have his gaze 'lap' round her for ever. The yearning it attributes to Eurydice can also be explained as a projection of a *male* desire to be thought the centre of a woman's universe.

The following section returns to France to consider how painters of the Second Empire continued to be fascinated by the myth.

French Painting in the Second Empire: Failures and Successes

We have seen how the tendency of painters to identify with Orpheus often resulted in works of dubious taste. This tendency continued during the Second Empire.

An example of this is provided by Charles Jalabert. *Nymphs Listening to the Songs of Orpheus* (1855) shows the brightly lit 'nymphs', in various states of academically acceptable undress, ostensibly listening to Orpheus, who sits in shadow.[42] The female figures are well painted. The tones are well handled. The titillation borders on pornography. In similar fashion, Émile Lévy's *The Death of Orpheus* (1866) shows the demi-god soon after he has been beaten to the ground by a group of sensuous and half-naked young women, one of whom is about to decapitate him.[43] Orpheus lies as if in erotic exhaustion, depicted with his arms stretched and his knees slightly bent, as if he has just been taken down from a cross. Everything is well rendered. The painting is striking. It has only two faults. It adds *nothing* to our understanding of the moment it depicts, and it is a ludicrous and tasteless blend of saccharine eroticism and inappropriate religiosity.

Altogether more interesting is Camille Corot's deeply atmospheric treescape, *Orpheus Leading Eurydice from the Underworld* (1861).[44] In subdued tones, it depicts the melancholy of an early winter morning. In the middle distance, a group of ghostly figures mourn the death of Eurydice. In the foreground, Orpheus, holding his lyre aloft, leads an untroubled Eurydice by the hand along a woodland path. The ambivalence is strangely poignant. Does the painting represent the moment *before* he turns? Or is he leading her to a Ballanche-inspired redemption?

An equally surprising response to the myth is provided by Gustave Moreau. About 1860, he began working on the figure a young woman in an embroidered costume set against a rocky landscape. She is holding a richly decorated lyre on which lies the head of Orpheus. In 1864, he produced a striking gouache. The following year, he produced an oil painting of the same theme, set now in a fanciful pastoral landscape. He exhibited is as *Orpheus* at the Paris *Salon* of 1866, where it was promptly bought by the state for 8,000 francs, a high price for a still little-known painter.[45] Despite the glowering clouds, it is a luminous work. Wrapped in a world of her own, the girl gazes down at the head with a curious mix of tenderness and indifference. It is strangely haunting—perhaps because Moreau so obviously identifies with an Orpheus who finds his Eurydice only in death.

Five years later, the Second Empire came to an ignominious end. Napoleon III had tried to extend French influence abroad (Mexico, Indochina), but he had neglected the defence of France. In 1870, when French forces foolishly invaded Germany, the Prussian army was quick to retaliate—and with devastating effect. Napoleon III had no option but to surrender. A sick man, he fled to exile in Chislehurst (south-east of London). While the German army besieged Paris and the Paris Commune bravely resisted, the long-hoped-for unification of Germany was finally agreed. It was soon followed by the Treaty of Frankfurt (1871), which imposed humiliating conditions on France.[46]

Orpheus in the Late Nineteenth Century

Meanwhile, during the Third Republic, Parisians continued to flock to the annual *Salon*; the myth of Orpheus and Eurydice continued to be a popular subject; and painters continued to express their ill-digested identification with Orpheus.

Gustave Courtois' *Orpheus* (1875) is a small, early work, more than twice as wide as high.[47] It shows the head of Orpheus and his lyre, half-sunk on a sandy beach—everything well executed, but precious. His friend, Pascal Dagnan-Bouveret, painted his own version of the myth: *The Grief of Orpheus* (1876).[48] Neither work contributes to an understanding of the myth. Even the greatest stumbled. In his mid-seventies, Victor Hugo wrote a short poem on Orpheus, whom he envisages as the carrier of all deeply felt male love—and, inevitably, with whom he identifies.[49] The poet had forgotten not only that the myth *begins* with the death of Eurydice, but also that bombast makes for poor poetry.

In 1881, the French government passed its sponsorship of the annual *Salon* to the Société des Artistes Français. It hoped that this would launch a new era in French painting. In the event, the *Salons* of the 1880s all-too-often sounded new lows in tastelessness, as illustrated by two paintings of the childhood of Orpheus, both painted in 1884. In the centre of Edouard Rosset-Granger's *Orpheus Singing* stands a naked teenage Orpheus, playing his lyre to a tiger, a fulsome studio-nude, and doves hovering above. Georges Callot's *Education of Orpheus* (1884) is even more ridiculous.[50] A nude Calliope, lying on her back, the light falling on her breasts, is idly playing a lyre while a swan amorously caresses the instrument. Standing behind her is her chubby young son, Orpheus, his head raised as if he were awakening to a love of music. *Risqué* titillation? or pornography? It defies belief that an artist could paint such rubbish—or that a buyer could want it.

But even as academic art was sounding new depths, new kinds of painting were beginning to emerge—and Orpheus is also central to this new development.

Esotericism and Symbolism: Orpheus and the Birth of Modern Art

The most successful of these developments was Impressionism and yet, in one respect, the Impressionists were surprisingly conventional. They employed a freer technique and showed a new interest in light, but like all academic artists of the time, they painted what they saw before them: whether landscape or cityscape, grain stack or cathedral, human figures or still life. For this reason, some prefer to date the beginnings of modern art to the 1880s, when a handful of artists began to proclaim that the tradition of mimesis (the representation and exploration of the visible world) was exhausted. Their purpose was to explore *not* what they saw before them, but something they saw in their 'mind's eye'. They became known as symbolists.

Symbolism was born of several recent tendencies. They include the claims of Ballanche, the rapid growth of interest in the esoteric and the occult (Eliphas Lévi), in spiritism (Allan Kardec), in theosophy (Madame Blavatsky), and the increasing interest in psychology (Herbert Spencer, Wilhelm Wundt, William James). Symbolism owes something to all these developments. In 1886, Jean Moréas announced that its purpose was to explore 'primordial ideas'; that is, to re-sacralise art.[51]

Many artists who are now identified as symbolists showed little interest in the label. Following the Franco-Prussian War, Odilon Redon settled in Paris, where he was soon producing startling lithographs (*Eye Balloon*, 1878) and charcoal drawings (*Smiling Spider*, 1881).[52] He repeated motifs obsessively: for example, heads without bodies, women's heads, men's heads, heads resting in a bowl, heads held aloft, grinning heads, sad heads. They are suggestive of dreams, in which they anticipate surrealism.

The Head of Orpheus (1881) is a large charcoal drawing on blue laid paper.[53] To the left, the head, resting on a lyre, is floating down a wave into a sea trough. As it does so, Orpheus looks up, open-mouthed, as if he were crying 'Eurydice! Eurydice!' Redon returned to this haunting image in several later works, including a richly coloured and very striking pastel (see front cover), and a more subdued oil on cardboard, in both of which the head seems to have come ashore by a rock or mound.[54] They are all mysteriously haunting.

His contemporary, Auguste Rodin, was similarly obsessive. In 1887, he began working on small plaster models for a sculpture on the climactic moment of the same myth.[55] In 1893, he carved it in marble. The two figures are emerging from Hades. Orpheus has just become flesh. Eurydice, behind him, is still a shade—and she is yearning to be reunited with him. The work depicts that moment, just before the catastrophe, when Orpheus can no longer feel her breath on his neck and is about to turn. There is no lyre. For the figures serve as a metaphor for the difficulty of translating into art an idea drawn from the imagination.

Joséphin ('Sâr') Péladan was an attention-seeking charlatan who played an enormous role in changing attitudes toward visual art.[56] One of those who fell under his spell was Jean Delville, whose early *Orpheus* (1893) remains perhaps his best-known work. It shows the singer's head, eyes closed, lying on a richly jewelled lyre (modelled on the one in Moreau's *Orpheus*) which has come to rest on a shore with pebbles and seashells.[57] The entire painting is blue, except for the watery glow of moonlight on the face, which is modelled on the artist's wife. Orpheus is resting in calm repose, consumed by his own androgyny, which suggests an unexpected ending to the familiar myth. Orpheus has become *fused* with the Eurydice for whom he yearned.

In 1892, Alexandre Séon, a pupil of Puvis de Chavannes, painted a striking portrait of Sâr Péladan. According to an art critic who knew him well, 'he received confidences from Orpheus; he shared the god's dreams and his despair; and he records these in his works with a lapidary simplicity'.[58] Sometimes, this lapidary simplicity served him well. *The Lamentation of Orpheus* (1896) remains the best known of his various renderings of the myth.[59] The beach, the cliffs, and the seashore are all deliberately stark, flattened, and bare of shadow. The disconsolate demi-god, a grey-blue cloak draped across his hips and legs, is lying on the sand, his right arm raised across his eyes to hide his grief. With his left hand, he clings to his lyre. The painting vividly illustrates his hopeless, but poignant despair.

Symbolism encouraged artists to look inward and to depict their *inner* concerns. Predictably, this produced some truly awful art: precious, pretentious, and mawkish.[60] And yet, its importance cannot be exaggerated. For its break with realism paved the way for *modern* art.

Conclusions

Part one has looked at versions of the myth of Orpheus and Eurydice that span almost 2,000 years. It illustrates how, throughout these years, writers and other artists turned to the myth to explore concerns that intrigued them. The surprise is to discover how very different these concerns have been. This suggests that a myth is not defined by a single story. It is defined by the sum of all the concerns that successive generations of writers and other artists have found to be harboured in the myth.

Inevitably, these concerns reflect significant aspects of the time in which each work was produced, and the history of these concerns thus provides intriguing snapshots of the evolution of Western culture—from its interest in moral philosophy (the Augustan myth, Boethius), through its insistence on Christian allegory (the medieval myth), its exploration of human love (during the Renaissance), to its determination to call out unacceptable personal and social behaviour (the Enlightenment).

During the long romantic period, for the first time, writers and other artists project their *personal* concerns into the figure of Orpheus. Undigested, this tendency often leads to self-indulgent and tasteless works. But when the author is driven by something beyond adolescent posturing, or the intensity of their personal quest or theory, an aesthetic or critical distance allows them to produce works that still speak to the reader/viewer today: for example, such unforgettable works as those by Novalis, Nerval, Moreau, and Redon.

Part Two of this study spans only just over a hundred years—and yet, it reveals an even greater variety in the concerns that characterises recent and contemporary versions of the myth.

Notes

1 And yet, France retained the administrative *départements* set up in 1790, as well as several initiatives established by Napoleon, including his reforms to civil law (the *Code Civil*, or Napoleonic Code), finance (the Banque de France), education (the *lycées*), and recognition of public service (the *Légion d'honneur*).

2 For example, Mrs. Gaskell, *North and South* (1854–1855).

3 For a discussion of romanticism, see, for example, J. Barzun, *Classic, Romantic, and Modern*, Chicago: University of Chicago Press, 1961; M. Brown, 'Romanticism and Enlightenment', S. Curran (ed.), *The Cambridge Companion to British Romanticism*, 2nd ed., Cambridge: Cambridge University Press, 2010, pp. 34–55.

4 Wordsworth, 'The Two-Part Prelude' (1799, line 67), 'Home at Grasmere/The Prospectus to *The Recluse*' (1800/1806, line 989), *The Prelude*, Book 1 (1805, line 351; cf. 1850, line 347).

5 Wordsworth, 'Essay, Supplementary to the Preface', in *Poems*, 2 vols., London: Longman, Hurst, Rees, Orme, and Brown, 1815, vol. I, p. 371.

6 J. Réattu, *Orphée aux Enfers devant Pluton et Proserpine*, Arles: Musée Réattu.

7 See V. van Gogh, letter of 24 February 1888 (to Theo), in *The Letters: The Complete Illustrated and Annotated Edition*, ed. Leo Jansen, Hans Luijten, and Nienke Bakker, *vol. 4: Arles, 1888–1889*, London: Thames & Hudson, 2009, p. 14.

8 Charles Landon, *Les Regrets d'Orphée*, Alençon: Musée des Beaux-Arts et de la Dentelle.

9 Pierre Narcisse Guérin, *Orphée au tombeau d'Eurydice*, Orléans: Musée des Beaux-Arts.

10 Ary Scheffer, *La Mort d'Eurydice*, Chateau de Blois: Musée des Beaux-Arts.

11 Novalis, *Philosophical Writings*, tr./ed. M. Mahony Stoljar, Albany, NY: SUNY Press, 1997.

12 See W.A. Strauss, 'Novalis: Orpheus the Magician', chapter 2 in *Descent and Return: The Orphic Theme in Modern Literature*, Cambridge MA: Harvard University Press, 1971, pp. 20–49.

13 Novalis, *Henry von Ofterdingen*, tr. P. Hilty. New York: Frederick Ungar, 1964. The original Heinrich von Ofterdingen was a poet/singer who, in 1207, competed in the legendary singing contest at Wartburg Castle, in Eisenach (Germany). Today, the event is best known from Wagner's later opera, *Tannhäuser* (1845).

14 A resonant phrase, borrowed, for their novels, by Ursula K. Le Guin (*Always Coming Home*, 1985) and by Thomas Lang (*Immer nach Hause*, 2017), about the young Hermann Hesse.

15 My paraphrase, see 'Tieck's Notice on the Continuation of Novalis' "Heinrich von Ofterdingen" (1802)' available on Wikisource.

16 A witty parody of this tradition is *Fleur bleue* (1937), a song by Charles Trenet.

17 Artists who painted her in her twenties include Jacques-Louis David (1800, Louvre) and François Gérard (1801, Musée Histoire de Paris, Carnavalet), and who sculpted her later, Antonio Canova (1819–22, Musée des Beaux-Arts de Lyon).

18 See A. Kettler (ed.), *Lettres de Ballanche à Madame Récamier (*1812–1845*)*, Paris: Honoré Champion, 1996.

19 Pierre-Simon Ballanche, 'Essai sur les institutions sociales', in *Œuvres complètes*, Paris: Bureau de l'Encyclopédie des connaissances utiles, 1833, vol. 2, p. 71.

20 Pierre-Simon Ballanche, 'Palingénésie sociale', in *Œuvres complètes*, Paris: Bureau de l'Encyclopédie des connaissances utiles, 1833, vol. 4, p. 10.

21 Pierre-Simon Ballanche, 'L'Homme sans nom', in *Œuvres complètes*, Paris: Bureau de l'Encyclopédie des connaissances utiles, 1833, vol. 3, p. 163.

22 Pierre-Simon Ballanche, 'Palingénésie sociale', in *Œuvres complètes*, Paris: Bureau de l'Encyclopédie des connaissances utiles, 1833, vol. 4, p. 96, cf. p. 98.

23 Their grave, with a single tombstone, is in the cimetière de Montmartre (cimetière du Nord), Paris.

24 C. Baudelaire, 'Correspondances', in *Les Fleurs du mal* (1857), in *Œuvres complètes*, 2 vols., ed. C. Pichois. Paris: Gallimard, 1975, vol. 1, p. 11.

25 All four paintings are now in the Museu de Arte, São Paulo, in Brazil. Summer is on the myth of Actaeon and Diana; autumn/fall, on Bacchus and Ariadne; and winter, on Juno and Aeolus.

26 The first part only: the second part of *Faust* was not published until 1832.

27 See 'El Desdichado', in Gérard de Nerval, *Œuvres,* tome I, ed. A. Béguin et J. Richer, Paris: Gallimard/Pléiade, 1966, p. 3. The title was borrowed from Walter Scott's *Ivanhoe* (1819), ch. 8, where it is translated as 'Disinherited'.

28 See W.A. Strauss, 'The Seasoning of Hell: Nerval', in *Descent and Return: The Orphic Theme in Modern Literature*, Cambridge, MA: Harvard University Press, 1971, pp. 50–80.

29 Gérard de Nerval, *Œuvres complètes,* ed. J. Guillaume et Claude Pichois, Vol. III, Paris: Gallimard-Pléiade, 1993, pp. 693–756.

30 C.G. Jung lectured on *Aurélia* in 1942, and again in 1945 (see C. G. Jung, *On Psychological and Visionary Art: Notes from C. G. Jung's lecture on Gerard de Nerval, 1945*, ed. Craig E. Stephenson, tr. Richard Sieburth, Princeton: Princeton University Press, 2015). Since then, *Aurélia* has received considerable attention: for example, Gabrielle Chamarat, *Lucidité de Nerval*, Paris: Classiques Garnier, 2019.

31 See C.G. Jung, 'A Study in the Process of Individuation' (1950), in *CW* 9.i (*The Archetypes and the Collective Unconscious*), 1969, p. 351.

32 See Baudelaire, 'Le Cygne', *Œuvres complètes*, ed. C. Pichois, Paris: Gallimard/Pléiade, 1975, p. 85.

33 In prose, a scathing pamphlet (Victor Hugo, *Napoléon le petit*, Paris: J. Hetzel, 1852); in verse, an equally scathing poem ('Napoleon III', in *Les Châtiments*, Paris: Henri Samuel, 1853).

34 P. Séguin, *Louis-Napoléon le Grand*, Paris: Grasset, 1990.

35 J. Offenbach, *Orphée aux enfers*, Opera National de Lyon, cond. Marc Minkowski, France 2/TDK, 2002.

36 D. Charlton (ed.), *E T A Hoffmann's Musical Writings: Kreisleriana, the Poet and the Composer*, Cambridge: Cambridge University Press, 1989; A. Chantler, *E.T.A. Hoffmann's Musical Aesthetics*, Aldershot: Ashgate (now Routledge), 2006.

37 Liszt, *Symphonic Poems*, no 4, Orpheus.

38 F. Leighton, *Orpheus and Eurydice*, London: Leighton House Museum.

39 R. Browning, 'Eurydice to Orpheus: A Picture by Leighton' (1864), included in '*Dramatis Personae*' in *The Complete Poetic and Dramatic Works of Robert Browning*, ed. H.E. Scudder. Cambridge, Mass.: Riverside Press, 1895, p. 395.

40 *Poems of Robert Browning 1833–1865*. London: Cassell, 1907, p. 611.

41 A. Brookner, *Look at Me*, London: Jonathan Cape, 1983; J. Egan, *Look at Me*, New York: Doubleday, 2001.

42 C. Jalabert, *Nymphs Listening to the Songs of Orpheus*, Baltimore, MD: Walters Art Museum.

43 É. Lévy, *La Mort d'Orphée*, Paris: Musée d'Orsay.

44 C. Corot, *Orpheus Leading Eurydice from the Underworld*, Houston, TX: The Museum of Fine Arts.

45 G. Moreau, *Orphée*, Paris: Musée d'Orsay. In English, the painting is sometimes called *Young Thracian Girl Carrying the Head of Orpheus*.

46 The terms were calculated as proportional to those that Napoleon had imposed on Prussia in the second Treaty of Tilsit, 1807, when Prussia was forced to cede territory to its neighbours, and to pay a humiliating tribute: see A.J.P. Taylor, *Bismarck: The Man and the Statesman*, London: Hamish Hamilton, 1955, p. 133.

47 G. Courtois, *Orphée*, Pontarlier: Musée Municipal.

48 P. Dagnan-Bouveret, *La Douleur d'Orphée*, Mulhouse: Musée des Beaux-Arts.
49 V. Hugo, 'Orphée', J. Truchet (ed.), *La Légende des Siècles*, Paris: Gallimard/Pléiade, 1950, p. 495.
50 G. Callot, *L'Éducation d'Orphée*, Châlons-sur-Marne: Musée Municipal.
51 Jean Moréas, 'Le Symbolisme', *Le Figaro*, 18 September 1886, Supplément littéraire, pp. 1–2. For a fuller account, see Dorothy M. Kosinski, *Orpheus in Nineteenth-Century Symbolism*, Ann Arbor: UMI Research Press, 1989.
52 Odilon Redon, *Œil-ballon*, New York: Museum of Modern Art; *Araignée souriante* (Musée d'Orsay (but kept at the Département des art graphiques, Musée du Louvre).
53 Odilon Redon, *Head of Orpheus*, New York: Museum of Modern Art.
54 Odilon Redon, *Orpheus*, a pastel (Cleveland Museum of Art), and *Orphée*, an oil on cardboard which featured in the Armory Show in 1913 (Musée Fabre de Montpellier).
55 A. Rodin, *Orpheus and Eurydice*, marble, New York: Metropolitan Museum of Art.
56 For a succinct introduction to this influence, see P. Julian, *Dreamers of Decadence: Symbolist Painters of the 1890s*, tr. R. Baldick. London: Pall Mall, 1971; also, *Mystical Symbolism: The Salon de la Rose+Croix in Paris, 1892–1897*, ed. V. Greene, New York: Guggenheim Museum, 2017.
57 J. Delville, *Mort d'Orphée*, Bruxelles: Musées Royaux des Beaux-Arts de Belgique.
58 C. Saunier, 'Alexandre Séon', *La Revue blanche* 25 (mai-août 1901), pp. 303–304.
59 A. Séon, *Lamentation d'Orphée*, Paris: Musée d'Orsay.
60 As illustrated (presumably unintentionally) by the recent exhibition, *Mystical Symbolism*, 2017.

Part II

Eurydice, or Unbearable Loss

Chapter 7

Orpheus and Eurydice, Dissociative Tendencies, and Self-Transformation

Early Twentieth-Century Modernism

The new century was much like the old. It promised the wealthy all the luxury and leisure to which they felt entitled, but for most of the population, it offered only hunger and hopeless struggle. Britain was typical. In 1900, a mere 17,000 people owned two-thirds of the nation's wealth, 90% of the population died without *any* recorded property, and millions lived in abject poverty.[1] Western leaders continued to brush this grotesque inequality under the carpet. They were still giddy with dreams of empire, even though, for many, the dreams had turned sour. In India, administrative failures were leading to repeated famine. In Africa, in its determination to win the Second Boer War, Britain adopted repugnant methods.[2] And in North America, indigenous peoples were still being hounded into reservations. Colonialism had always been the triumph of might over right. Its failures and atrocities made it abhorrent.

In June 1914, Europe sleepwalked into the hopeless obduracy of the First World War.[3] Twenty million lost their lives to little purpose, for the 'war to end war' was concluded by a series of agreements that *invited* further conflict.[4] The European Allies carved the Ottoman Empire to suit not the peoples of the Middle East, but themselves. Led by France, still bitter about the Treaty of Frankfurt, they imposed humiliating terms on Germany, which naturally stirred resentment. And the reluctance of Western leaders to listen to the concerns of non-Western powers ensured that the League of Nations (1920) was dysfunctional from the outset.

Meanwhile, during its brutal civil war (1917–1922), Russia lost control of most of its Western Empire, including Finland, Estonia, Latvia, Lithuania, most of Belarus, and Ukraine. About ten million—mostly civilians—lost their lives and the economy collapsed. But, for the first time in Western history, the 'people' had decisively overthrown their 'masters'. As had happened following the French Revolution, Western leaders quickly determined to prevent such a revolution breaking out in their own country.

This chapter looks at a selection of versions of the myth of Orpheus and Eurydice written during these tense and divisive years—years that coincide with early twentieth-century modernism.[5] It is in four parts. The first looks at two representations of Eurydice, including the first poem by a woman to re-imagine the myth in relation to a specifically female experience. The second examines the first versions

DOI: 10.4324/9781003519584-10

to associate the myth with the underprivileged and the marginalised. The third explores two very different dramatic works which explore pathological dissociation. And the fourth considers three works which explore the writer's need to produce a work of distinctive and significant art.

Re-Imagining Eurydice

Throughout the Western world, the second half of the nineteenth century witnessed increasing calls for equal suffrage. It was first granted in New Zealand (1893), then in Australia, Finland, Norway, and Denmark; next came the Netherlands and Russia (1917), the United States (1920), and the United Kingdom (1928). This sea-change in social attitudes coincides with two landmark representations of Eurydice.

Rilke: Eurydice Surprised by Orpheus

Rainer Maria Rilke was born in 1875, in Prague, into a privileged but troubled family. In 1901, while living in an artist's colony in Worpswede (near Bremen, North Germany), he met and married Clara Westhoff, a sculptor. Soon after, while on a visit to Naples, he became fascinated by a Roman copy of a Greek relief from the fifth century BCE.[6] It shows three standing figures: Hermes (left) who is holding Eurydice (centre) by the hand while she is looking toward Orpheus (right), and both are looking down, in obvious distress. The sculpture triggered one of the most striking lyrics in Rilke's *New Poems* (1907).

'Orpheus. Eurydice. Hermes' illustrates a moment shortly *after* Orpheus has turned, but *before* Hermes has insisted that she return to the underworld for ever. It begins with the three figures slowly wending their way upward, out of the underworld. They are represented as both *porphyry* (rock) and as the *blood* (liquid) that flows through human veins—a contrast of metaphors which suggests that the poem explores a tension between opposite tendencies and attitudes.

Vibrant with determination, Orpheus strides upward. His sight runs ahead of him 'like a dog', while his hearing (intent on ascertaining whether Hermes and Eurydice are following) trails behind 'like a scent'. Impatient and restless, he is defined by his yearning to be somewhere *else* and his longing for someone *other*. In contrast, Eurydice is completely absorbed in her own concerns. She has forgotten Orpheus. She is no longer *his* 'blond wife'. When Hermes tells her, he has turned, she is taken aback. '*Who?*' she asks. She has attained 'a new virginity'. She is 'turned in on herself' (*Sie war in sich*), in her own experience, her own process, like a woman about to give birth.

Browning's identification with Eurydice reflects male insecurity. In contrast, Rilke's poem contrasts two aspects of creativity. Eurydice embodies the artist's need to be deeply in tune with their inner experience. While Orpheus represents their need to bring this experience to the surface and to translate it into form. The poem expresses a doubt as to whether he can do this.

A decade after it was written, a young woman turned to the same myth to express an emphatically female experience.

Hilda Doolittle [H.D.]: The Myth of Eurydice and Orpheus

Until the early twentieth century, relatively few women had been drawn to the myth of Orpheus and Eurydice—and understandably. For why would a woman be drawn to a myth in which all the attention is on the male hero, and the female figure dies, not once, but twice? Several women had produced accounts of the myth, but their works do not appear to explore a *specifically* female experience.[7] The American poet and novelist, Hilda Doolittle, better known by her initials, may be the first woman to re-imagine the myth from a *woman*'s point of view.

H.D. was from a Moravian community in Pennsylvania. She was a schoolfriend of Ezra Pound. In 1911, she moved to London where he ensured that she played a prominent role in the Imagist movement. Her work, however, is both more personal and more committed than 'imagism' suggests. Her entire life can be seen as a quest for fulfilment in an indifferent, if not alien world. 'Eurydice' (1917) belongs to a group of autobiographical poems ('Amaranth', 'Eros', and 'Envy') written during the depression into which she fell after she gave birth to a stillborn child, a depression made worse by the discovery that her husband was having an affair with another woman.

She turned to the myth of Orpheus and Eurydice to help her come to terms with her husband's double betrayal: first, the betrayal that plunged her into the 'hell' of depression; and, secondly, the betrayal represented by him descending into her 'hell' to seek her, but without really knowing what he wanted. She reproaches him for offering her the hope of renewed joy when he hasn't the strength of determination to bring this about. If she mourns, it is not for him, but only for the loss of what he has robbed her of: the brightly coloured flowers of Spring which represent not only her joy in the upper world, but also her lost child.

She has lost the 'earth', its 'flowers', and 'live souls' not because of a third party (Aristaeus, a snake in the grass), but because *Orpheus* is so self-centred that he has been careless of *her* needs and feelings.

Whereas the traditional figure of Orpheus embodies a man who *refuses* to accept what fate has dealt him, H.D. *accepts* her fate with courage. In the final section, she resigns herself to her lot with a ringing assurance. She is contemptuous of *his* hell, because he cannot understand the value of the flowers which are a metaphor for the inner joy of life. She prefers her own hell:

At least I have the flowers of myself
and my thoughts — no god
can take that!
I have the fervour of myself for a presence
and my own spirit for light.[8]

Traditionally, Orpheus is overcome by despair. H.D.'s 'fervour' underlines her determination to survive, to be resilient. Her poem makes clear that, when *felt* from a woman's point of view, the myth harbours significantly different implications from versions written by men. This was in 1917. Not until the middle of the Second World War would another woman writer respond to the myth from such an emphatically female perspective. Caroline Gordon would be the first to refer to it as the myth of 'Eurydice and Orpheus'.

Meanwhile, two other striking versions of the myth were produced, and they explore not their author's personal concerns, but their *social* and *political* concerns.

Orpheus and Social Marginalisation

While the First World War was grinding to its conclusion, writers and other artists were struggling to find a language to describe the brave new world in which they found themselves. One of these was Isaac Lang, better known by his pseudonym.

Yvan Goll: Orpheus and the Hopeless Longing of the Underprivileged

Yvan (or Iwan) Goll was from Alsace-Lorraine, and he wrote with equal fluency in German and French. He also moved easily in artistic circles. In the final years of the war, in German, he composed 'Der Neue Orpheus' (1918). After the war, he revised it and translated it into French as 'Le Nouvel Orphée' (1923), in which version it was published in a collection with illustrations by Robert Delaunay, Georg Grosz, and Fernand Léger.[9] Two years later, Kurt Weill set a section of the German text as a cantata for soprano, solo violin, and orchestra (opus 16)—and its first performance was conducted by Erich Kleiber.

'The New Orpheus' is overtly socio-political, but it carries strong psychological implications. Orpheus is depicted as the modernist artist who would like to rescue Eurydice—that is, all those whose lives are spent in repetitive, thankless, and mind-numbing jobs. The poem juxtaposes a vivid sense of the banality of everyday life with a yearning for another freer, richer mode of being—but with an intriguing distinction. It suggests that, to fill the vacuum of their lives, the middle classes can always turn outward, for their money allows them to breathlessly pursue one novelty after another, careless of what can be learned from each experience. In contrast, the working class needs must be satisfied with fewer pleasures, which they therefore invest with deeper significance. In this way, they retain an instinct for life which often evades those more privileged than they are.

Orpheus is introduced as a 'collector of stars'. He breathes the pure oxygen harboured on 'mountain peaks' and in 'forests inhabited by nymphs'. He cannot understand that others find it difficult to breath the refined air in which he lives. Consumed by his own longing, he is unaware of the pain of modern humankind. He shudders to see a person who is imprisoned in their body and has nothing to guide them. And yet, the text reminds us, these other human beings also have their mystery: their longings, *their* Eurydice. And they recognise Orpheus, for nothing can equal his music, which orders the harmony of the spheres and of the human heart.

For Orpheus makes the lives of the underprivileged endurable. He delivers them from tedium and informs them of their humanity. He is the shy piano teacher who rescues a young girl from her mother's stifling anxiety. He is the entertainer crooning in nightclubs. He is the scrawny organist in a suburban church. He is the celebrity who plays to packed houses. And he is always, always looking for Eurydice. One day, never having found her, in the middle of an interview, he shoots himself.

Never mind the histrionic ending. 'The New Orpheus' is the first version of the myth to explore not the yearning of a young man for a dearly-loved young woman, but the yearning of all those, especially women in low-paid jobs, who seek a respite from their inner emptiness in an experience (most often, music) which they associate with Orpheus—for Orpheus *reflects* their yearning, because he too is consumed by his own impossible longing. That is, following Ballanche, but very differently, Goll sees the myth as a combination of psychological and sociological factors. A few years later, a French chamber opera became the first version to present the myth as a tragedy about marginalised *communities*.

Lunel and Milhaud: Orpheus and the Intense Passions of the Marginalised (France)

Darius Milhaud was born into a well-to-do French Jewish family from Aix-en-Provence, in the south of France. His compositions, often small-scale, span an impressive range of forms and styles, including the syncopated rhythms of both Brazilian music and American jazz. In his late twenties, he produced the music for three ballets whose zany scenarios were devised by Jean Cocteau.[10] The two men had much in common—and yet, they held very different views about myth.

Milhaud held that myths reflect the restricted vocabulary, and the intense and often violent passions that can erupt quickly in small and isolated communities. So, when it came to planning an opera based on the myth of Orpheus, he turned to Armand Lunel, an old school friend and one of the last known speakers of Shuadit (a Jewish-Provençal dialect).

The Misfortunes of Orpheus (*Les Malheurs d'Orphée*), first performed in Paris in May 1926, is a chamber opera which lasts only thirty-five minutes.[11] It is set in the Camargue (south of France), an area of sun-soaked and wind-swept marshland famous for its wild horses, its flamingos, and the Romani festival held each year in Les Saintes-Maries-de-la-Mer. There are three short acts or *tableaux*.

Orpheus is a bonesetter and folk-healer who lives on the edge of a small village whose residents are wary of him. He has fallen in love with Eurydice, a young woman from a nearby Romani encampment, but he is afraid of the possible repercussions of their relationship. Meanwhile, Eurydice's friends warn her not to get close to anyone outside their tight-knit community. The couple plight their love—whereupon Orpheus accepts the advice of his friends and flees to the mountains.

The second tableau represents how both protagonists lose something of themselves when they retreat from their social reality. Eurydice quickly wastes away and dies of an unnamed illness. Orpheus, surrounded by a wolf, fox, bear, and boar, laments her death. Paul Collaer has described it as one of the most 'starkly beautiful' moments in twentieth-century music.[12]

In the final tableau, Orpheus is alone: even his animals have deserted him. Eurydice's Romani sisters enter. Making accusations that veer between hysteria and desire, they finally attack him. He makes no effort to defend himself and dies, the victim of his and Eurydice's mutual inability to secure the acceptance of their relationship by their respective communities.

The Misfortunes of Orpheus is a fable with the raw immediacy and luminous textures of a religious play. It unfolds between two realities. On the one hand, it insists on the *social* reality of the two equally marginalised groups. On the other, it resists the banal objectivity of realism. It is the first major adaptation of the myth to explore the deep-rooted passions and suspicions that can be triggered in isolated communities.

In contrast, we turn now to two versions of the myth which explore different forms of narcissistic obsession.

Orpheus and the Perils of Self-Absorption

In 1914, Freud distinguished between two kinds of narcissism. Primary narcissism refers to a necessary stage of growth in which a child develops a healthy sense of self-worth and independence. Secondary narcissism refers to the obsessive behaviour of adults who are so consumed by their private concerns that they lose their footing in their social reality.[13]

The following pages look at two works, both of which probe the destructive nature of excessive secondary narcissism. Kokoschka's play illustrates the violence of self-centred emotions, while Malipiero's chamber opera explores the impact of these on society.

Kokoschka and Krenek: Orpheus and the Violence of Self-Centred Emotions

Oskar Kokoschka was born in a small Austrian town into an unstable family of Czech origin and modest means. In Vienna, although he studied under Gustav Klimt, he took no interest in the fashionable *Jugendstil* (Youth Style, a version of Art Nouveau). In 1909, he published *Murder, Hope of Women*, sometimes described as the first 'expressionist play'.[14] Three years later, he began an affair with Alma Mahler, the widow of Gustav Mahler, who had died two years earlier. He was impossibly possessive; she was impossibly difficult.[15]

As their relationship fell apart, he turned to painting to express his confused emotions. *The Bride of the Wind* (1913/1914) is a large, striking canvas.[16] It shows two lovers lying as if on a bed caught in a sickly, storm-tossed sea. The man stares upward in an agony of unconsummated doubt, while the woman sleeps peacefully on his shoulder.

As soon as war broke out, Kokoschka volunteered to serve in the Austrian army. While at the Russian front, he was badly wounded. As he recovered, he suffered from hallucinations, many of them haunted by Alma. He wrote them down as they came to him, and they became the basis of a play in which he turned to the myth of Orpheus and Eurydice to explore his difficulty in accepting that Alma had had enough of him.[17]

Orpheus und Eurydike was first performed in February 1921, in Frankfurt.[18] It was not the success he hoped for. He thought it might be improved by having incidental music. He turned to Ernst Krenek, a talented young composer, and they soon agreed that the play should be translated into an opera. Meanwhile, Krenek had fallen in love with Alma's teenage daughter, Anna Mahler. They married, and as *their* marriage imploded, Krenek turned to Kokoschka's play. With the help of Eduard Erdmann, he tightened the action into a libretto surprisingly faithful to his source.[19] And he soon completed the score.

The play is marked by histrionic bitterness and is rarely revived. Krenek's tighter opera blends atonality with late romanticism, and has some wonderful moments, especially for Eurydike. Krenek regarded it as amongst the best of his early works.[20] It premiered in Kassel, in November 1926.

Only Orpheus and Eurydike belong to a social reality. The other characters, including Psyche (Eurydike's younger sister-cum-guardian angel), three Furies, and various personifications of Hades belong to an imaginal reality. In the first scene, Eurydike is apprehensive about her relationship with Orpheus. Reflecting this, Psyche *inadvertently* lets the Furies into Eurydike's bedroom, which results in the blinding of Cupid. The Furies allow Eurydike a farewell meal with Orpheus before holding her in their arms as she dies.

Five years later, Psyche leads Orpheus into Orcus (the underworld) and warns him never to mention the time Eurydike spent with Hades. Inevitably, he can't resist asking and insisting on an answer. Eurydike finally admits that Hades seduced her, whereupon, seized by jealousy, he goes mad and kills her.

Two years later, Orpheus returns to his home: it is in ruins. He finds his lyre, but its sound is so grotesque that it enrages a group of women who hear him play. They hang him. Meanwhile, to atone for her mistake, Psyche has spent seven years filling a jug with her tears in the hope they will restore Cupid's eyesight. As Orpheus frees himself from the noose, Eurydike's spirit begs him to release her from *his* passion. Laughing insanely, he tells her that his love is really hatred, whereupon *she* suffocates him. In a short coda, Psyche holds a lyre, and a chorus of youths explain how egocentricity will give way to love and brotherhood. She is finally able to return to Cupid.

Although hardly obvious, the driving concern of both the play and the opera is Kokoschka's yearning for closure. He appears to have thought the reunion of Psyche and Cupid would allow the audience to forget the hate-filled deaths of Orpheus and Eurydice. In the opera, Krenek's music almost achieves this.

Alma was the love of Kokoschka's life: he never got over her. In contrast, by the time of the opera's first performance, Krenek was already divorced from Anna and finishing the boisterous, jazz-inspired *Jonny spielt auf* (Jonny Swings), which premiered three months later and was a runaway success. Its most catchy numbers—such as 'Leb wohl, mein Schatz' (Farewell, my dear)—were on everyone's lips. Kokoschka must have wished that he could have been as resilient.

Meanwhile, in Rome, an Italian composer turned to the same myth to explore how individuals have become so consumed by their personal obsessions that *society* has become dissociative.

Malipiero: Orpheus, Dissociative Individuals, and a Dissociative Society

Gian Francesco Malipiero came from an aristocratic and musical family in Venice. While studying in Paris, he was introduced to works by his contemporaries, including Schoenberg, Berg, and Stravinsky. He soon became a well-respected composer and musical scholar.

The term dissociation usually refers to an *individual's* pathological detachment from reality, whether the reality of their personal experience (their situation, a relationship), or the reality of their social world (indifference to, or unreal notions about). In contrast, Malipiero's *L'Orfeide* offers a searing indictment of the dissociative tendencies of modern *society*.

L'Orfeide was first performed in the old Stadttheater Düsseldorf (Germany) in late 1925.[21] It is in three acts—but they were *not* conceived in the order they have in the opera. In 1920, the second part, 'Seven Songs', was performed as a complete work. He then added the third part, 'Orfeo, or the Eighth Song', to illustrate that his subject has a long history. And finally, for the same reason, for the *first* part of his opera he turned to characters from the *commedia dell'arte* (a form of semi-improvised comedy based on human types which became popular in Italy in the sixteenth century).

Act 1: 'The Death of the Maskers' is set in a large bare room. At the back is a wardrobe. An impresario with a black gown and huge owl-eyed spectacles introduces seven of the characters from the *commedia dell'arte*. Conspicuously *absent* from these characters are the lovers (who feature at the heart of every *commedia dell'arte* performance, and who are always united at the end). That is, the focus of the opera is on those characters who, each in his own way, thinks only of their own concerns, always opportunistic, and often predatory.

The introductions are rudely interrupted by a figure dressed in red, wearing a hideous mask, and brandishing a whip. He drives the impresario out, shuts the characters in the cupboard, and then unmasks. He is Orpheus—and he calls for a fresh cast of characters. The implication is that the world *prior* to the First World War may also have been dominated by self-interest and greed—but at least it was not dissociative. As the curtain closes, Harlequin (who is defined by his cunning, and yet always ends as a victim of his own appetites) escapes.

Act 2: ('Seven Songs') consists of seven miniature tableaux-operas set in a contemporary, post-war social reality. Each is devoted to one of the *new* types introduced by Orpheus, and they each illustrate different expressions of psychological dissociation. For example, in 'Vagabonds', a young woman is looking after a blind and elderly guitarist. A young singer/storyteller enters and woos her. After a few moments, they leave a few coins for the blind man and abandon him.

The common theme of the seven miniature operas is *loss*: loss of empathy (The Vagabonds; Vespers); loss of belief (The Return); loss of reason (The Drunkard); loss of connection (The Serenade); and loss of decorum and decency (The Bellringer; Dawn on Ash Wednesday)—in other words, the *loss* of that part of a person's human nature which allows them to see *beyond* their own self-interest. The suggestion is that the new age is characterised by both individual and social dissociation.

The third act, 'Orpheus', is a *tour de force*. The stage is divided into four separate spaces: (1) an eighteenth-century marionette theatre in which a puppet Nero indulges in one monstrosity after another. This play is watched by (2) a privileged audience, including a king and queen, in eighteenth-century costume and who sit unmoved throughout; (3) an audience composed of elderly people, also in eighteenth-century costume, but who are increasingly horrified by what they are watching; and (4) an audience, composed entirely of children in modern dress, who loudly applaud every monstrosity. Suddenly, all four stages fall into darkness.

The lights come on again. Orpheus enters, now dressed in white. With scathing irony, he praises the eighteenth-century audience for having been untouched by Nero's crimes. He then begins a song in which he asks the audience 'to bear witness to the funereal homage that I celebrate today'. By the time he finishes, everyone on stage has fallen asleep, except the queen. She rises; Orpheus leaps to join her; they kiss and leave together.

Malipiero is not concerned with Nero, whose monstrosities are a given. He is concerned with the *response* of the different audiences to the puppet play: the audience in the 'stalls' (who fall asleep), the old people (who are scandalised, but impotent), and by the children (who applaud every vicious act). The common denominator is a pathological dissociation which he attributes to two tendencies: first, to the excessive attention that the privileged classes of the eighteenth century gave to their own entertainment, which blinded them to the real plight of the poor; and (2) to the misplaced admiration and the delight in cruelty of children whose ethical conscience is still unformed and who 'know not what they do'.[22]

L'Orfeide is a masterpiece of modernist opera, both emphatically political *and* emphatically psychological. It offers a blistering picture of society's inability either to identify its own dissociative tendencies, or to recognise its own moral vacuum. The opera is as relevant today as it was a century ago.

The last part of this chapter explores another new concern of the time: the struggles of the creative artist.

Orpheus and Self-Transformation through Art

One of the defining characteristics of modernist writing is its keen interest in the source of poetic creativity. In the following pages, we look at three works, each in a different genre: a modernist poem, a dadaist play, and an experimental film.

What they have in common is their author's association of Orpheus not only with creativity, but also with the need for self-transformation.

Rilke was in his late forties when he was once again reminded of the myth.

Rilke: Orpheus, the Need to Listen, and Self-Transformation

In 1912, Rilke sank into depression. He was invited to stay at Duino Castle (on the Adriatic, near Trieste), where he began what is perhaps his greatest work, the *Duino Elegies*. But he could not finish it. The war intervened, during which he lost his home in Paris. But even after the Armistice, he felt unable to produce the masterpiece he yearned to write. In July 1921, a friend rented a fortified manor house for him (the Château de Muzot, near Sierre, in Switzerland). Rilke wanted to finish the *Duino Elegies*. For six months, nothing came. Then, on 2 February 1922, he suddenly rediscovered his creative voice. He finished the *Duino Elegies*—but only *after* beginning a sequence of sonnets loosely held together by the figures of Orpheus and a young unnamed girl dancer. Although all are sonnets, the most striking thing about them is their variety.

Three things seem to have triggered the new work. First, Rilke had recently acquired a small engraving of Orpheus playing a lyre. Secondly, he had recently re-read the works of Paul Valéry, who had broken out of an even longer creative hiatus by writing 'La Jeune Parque' (1917), a poem in which he projects himself into the thoughts of a young woman idly reflecting on the significance of life. And thirdly, the teenage daughter of an acquaintance of his died of a glandular disease. Rilke had seen Werna Knoop only once, long before: all he could remember about her was that she loved dancing.

Sonnets to Orpheus is in two parts. Part One begins with the poet becoming aware of Orpheus and the miracle of the music he embodies. Consciousness, he tells us, begins with *listening*. The lyre of Orpheus is able not only to tame wild beasts; it allows individuals to *imagine* the world. It transforms a bare hillside into civilisation. In the second poem, the poet no sooner becomes aware of a girl sleeping in his *ear* than her image begins to fade. Whilst 'Orpheus' might be able to follow her, he asks, how can *he* follow Orpheus? The answer is: only by discovering the right kind of song. The wrong kind of song is equated with the yearning of an adolescent. The right kind, which partakes of the god's inspiration, is one in which 'song is being'.

Rilke refers to the Arabian constellation of the Rider as a symbol of man's divided nature: the earth-bound horse guided by spiritual man. If we are to fuse the two realms in ourselves, we must long, not to *escape* the earth, but rather, to become unfettered by its superstitions—to sing its praise and to enjoy its fruit to the point where we *become* the sensual ecstasy which it engenders. In the penultimate poem of the first part, the girl dancer dies as if frozen into a sculptor's bronze. In the following poem, although Orpheus is torn apart by the Maenads, his spirit is disseminated through all nature.

Part Two consists of an extended meditation on the nature of creativity. It has an even freer structure and is even more varied in its formal experiments. It consists of a wide-ranging meditation on the relationship between poetry and transformation. Rilke tells his readers to 'Be like a ringing glass, resounding even as it shatters'[23]. That is, we should not wait for experience to happen by chance. At every moment, we must be engaged in experiencing life to the full—whilst simultaneously putting it behind us. We must move on and allow transformation to change us inside and outside. If drinking from the cup of our most painful experience is too hurtful to be contemplated, then we must transform ourselves into wine. In relation to the motionless earth, we should become a roaring torrent; but, if we are next to a roaring torrent, we must just *be*.

Sonnets to Orpheus is not without its problems. Its imagery is sometimes effete; it sometimes surrenders the sense to the sound. And yet the sequence is overwhelming. It is an astonishing expression of the creative imagination. It is about the need to connect with the essential core of human experience which gives life and poetry their meaning.

Rilke envisages Orpheus as the poet who has 'eaten the poppy with the dead'. But this is partly misleading, for the 'other' realm to which he refers is *not* death, but a 'deeper' inner reality. Orpheus is a mediating symbol whose function is to encourage human beings to plunge into themselves, for only by recognising their *inner* world can they experience the *outer* world in a richer and more meaningful fashion. Only by *listening* to the heartbeat of the world can one hope to transform oneself.

Some four years later, Jean Cocteau produced his first version of the same myth, and his primary concern is also a yearning to discover his authentic poetic voice.

Cocteau: Orphée (the Play) and the Longing to Produce a Significant Work

Jean Cocteau was born in July 1889 into a privileged middle-class family. His father committed suicide when he was nine; his mother was an absentee socialite with a love of theatre and music. He grew up mostly alone, observing and taking everything in. And yet, from an early age, he moved easily amongst the rich and the fashionable, and the writers and artists whom they lionised.

He met and collaborated with many of the most imaginative artists of the time, including painters (Picasso, Modigliani), composers (Satie, Milhaud, Poulenc), and choreographers (Massine, Fokine). Cocteau was everywhere—and yet, what he most wanted was to produce a distinctive work of his own.

In the early 1920s, his partner, the poet and novelist Raymond Radiguet, died of tuberculosis and Cocteau took solace in opium. Jacques and Raïssa Maritain helped him to overcome his dependence and to 'accept God'. He was in his late thirties when he wrote his first major response to the myth of Orpheus and Eurydice.

Orphée (1926) is a boulevard comedy coloured with Dadaist humour. It had a set designed by Jean Hugo (great grandson of Victor Hugo) and costumes by Chanel. It begins with Orpheus feeling trapped in a stifling middle-class world, as if he and his wife Eurydice are dead without realising it. He is obsessed with discovering both a new mode of being and a new medium of expression. He keeps a horse because he imagines that it once tapped out a phrase which he is planning to submit in a forthcoming poetry competition.

Determined to end Orpheus' obsession, Eurydice has written to Aglaonice (a Bacchante), asking her for poison with which to kill the horse. Aglaonice sends her the poison in a sugar lump (which the horse refuses to eat) and asks her to return a compromising letter in the envelope she encloses. When Eurydice licks the envelope, too late, she learns that it is poisoned. She dies.

Death (a young woman in a pink evening dress and a fur stole) enters *through* the mirror, accompanied by two men dressed like surgeons. She gives the horse the sugar lump. Orpheus returns, realises what has happened, and vows to recover Eurydice, even if it be from hell. Heurtebise suggests he wears the rubber gloves left behind by Death's assistants. Orpheus then steps through the mirror.

Orpheus and Eurydice reappear through the mirror. They argue. When he looks at her, she disappears. He reads a letter in the mirror. Aglaonice has discovered that the first letter of each word of Orpheus' poem form an offensive word.[24] She has sent her Bacchantes to kill him. He steps offstage and is stoned to death.

His head is thrown back onto the stage: it wants to know where its body is. Eurydice enters through the mirror to reassure the head. A police commissioner arrives and begins to question Heurtebise, failing to realise that his questions are being answered by the head of Orpheus. Eurydice and Orpheus appear briefly through the mirror and invite Heurtebise to join them. The commissioner leaves.

In the final tableau, Orpheus and Eurydice return through the mirror and look around as if seeing their home for the first time, whereupon Orpheus offers a prayer of thanks to God for having opened his paradise to them, and for having saved Eurydice because she killed the devil (the horse); also, for having saved him 'because I love poetry and You are poetry'. After the '*ainsi soit-il*' (Amen), they finally sit down to dinner.

The play has many amusing moments, but it lacks an over-arching purpose— and the ending is embarrassing (especially given that Cocteau's conversion was short-lived). And yet, it makes at least four intriguing contributions to the myth.

1 The *frame story* is not about Orpheus yearning for Eurydice; it is about Orpheus' longing to discover a significant poetic language which he can call his own.
2 Eurydice tries to protect Orpheus from himself: that is, from his obsession with poetry.
3 Despite the insistence on death, the underworld (borrowing from Celtic tradition) is a *parallel* universe. At the end, Orpheus and Eurydice are once again a typical middle-class couple.
4 Most importantly, it is the first version of the myth in which Orpheus feels 'trapped'—as if he wants to escape the *myth* with which he is associated.

It was the first of several brilliant responses to Greek literature by French writers of the time.[25] They include André Gide's *Oedipe* (1930), Cocteau's *The Infernal*

Machine (1934), Jean Giraudoux' *The Trojan War Will Not Take Place* (1935) and *Electra* (1937), as well as three great responses to the German Occupation: Jean Anouilh's *Eurydice* (1941), *Antigone* (1942), and Jean-Paul Sartre's *The Flies* (1943).[26]

Meanwhile, Cocteau recognised that he had failed to deal persuasively with his hero's yearning to create. It was not long before he returned to Orpheus.

Cocteau: The Blood of a Poet, *Self-Awareness*, and Creativity

In 1930, Cocteau began work on a play about a poet who would walk through a mirror and explore the riddle of creativity. Charles de Noailles (who was already financing *L'Age d'or*, a surrealist film by Luis Buñuel and Salvador Dali) promptly offered him a million francs to translate it into an experimental film.[27]

The Blood of a Poet (Le Sang d'un poète, 1930) grew out of his earlier play (*Orphée*); it too explores the origins of *unbearable loss* and *impossible yearning*; and it ends with a categoric reference to Orpheus. Its metaphors, however, suggest not Dadaism, but Surrealism. It has music by Georges Auric, and it consists of four episodes, each of which explores a challenge faced by a creative artist.

The first episode ('The Wounded Hand, or the Scars of a Poet') begins with the poet/artist drawing a head. When its lips begin to move, as if trying to speak, he tries to rub them out. They appear on his hand. He dips his hand in a bowl of water. When the lips ask for air, the poet holds his hand outside a window. The following day, he sticks the lips onto a plaster statue, whereupon the narrator comments, 'After their secular sleep, it is not crazy to awaken statues'.[28] The suggestion is that it takes many frustrating experiments before artists can produce a work that 'speaks' in the way they want it to.

The second episode ('Do Walls have Ears?') begins with the narrator asking: 'Do you think it that easy to get rid of a wound?' The statue instructs the poet to walk through a mirror, whereupon he finds himself in the corridor of a hotel, struggling to walk as if he were in an apprehensive dream. Outside each room, he bends down and peeps through the keyhole to penetrate the life inside. Each room suggests a different element of Cocteau's personality: his abhorrence of war (The French intervention in Mexico) and gratuitous executions, whether in wartime or peace (Room 17); his need to testify to his own cravings (opium) and mistakes (Room 19)[29]; the need for children to resist the repressive conformity expected of them (Room 21); and his struggle to come to terms with his own conflicting sexual tendencies (Room 23). Horrified by his own confusions, he dives back through the mirror.

The third episode ('The Snowball Fight') explores how the dreams and hopes of a child are worn away by bullying at school, which can scar a person for life. A boy is struck by a snowball/stone.

The fourth episode ('Profanation of the Host') is set in a theatre, with a small audience. It begins with blood spilling from the boy's mouth. Suddenly, next to his corpse, a card table and two players appear: a woman (the statue) and the poet. The episode suggests that individuals spend their lives trying to recover themselves as they were *before* they were hurt in childhood, and that they will cheat to prevent any further hurt. But every time they cheat—whether others or themselves—they disrespect the religion in which they were born.[30] Ashamed that he has cheated, the poet shoots himself. As the spectators applaud the death of the poet, the woman once again becomes a statue. The suggestion is that both life and art require the courage to cheat and to be hurt.

The epilogue shows the woman descending some steps. A bull, covered with a torn map of the world, is waiting. As they exit, the camera closes on its horns, which become the two sides of the lyre of Orpheus. The final image is of the statue lying beside the lyre and a globe.

Few films explore such a broad range of concerns: the poet's convictions (his pacifism; his need to resist even the well-meant expectations of others), his anxieties (the need for art to speak to the viewer); and his own tendencies (his need to wrestle with his demons, especially those that stem from childhood traumas); and his yearning to recover the integrity he had before he was scarred and felt the need to cheat. Although art of necessity involves sleight of hand, the film suggests that the artist must always be 'sincere'. In *The Blood of a Poet*, Cocteau explores the concerns that define him—concerns that include the metaphors of loss, longing, descent, and despair that lie at the heart of the myth of Orpheus and Eurydice—and his *need* to transform them into both art and greater self-awareness.

Conclusion

Until the end of the nineteenth century, behind almost every version of the myth of Orpheus and Eurydice one could discern the *story* told by Virgil. From the beginning of the twentieth century, this is no longer the case. More obviously than before, new versions of the myth explore the *metaphors* that its authors associate with the myth. And by doing so, they 'find' a startling range of new concerns at its heart.

- The artist's need to understand their inner world if they are to translate its intuitions into creative form (Rilke).
- The experience of a woman who has been plunged into an underworld by 'Orpheus', and her realisation that this requires her resilience (H.D.).
- The intense anxieties and suspicions that can arise in isolated and marginalised communities and that can easily lead to preventable tragedy (Lunel and Milhaud).
- The intense emotions of the underprivileged, and their sense of exclusion from 'something' for which they hopelessly yearn (Goll).
- The artist's failure to come to terms with turbulent and violent feelings triggered by the hurt of being abandoned by a partner (Kokoschka).
- The conviction that Western society has become characterised by deep-rooted dissociative tendencies, both personal and collective (Malipiero).
- The need a poet has to be both in tune with themselves and with the world around them if they want to write a significant work (Rilke).

- The writer's feeling that he is 'trapped' inside the myth that fascinates him (Cocteau, *Orphée*).
- The author's need to reflect on the riddles of individual identity and their relation to his creative impulse (Cocteau, *The Blood of a Poet*).

By the time the last of these works was first shown, in 1932, the Wall Street Crash had thrown the Western World into confusion. Writers and other artists turned to the myth with a new purpose: to *testify* to their concerns about the increasingly dysfunctional societies in which they found themselves.

Notes

1 See L.C. Money, *Riches and Poverty*, London: Methuen, 1905.
2 Atrocities committed by the British during the Boer War include confining women prisoners in concentration camps (in which over 26,000 women and children perished), and deporting men to prisoner of war camps overseas (where about 20,000 died). See B. Nasson, *The Boer War: The Struggle for South Africa*, Cape Town: Tafelberg, 2010/ Cheltenham: The History Press, 2011.
3 C. Clark, *The Sleepwalkers: How Europe Went to War in 1914*, London: Allen Lane, 2012.
4 'After the "war to end war" they seem to have been pretty successful in Paris at making a "Peace to end Peace"' (A.P. Wavell, an adjutant at the Supreme War Council in Versailles): see D. Fromkin, *A Peace to End All Peace: The Fall of the Ottoman Empire and the Creation of the Modern Middle East*, New York: Henry Holt, 1989.
5 Modernism is another elastic term. For twentieth-century, or Anglo-Saxon modernism, see Michael Levenson (ed.), *The Cambridge Companion to Modernism* (1999), 2nd ed., Cambridge: Cambridge University Press, 2011. But in Europe, modernism is usually dated from about 1850: see P. Lewis (ed.), *The Cambridge Companion to European Modernism*, Cambridge: Cambridge University Press, 2011.
6 *Orfeo Euridice e Mercurio*, in the Museo Archeologico Nazionale di Napoli. Ironically, Rilke might have seen the relief in Paris, as there is an early Greek copy of the same relief in the Louvre (Ma 854).
7 For example, Christine de Pisan in *L'Épitre d'Othéa à Hector* ('The Epistle of Othea to Hector', 1400), paintings by Angelica Kauffman (1782) and Henrietta Rae (1887), Isadora Duncan's modern ballet, *Orpheus Mourning the Death of Eurydice* (1902), and Maude Allan's ballet, *Orfeo* (1910).
8 'Eurydice', from *Some Imagist Poets 1917: An Annual Anthology*, Boston, MA: Houghton Mifflin, 1917, p. 35, reprinted in H.D., *Collected Poems, 1912–1944*, ed. Louis L. Martz. New York: New Directions, 1983/Manchester: Carcanet, 1984, p. 55, © 1917 by Hilda Doolittle.
9 Y. Goll, *La Chaplinade, Mathusalem, Paris brûle, Le Nouvel Orphée, Astral, Édition du Matin*, Paris: Éditions de la Sirène, 1923. See also, J. Phillips, *Yvan Goll and Bilingual Poetry*, Stuttgart: Akademischer Verlag Hans-Dieter Heinz, 1984.
10 *Le Bœuf sur le toit* (1920), *Les Mariés de la Tour Eiffel* (1921), and, for Diaghilev's Ballets Russes, *Le Train bleu* (1924).
11 Darius Milhaud, *Les malheurs d'Orphée* and *Le pauvre Matelot*, Orchestre de l'Opéra de Paris, cond. Darius Milhaud, 1956 (CD).
12 P. Collaer, *Darius Milhaud* (1947), tr. and ed. J. H. Galante, London: Macmillan, 1988.
13 S. Freud, 'On Narcissism: An Introduction' (1914), in *The Standard Edition of the Complete Psychological Works of Sigmund Freud*, ed. J. Strachey and A. Freud, 1953-1974, vol. XIV, pp. 67–102.

14 The play was sufficiently successful for him to later revise as a libretto for *Mörder, Hoffnung der Frauen* (1921), a one-act opera by Paul Hindemith.

15 O. Hilmes, *Malevolent Muse: The Life of Alma Mahler* (2004), tr. D. Arthur, Lebanon, NH: Northeastern University Press, 2015.

16 O. Kokoschka, *Die Windsbraut*, aka *The Tempest*, Basel: Kunstmuseum.

17 See J.E. Bernstock, *Under the Spell of Orpheus: The Persistence of a Myth in Twentieth-Century Art*, Carbondale: Southern Illinois University Press, p. 66.

18 O. Kokoschka, *Plays and Poems*, tr. M. Mitchell, Riverside, CA: Ariadne Press, *c.*2001. Also, O. Kokoschka, *My Life*, New York: Macmillan, 1974, p. 96; see also, p. 117.

19 Surprising, because at the time Krenek was working on a comic opera, *Der Sprung über den Schatten* (The Leap over the Shadow), which parodied not only psychoanalysis, but also expressionism: it was first performed in Frankfurt in 1924.

20 E. Krenek, *Orpheus und Eurydike* (op. 21). Live recording: ORF-Symphonie Orchester, Wien, cond. P. Steinberg (Salzburg Festival, 1990), CD on Orfeo.

21 The Stadtheater was bombed during the war and rebuilt in the 1950s as the Opernhaus Düsseldorf, home of Deutsche Oper am Rhein. For CD, G.F. Malipiero, *L'Orféide*, Orchestra of the Maggio Musicale Fiorentino, cond. H. Scherchen, 1966, Buzançais, France: TAHRA, 1966.

22 Jesus, on the cross, at Luke 23:34.

23 My translation.

24 The capital letters of the phrase *Madame Eurydice Reviendra Des Enfers* = *merde* (shit).

25 Paul Claudel's *Protée* (1913) is earlier, but Cocteau's play, with its wit and its irony, had by far the greater influence.

26 See J.S. Williams, *Jean Cocteau*, Manchester: Manchester University Press, 2006, p. 112.

27 Cocteau had only made one very short experimental film before, in 1925: *Jean Cocteau fait du cinema*.

28 The statue is Lee Miller, who at the time was working with Man Ray; later, she became a famous war photographer.

29 Jean Cocteau, *Opium: Journal d'une Desintoxication*, Paris: Librairie Stock, 1930.

30 The title of the episode was controversial, for it suggested that the blood flowing from the boy's mouth was a rejection of the host (the bread/wafer consecrated during the Mass).

Chapter 8

Orpheus and Eurydice, Dysfunctional Times, and the Need to Testify

The Second World War

In 1929, the Wall Street Crash set off an international banking crisis that led to mass unemployment, poverty, and hardship throughout the Western world. In European manufacturing cities, many of those engaged in brutal factory conditions turned to communism, while fear of communism stirred a new kind of militarist right-wing populism.

In 1928, the National Socialist German Workers Party (the Nazi Party) had won only 2.6% of the votes cast. Hitler might have been forgotten. But the return of economic turmoil gave him a second chance. In 1930, the Nazis won 18.3% of the votes; in 1932, over 37%. In March 1933, Hitler was appointed Chancellor. He was determined to restore German pride, to build a German Empire to rival that of Britain, and to free the country from all undesirables. While Europe looked on in growing horror, he modernised his armed forces. In September 1939, drunk on dreams of empire, Germany invaded Poland.

The economic hardships triggered by the Wall Street Crash had consequences. On both sides of the Atlantic, an alarming number of communities slipped into dysfunctionality. And between the last years of the 1930s and the middle of the Second World War, several writers turned to an unexpected myth to express their views on this development.

This chapter looks at seven versions of the myth of Orpheus and Eurydice produced within a span of about as many years. It is in four parts. The first part considers two works that focus on the plight of Eurydice in an abusive society; the second, looks at two versions which illustrate an 'inner journey'; the third, explores a searing testament to her life by a young Jewish woman who casts herself as both Orpheus *and* Eurydice; and the fourth, discusses two versions of the myth set during the German occupation of France.

The Plight of Eurydice in a Patriarchal and Abusive Society

In the years following the American Civil War (1861–1865), the industrialised North experienced a remarkable economic boom. Shaken by its defeat and reluctant

DOI: 10.4324/9781003519584-11

to abandon its agricultural traditions, the South gradually fell behind. By the 1930s, many once flourishing communities had become backwaters.

In these pages, we look at two works. Both are written by Southerners, both are set in backwater southern communities, and both foreground the plight of women.

Tennessee Williams: Eurydice in a Dysfunctional Society

Thomas Lanier Williams III was the son of an alcoholic shoe salesman who was, in turn, abusive and absent. In 1938, he adopted the name Tennessee Williams.

Battle of Angels was premiered in Boston in 1940.[1] It was followed by several huge successes: *The Glass Menagerie* (1945), *A Streetcar Named Desire* (1947), and *Cat on a Hot Tin Roof* (1955). But all the while, Williams kept revising *Battle of Angels*, whose protagonist is a young and charismatic writer fleeing from justice. Seventeen years later, it remained much the same play (which is why it is considered here), but its protagonist was now a thirty-year-old *musician*.

Orpheus Descending was premiered in 1957.[2] The author described it as 'the tale of a wild-spirited boy who wanders into a conventional community of the South and creates the commotion of a fox in a chicken coop'.[3] But Val is neither wild-spirited nor a fox. He is a prematurely weary and disillusioned rooster who wanders into a coop filled with bitterly frustrated chickens. The play is about how the *chickens* want Val to lead them out of the coop and away from its oppressive, bigoted, abusive, and racist society.

The events of the play hinge on loaded backstories. Vee, who lives in fear of her bullying husband (Sheriff Talbot), finds solace in the church and in her crude paintings of her religious visions. The once-privileged Carol, ostracised for setting up projects to help African Americans, is now a depressed alcoholic. And the once-beautiful Lady, stuck in a marriage that has become hateful to her, is wasting away with frustration. Many years earlier, during the Prohibition years, her father had kept a clandestine confectionery (wine bar) where he served African Americans and allowed lovers to meet. When the Ku Klux Klan burned it down, the fire department refused its help, and Lady's father was burned to death. Soon after, the wealthy David Cutrere (Carol's brother) began to shower his attention on Lady, who was still in her teens at the time. But as soon as she became pregnant, he abandoned her to marry a 'society girl'. Lady quickly married Jabe Torrance—unaware that he had helped to start the fire that killed her father.

The play is set in the claustrophobic interior of a 'mercantile store' owned by the elderly Jabe Torrance, but managed by Lady, his younger wife. At the back of the store is a confectionery. The events begin when Val Xavier ('Orpheus'), thirty years old, wearing a snakeskin jacket and carrying a prized guitar arrives in this backwater underworld. Each of the three long-suffering women claims him. Vee because she gave him the lift which brought him into town, and she sees him as a Saviour. Carol because she thinks that she and Val have met before. And Lady, by offering him a job in the store. At the centre of the play is a tiny offstage backroom, in which, with Val, she finds a shabby respite from her frustration.

The last act takes place on the Saturday before Easter. Lady learns the truth of her father's death. Vee is struck blind by a vision of her 'Saviour', which she identifies with Val. Trying to shoot Val, Jabe kills Lady, who was shielding him. Sheriff Talbot's men set the store ablaze, Val burns to death, and Carol walks away into an uncertain future.

Tennessee Williams quickly realised that, even in its revised form, the play was a 'failure'. It was 'overwritten'.[4] Its genre was unstable. The social realism is undermined by the relentless insistence on images of stifling control, of the enormous consequences of small mistakes, of rain and fire, and of birds and hunter dogs. The suggestion of a parallel between Val and Christ is ill-judged. Val's homespun view that 'we're under a life-long sentence to solitary confinement inside our own lonely skins for as long as we live on this earth' has nothing in common with the Christian message. The play has been frequently performed and filmed twice.[5] And yet its histrionic excess means that productions are rarely successful.

Orpheus Descending reworks the views of Yvan Goll. It is about the frustrated emptiness of the lives of three women who seek to escape their pain through dreams they project onto a musician who is also searching for his Eurydice. It suggests that a society shaped by the self-centredness of abusive men produces a brutal, sexist, dysfunctional, and racist society.

Meanwhile, soon after the first performance of *Battle of Angels* in 1940, Caroline Gordon turned to the same myth to help her re-examine her convictions.

Caroline Gordon: Eurydice Re-Examines Her Assumptions

Caroline Gordon was born in 1895, on a farm in the south of Kentucky. She studied Greek at Bethany College (in West Virginia). While working as a journalist, she met the Fugitives, a group of poets and writers including John Crowe Ransom, Robert Penn Warren, and Allen Tate.[6] She married Tate, and for the next thirty years, they were central figures in American literary life. Her early novels are predominantly historical and naturalistic. They suggest a deep-rooted bond with the values of the Southern Agrarians, a group of writers—many of whom were part of the earlier Fugitives—who defended agriculture, tradition, and the importance of a religious humanism.[7] By the 1940s, Gordon was amongst the first to realise that they represented an outdated twentieth-century romanticism.

Caroline Gordon had a lifetime interest in the narrative structures of myth. She called them the 'constants' of fiction.[8] And like H.D. before her, she understood that the implications of a myth might be different for women and men. Her novel, *The Women on the Porch* (1944), fuses Gluck's rendering of the myth of Orpheus and Eurydice with the myth of Persephone (Proserpine) eating the pomegranate seed.[9]

The Women on the Porch is set in the early 1940s, shortly before the United States entered the Second World War. It is not only more tentative and more experimental, but also more complex and more personal than her earlier works. It illustrates how even individuals with similar backgrounds harbour different pasts within them. As it unfolds, the reader is taken further and further back in time through memories of the heroine's immediate past (married life in New York), her personal past (childhood in Kentucky), and the collective past of the American Civil War—all of which she must re-assess for herself in the present.

It begins with Catherine Chapman learning that her husband Jim, a professor of history, has been having an affair with a junior colleague. She promptly leaves him and sets off for her childhood home in Kentucky. That is—as for H.D.—Eurydice is swept into the underworld by 'Orpheus'. On arrival at Swan Quarter, she must struggle through undergrowth, which recalls the opening lines of Dante's *Inferno*. Catherine, age thirty-five, has lost her 'straight path' and finds herself in 'hell'. More to the point, she has embarked on a personal journey, the purpose of which is to establish what she truly believes, and what she wants to do next.

On arriving at her former home, Catherine finds three elderly women sitting on the porch: Old Catherine, Aunt Willy, and Cousin Daphne. Each represents a kind of failure: either to find a fulfilling occupation, or to consolidate a lasting relationship. They now exist in a twilight world of mistaken attitudes, missed opportunities, and tragic short-sightedness. They represent the fate of women who play no active part in their society. The most they can hope for is to have some passionate interest, like Willy's love of her favourite horse, or Daphne's hobby of collecting mushrooms.

Their neighbours represent an attempt to maintain traditional southern values. Elsie aspires to be the elegant mistress of a plantation. Catherine is briefly drawn toward her son, Tom Manigault, who is significantly younger than she is, but she gradually comes to realise that the values of the privileged agrarian South are fundamentally flawed, and that its dreams are outdated.[10]

The events hinge on her aunt Willy, who, many years earlier, saved a crippled foal from being shot. It grew up to be a prize-winning stallion called Red, which symbolises the spirit which prevents not only Willy, but also Catherine from being crushed. By riding Red, Catherine rediscovers confidence in her own worth, which she now must test.

In the closing pages, her husband Jim arrives and tells Catherine that his affair is over. He *expects* her to forgive him. When she admits that she was close to Tom, he almost strangles her. She escapes, but later they discuss their situation, whereupon her aunt Willy arrives to announce that Red has been electrocuted in a freak accident. The novel ends with Jim kissing Catherine and saying they will return to New York as soon as it is light.

Some readers see the ending as a sign of defeat. But this may be to miss the point. Catherine realises that she does *not* belong in the 'underworld' to which she instinctively fled. She must return to New York, which is her current *social* reality, and face her problems there. Caroline Gordon and Allen Tate divorced, remarried, divorced again, and yet remained deeply attached to each other. Meanwhile, soon after the publication of *The Women on the Porch*, John Crowe Ransom, widely regarded as the leader of the Agrarians, renounced *his* adherence to their views.[11] Caroline Gordon had led the way.

The following section considers two slightly earlier works. Both were written in Europe, and both were influenced by writers who held strong views about individual development, the evolution of consciousness, and the responsibility of the individual.

Orpheus and Self-Realisation

During the 1930s, partly owing to the weakening hold of collective Christianity, and partly to the dysfunctional turbulence of the times, many of the privileged turned to alternative spiritualities, including yoga and Zen Buddhism (D.T. Suzuki), spiritual philosophies (Rudolf Steiner, Gurdjieff), and therapies, both Freudian and Jungian. They hoped either to relieve their stress, to discipline their mind, to access a 'higher' world, to identify the origin of their difficulties, or to find a 'deeper' meaning to their life.

Two adherents to these alternative disciplines turned to the myth of Orpheus and Eurydice to illustrate an inner journey whose purpose was to obtain greater self-awareness: Owen Barfield (who was strongly influenced by Rudolf Steiner) and Alfred Wolfsohn (who was equally influenced by Jung).

Owen Barfield: Orpheus and the Evolution of Consciousness

Owen Barfield was born in London in 1898, into a non-conformist middle-class family. He studied English language and literature at Oxford University, where he met C.S. Lewis. Despite their differences (at the time, Barfield was discovering his spirituality, while Lewis was still a convinced materialist), they became close friends.

After graduating, Barfield became a lawyer and a writer. In 1924, he attended a lecture by Rudolf Steiner, who argued for the need to bring science and spirituality into harmony, and who held that the imagination guarantees the fullness of our human nature.[12] Steiner's ideas about self-awareness and the evolution of consciousness impressed Barfield deeply. He published *Poetic Diction* (1928), which is about how poetry expands the sense of the meaning which we find in the world. In the 1930s, he became a keen member of The Inklings, a group of friends, writers, and academics who met regularly to chat and to read their work in progress (e.g. early sections of Tolkien's *The Lord of the Rings*, begun 1937, or Lewis' *Out of the Silent Planet*, 1938).

Soon after, he developed an interest in myth, and Lewis suggested that he explore the story of Orpheus. The result was *Orpheus: A Poetic Drama in Four Acts*. It was written in verse, in the late 1930s.[13] And it was designed to illustrate Steiner's ideas about the evolution of consciousness: a journey of self-realisation from 'sleep into self'.[14]

The first act argues that infatuation is not to be confused with love. In the second scene, Eurydice explains that infatuation with the *idea* of the other is not enough. She still loves Orpheus, but she feels imprisoned by his constant songs about her.

She wants them to suggest the evolution of their *joint being in the world*, as if they were two parts of *one* whole. Orpheus cannot grasp what she means. His half-brother, Aristaeus, tries to force himself on Eurydice. While trying to escape, she is bitten by a snake and dies. That is, Aristaeus represents the tacit violence that lies at the heart of Orpheus' infatuation. He cannot see beyond the *idea* he has of Eurydice—and, metaphorically, this inability is responsible for her death.

This promising beginning is undermined by the remaining acts, which are built on the traditional reading of the ending of Virgil's epyllion. Barfield sees Aristaeus' exaggerated sacrifice of a bull as *sufficient* atonement for his attempt to rape Eurydice. Early in the play, Aristaeus represents the negative implications of Orpheus' infatuation. In the final act, his 'sacrifice' allows *him* to recover his bees, and for both Orpheus and Eurydice to proceed from Hades to the Elysian Fields. Despite some powerful lines, it is not clear what exactly Orpheus has learned, nor why the fate of Orpheus and Eurydice should be decided by Aristaeus.

Nonetheless, the play makes some powerful claims. Barfield implies that a renunciation of the ego is necessary for a mutual infatuation to be transformed into a shared sense of *agape*, by which he means not only a fulfilling bond between man and woman, but also the determination to be always making the world a better place.[15] For to love, he argues, is to be *part of a whole which serves a greater whole*. Barfield's play may not be persuasive, but some of its suggestions are.

Meanwhile, in Germany, Alfred Wolfsohn was working on an autobiographical essay on the same myth, and he was strongly influenced by the ideas of Carl Jung.

Alfred Wolfsohn: Orpheus, Voice Therapy, and Self-Awareness

In January 1933, when Hitler became Chancellor of Germany, there was an immediate purge of Jewish employees in all government-related institutions. In May, Kurt Singer persuaded the Nazi authorities to allow him to establish a Cultural Association of German Jews (*Kulturbund Deutscher Juden*). Its members were allowed to exhibit works and perform plays, recitals, and concerts—but *only amongst themselves*.[16] When Germany passed the Nuremberg Laws (1935), which redefined citizenship along racial lines, Jews could no longer be 'German': it became the Jewish Cultural Association (*Jüdischer Kulturbund*)—and for three short years, it continued to serve as a much-needed space in which some 70,000 members were able to exchange information and help all those who could to escape abroad.

Alfred Wolfsohn was born in 1896. Growing up in Berlin, he read widely, and learned to play both the piano and the violin. During the First World War, he was traumatised by his experiences at the front and suffered fits during which he sometimes lost consciousness. He also lost his voice. In the 1920s, he gradually recovered, but drifted aimlessly, until he found his way to the Jewish Cultural Association. Kurt Singer asked Paula Lindberg, a well-known contralto, to help establish him as a singing teacher. About 1937, he wrote an essay about the need for every individual to discover their authentic *voice*.

Orpheus, or the Way to a Mask is about a singer who loses his voice, who descends into an 'underworld' of suffering and confusion, slowly transforms his voice, and who returns to his social reality.[17] It consists of its author's reflections on moments in his life which had impressed him deeply. Wolfsohn had a keen visual memory. He repeatedly begins a new thought with the phrase 'I see myself'. He refers to his childhood, to his traumatic experiences in the trenches, and repeatedly and insistently, to wide-ranging works of art. He also refers to more recent memories, including conversations with friends and students. They are almost always designed to illustrate his views about how to resolve a difficulty.

He argues that vocal difficulties stem less from faulty technique than from deep-rooted psychological tensions related to the singer's whole personality. To overcome these tensions, the individual 'must go into oneself first, to be able to go outside oneself'. And they must recognise that the notions they encounter in their dreams or fantasies which *differ* from those they usually hold represent 'the inferior parts' of their own personality. For, 'to go into oneself also means [...] to come to terms with oneself'.[18]

Western literary culture is predominantly visual. Both Freudian and Jungian psychology emphasise imagery. In contrast, Wolfsohn emphasises *sound*. He describes the rapt inwardness of a person who is listening to music as 'dreaming' and suggests that listening to music also represents a 'listening to oneself'. His purpose is to understand what a person *hears* when they listen to music—to establish how they have been 'touched' or 'moved' by what they hear ('the music within')—and to ascertain how this reveals their inner personality.

As an essay, *Orpheus, or the Way to a Mask* is muddled. It rests on a tension between two very different, although not necessarily contradictory views. On the one hand, it suggests that great art originates in the genius of the artist. Borrowing from Jung (who became interested in alchemy in the 1920s), Wolfsohn wanted his students to 'search for the golden treasure in the depths [of their personality], to help cleanse [their voice] of its impurities, transforming its sound into the shining, illuminating power of gold'.[19]

On the other hand, Wolfsohn insists that the measure of great art is its reception. The analysis of the works of art to which he refers invariably hinges not on the work itself, but on the effect which the work produces in the viewer or audience. That is, he requires the *singer* to engage with their difficulties—and yet, the guarantee of their success is the response their singing produces in the *listener*.

Wolfsohn had barely finished *Orpheus* when *Kristallnacht* (9–10 November 1938) shattered the delusions of the countless German Jews who were still in Germany. They finally realised the horrific truth: none would be spared. Everyone tried to flee. Kurt Singer, Paula Lindberg, and her husband soon found their way to Holland. Wolfsohn escaped to England where, after the war, he became a successful singing teacher whose ideas attracted the interest of composers (Peter Maxwell Davies, Meredith Monk), actors/vocalists (Roy Hart), and voice theorists (Paul Newham).[20]

In *Orpheus*, Wolfsohn quotes from an essay by a fifteen-year-old girl who drew inspiration from music for her paintings. Wolfsohn wondered why she could not paint all that she felt in her soul. He then briefly refers to another, unnamed girl, who shows him a painting of 'Death and the Maiden'—*not* an illustration of the Schubert song, but a representation of her deeply felt 'yearning for an embrace, even if it is with Death'.[21]

This other girl was Paula Lindberg's stepdaughter: Charlotte Salomon—and Wolfsohn and his essay play a crucial part both in her life and in her extraordinary testament.

Eurydice Descends into Herself to Find Herself

Life? or Theatre? is Charlotte Salomon's account of how she did as Wolfsohn advised: she descended into herself 'to find what I had to find—namely, myself'.[22] Her aim was to recover her authentic voice—not her singing voice, but her voice as both *individual* and as *painter*. Her work explores the same metaphors that define the myth of Orpheus and Eurydice: unbearable loss, impossible longing, descent, despair, and self-awareness.

Charlotte Salomon was born in Berlin in 1917. She was nine when she was told that her mother had died from influenza; fourteen when her father, a well-respected surgeon, married Paula Lindberg (née Levi), a famous contralto; and sixteen when the Nazis came to power.[23]

Her grandparents promptly emigrated, settling in the south of France, where they found refuge with Ottilie Moore, a generous German American widow. Her father and stepmother stayed on—and soon paid the price. Her father was dismissed from the University Hospital (although he was promptly offered work at the Jewish Hospital) and her stepmother was now allowed to perform only at concerts mounted by the Jewish Cultural Association. In 1935, Charlotte was given a place reserved for Jewish students at an art school. Her work did not stand out. She might have become a book illustrator. Meanwhile, Kurt Singer had asked Paula to assess whether Alfred Wolfsohn might be qualified to teach singing.

Following the horrors of *Kristallnacht*, Charlotte was despatched to live with her grandparents in the south of France. A few weeks later, her father and stepmother escaped to Holland.

At Ottilie Moore's villa in Villefranche-sur-Mer, appropriately called *L'Ermitage* (= The Hermitage), Charlotte found her grandparents struggling to adjust to exile. Soon after her arrival, her grandmother first tried to commit suicide, and then succeeded. For the first time, she learned how eight other members of her family had also committed suicide. Before she could adjust to this revelation, along with 12,800 other German Jews, she and her grandfather were transported to Gurs, near Pau (in the foothills of the western Pyrenees). Owing to her grandfather's age and state of health, they were allowed to return to Nice, which was under Italian control.

Charlotte was beside herself with repressed confusions. One day, her grandfather snapped: 'O kill yourself!' Instead, she remembered Wolfsohn's advice: 'One has to plunge into oneself—into one's childhood—to be able to come out of oneself'. She decided to paint an account of her 'whole life'. She moved into a *pension* (boarding house) in Saint-Jean-Cap-Ferrat and for close to a year and a half, she painted tirelessly—all the time, either singing or humming quietly to herself.[24]

Charlotte Salomon: Her 'Personal Myth'

Life? or Theatre? consists of 769 gouaches painted on paper of about 10 × 13 inches, many of which have an overlay with text. It is introduced by a title page and five pages of painted text; and it ends with nine more pages of densely painted text.[25]

Over most of the early gouaches there is a sheet of tracing paper, on which Salomon has written a commentary on the episode depicted beneath. But for most of the work, she painted text *into* the paintings, often a sustained conversation. Intermittently, the viewer is asked to look at a painting with a specific tune in mind. The tunes come from wide-ranging sources, including *Lieder* (art songs), arias from oratorios, operas, operettas, and popular songs of the time. That is, the viewer must closely examine the paintings and assimilate the accompanying text, often while recalling a specific piece of vocal music. And the choice of music is often deeply ironic.

As Salomon worked, she developed a succession of highly individual styles. The early sheets are painstakingly composed and painted. They resemble cartoon strips or a storyboard for a film. A single sheet of paper might illustrate anything between three and twenty-five separate *scenes*. As the work progresses, she seeks to get 'inside' the characters of whom she writes: 'I became all the characters who appear in my play. I learned to travel all their paths and became all of them'.[26] Some paintings consist only of their *heads*: sometimes as many as sixty-four heads of the same character on a single sheet. Other paintings show horizontal bodies, while others show standing figures that seem to float rather than to grip the ground.

The story Salomon tells includes family deaths, her unhappy adolescence, and the horrors of Nazi policies. And yet, she recounts these events with such a laconic distance that it is sometimes impossible not to gasp in shock or even to smile at her account. Even the main characters are given wicked fictional names:

The relative/friend	Their fictional name	Its possible connotations
Her grandparents: (family name, Grunwald)	Dr and Mrs Knarre	*knarre* = rattle, or rachet; as adj. = rasping or grating.
Her father (family name, Salomon)	Dr Kann	*kann* = capable; but *kann sein* = maybe or possibly, suggesting dithering.
Paula Lindberg	Paulinka Bimbam	Paulinka is a diminutive of Paula; but *linkisch* = awkward, clumsy, and as an adj. *link* suggests underhanded, or double-crossing; *bimbam* = ding-dong.
Alfred Wolfsohn	Amadeus Daberlohn	Daberlohn is suggestive of having neither money nor salary; also, meriting neither reward nor punishment.

Figure 8.1 The Main Characters: Their Real and Fictional Names.

Salomon describes her work as a 'three-coloured' *Singespiel*, a word which can mean either a *play with music* or a *comic opera*.[27] The three 'colours' to which she refers are not only the primary colours she uses throughout (red, yellow, blue), they also suggest the three distinct media she employs (writing, painting, and music). By extension, the phrase further suggests the three distinct 'levels' on which her story unfolds (the personal, the family, and the socio-historical). And the work is also in three sections: Prelude, Main Section, and Epilogue.

The Prelude consists of over 200 paintings, almost all of which have an overlay with a pithy text. It consists of a family history in two 'acts'. Its subject is the suffocating effect of family silence. Salomon depicts her family members as wrapped in their own concerns, and she paints herself as awkward, as confused, as prey to longings, rages, and hurt.

The first act spans events pertinent to Charlotte's childhood (1913–1932). Its purpose is to show how her childhood was lost to the gnawing despair which gripped the Jewish community.[28] She grows up surrounded by a pervasive feeling of unbearable loss.

She describes the few happy moments from her own childhood; how her father marries Paulinka; how, at first, she adores her stepmother; but how they soon begin to quarrel. She then describes her stepmother's past as if *from Paulinka's perspective*, and in doing so, she uncovers not only Paulinka's unpredictable, illogical, and insensitive nature, but also her own. She then projects herself into Mrs Knarre, her grandmother. She identifies with the tragic events and suicides which have run through her life, and she wonders at the courage needed to assimilate them.

The second act covers events pertinent to her late teens. It begins on 30 January 1933, the day that Hitler became Chancellor, and it illustrates the effect this had on 'souls which were both human and Jewish'. A giant placard invites Germans to take their revenge on Jews. Dr Kann loses his post; Paulinka gives a concert to shouts of '*Raus! Raus!*' (Out! Out!). Singsong goes to the Ministry of Propaganda (*sic.*) to obtain permission to establish the Jewish Cultural Association. Meanwhile, Charlotte develops an interest in art. But she is beginning to feel that Paulinka is suffocating her. So ends the Prelude.

Salomon introduces the main concern of her work with a flourish: 'Now our play begins!'

The 'play' is composed of 468 paintings that span events from about 1935 to early 1939: that is, when Salomon was in her *late teens*. Its primary concern is the role of *devious manipulation*, first in Daberlohn's attempted seduction of Paulinka and, later, in his shoddy treatment (and possible seduction) of Charlotte.[29] It is divided into two parts.

The first part begins with Daberlohn (Wolfsohn) arriving at the Salomon apartment with a wonderfully ironic recommendation by Singsong (Kurt Singer). Two hundred and twenty-three paintings are given to the relationship between Paulinka and Daberlohn, who are both in their late thirties/early forties. Although Salomon loved Wolfsohn to distraction, she depicts Daberlohn in droll and scornful rhyme, and as madly conceited, scheming, and unscrupulous. He plans to 'redeem'

Paulinka and to make her the greatest singer in the world—but only *if* she allows him to seduce her. He begins by lending her his 'book' (= *Orpheus, or the Way to a Mask*).

Salomon paints Daberlohn's head repeatedly. At first, only four heads on a sheet; later, several dozens of heads on a single sheet of paper. Their changing expressions reflect his determination to anticipate Paulinka's every resistance. And depictions of Paulinka's head reflect her uncertainty. The struggle between them becomes an acutely observed psychodrama. And yet, Charlotte soon realises that *she* is beginning to absorb Daberlohn's dogmatism.

A whole chapter is given to reworking a section from Wolfsohn's *Orpheus*—as a conversation between Daberlohn and a sculptor who has just finished a work entitled 'I will not let you go, unless you bless me' (Genesis 32: 26). Daberlohn imagines Paulinka as Orpheus (i.e. as Orfeo in Gluck's opera), and himself as a 'sculptor' modelling her head, helping her to discover her soul, her true 'golden' voice—for *his* enjoyment.

After 420 paintings, we finally come to the centre of the work: the even more tortuous relationship between Charlotte and Daberlohn.

Chapter 7 ('A Young Girl') begins the story of Charlotte's 'unhappy love'—but told from *Daberlohn's* point of view. Salomon reveals the ruthlessness of his constant manipulation of her, the way he toys with her vulnerability, and his deliberate attempt to confuse, to hurt, and to humiliate her. One day, they are lying on a riverbank. She is motionless 'as if she had nothing to do with it'. He seeks to 'implant something of himself into her'. Whereupon he reflects, 'quaint little creature', then adds, out loud, 'let's go home'. Disgusted with him, she considers suicide.

Throughout, Salomon depicts herself as Eurydice in an underworld of unbearable confusion and pain—clinging to a mad belief that this unlikely Orpheus will rescue her. It makes painful viewing/reading. Meanwhile, Daberlohn completes his book.[30] He feels resurrected, as if he can begin his life anew. His narcissism knows no bounds. He continues to pester Charlotte, who announces that she cannot stand living at home anymore. A friend expresses concern that Charlotte is incapable of looking after herself; that she doesn't know her own mind. Arrangements are made for her to join her grandparents in the south of France.

The Epilogue is composed of 94 gouaches, and eight sheets of text. As soon as Charlotte arrives in Villefranche-sur-Mer, her grandfather wants her to earn her keep as a maid. Her grandmother wants to see her married. There are a few brightly coloured pages. Then, in September 1939, her grandmother tries to commit suicide. There follow five chilling gouaches which describe how, for the first time, Charlotte learns that her mother committed suicide, that there have been eight other family suicides. This is the fifth time her grandmother has made the attempt. Soon after, when her grandmother jumps from a window to her death, Charlotte is devastated. She prays: 'Dear God, please don't let me go mad'.

Charlotte and her grandfather are sent to Gurs, in the Pyrenees. Owing to his age, they are allowed to return to Nice where she ponders: 'a little education, a few laws, and inside, a vacuum—that is what humankind has now become'. When she remarks to her grandfather that she thinks the whole world needs to be put together again, he tells her: 'O kill yourself! Put an end to this babble'. This is the final gouache.

Salomon probably thought that by following Daberlohn's advice—that by re-collecting her life as she has, and by consciously re-living her pain—she would obtain a measure of calm. Sadly, this isn't the case. In 1942, having completed her project, Salomon returned to live with her grandfather in Nice. But despite her lucidity as an artist, she remained unaware of the extent of her own confused dogmatism and her own mental fragility. In February the following year, her grandfather collapsed and died, apparently of natural causes. As he was dying, Salomon wrote a rambling "Letter to Daberlohn" in which she reiterates the love she has for him (Wolfsohn)—and she confesses to having poisoned her grandfather.[31] It is a chilling possibility.

Her work, however, should not be judged by her action, whether real or imagined. It should be assessed for what it is: an attempt to discover a belief in the value of what she has suffered and a meaning to her life. As Eurydice, she has died a little every day of her life, not because she wasn't loved, but because so few people had ever really *listened* to her. Her *Singespiel* recalls Rilke's suggestion that true consciousness begins with *listening*, not only to others, but also to one's deeper self. It illustrates how no one *listens* to anyone else. Her grandparents do not listen to each other. Her parents live in worlds of their own. Her father and Paulinka live on separate planets. Neither listens to Charlotte. Daberlohn listens only to the throbbing of his own desires. The Nazis do not listen to souls that are 'both human and Jewish'. Everyone is too busy with their own obsessions to listen to anyone else.

Life? or Theatre? recalls Malipiero's *L'Orfeide*. For Salomon sees individual self-centredness as so pervasive that it signals a collective dissociation. As she writes: 'I saw the whole world fall apart before my eyes; I saw it turn to chaos. [...] What was playing out inside me so gruesomely was being played out in a large way in the world'.[32] Her work is a disturbing testament to the relation between the dysfunctional behaviour of individuals and the horrendous dysfunctionality of the times.

The work is not (as it was first presented to the public) a 'diary in pictures'.[33] It is an exercise in artistic and imaginative re-collection.[34] It is confessional literature: it *testifies* to its author's harrowing life. It is the first work to turn to the myth of Orpheus and Eurydice to represent the artist's own 'personal myth': the myth with which she has had to engage to find out how it both shaped and, owing to her own determination, also helped her to make sense of her life.[35]

Life? or Theatre? is a mind-numbing achievement. It is the first version of the myth in which its author represents herself as *both* mythic figures. She is *Eurydice* who has 'died' and who inhabits an underworld of confusion and pain, who yearns for love and to recover greater mental stability. She is also *Orpheus*, who must 'descend' into the underworld of *her* defining memories—those of her family, her childhood, her teenage experiences, including her infatuation with Wolfsohn, the central experience of her life—if she is to recover her sense of self, that is, of her inner *Eurydice*. Few artists have depicted more vividly, or more disturbingly, the cruelty of manipulation and the damage it can do to a young woman and her emotional growth.

As she was painting it, two other striking versions of the myth of Orpheus and Eurydice were being written—and they too are set during the German occupation of France.

Orpheus and the German Occupation of France

In May 1940, German forces crossed the French borders. Within weeks, France was forced to sign an armistice. It was a national humiliation. The German Occupation of the north and the west coast was traumatic. Suspicion and distrust undermined all social interactions. Hitler had his revenge for the humiliating terms imposed on Germany at Versailles.

These dire conditions triggered several literary masterpieces, including two striking versions of the myth of Orpheus and Eurydice. Both explore the relation between time, memory, and an idealised Eurydice-figure. One is a play by a young Frenchman; the other, an American film set in Vichy-administered Casablanca.

Jean Anouilh: Eurydice and the Repression of History

Jean Anouilh grew up in a poor family in south-western France. Following his move to Paris, he met Giraudoux and Cocteau, both of whom encouraged him to write.[36] In 1937, he enjoyed his first success: *The Traveller without Luggage* (*Le Voyageur sans baggage*).

Eurydice, which contrasts stark realism with fantasy, was first performed in mid-December 1941, at the Théâtre de l'Atelier in Montmartre.[37] That is, Anouilh knew that in the audience there would be intelligent, well-read German officers, hungry to lap up the latest French culture. In the traditional myth, Orpheus longs for something which he has *lost*. Anouilh's Orpheus longs for something he has *never had*.

The play opens in the cafeteria of a provincial railway station. Orpheus is a young violinist, inexperienced in both life and love. He plays on street corners with his father, a pitiful, money-grubbing, second-rate harpist. Eurydice is an actress with a small travelling theatre company, including her facile and pretentious mother. They become instantly infatuated. Both are ashamed of their parents. Both want to escape their poverty and background. Both are yearning for love, for happiness, for their *own* life, but they are weighed down by the combination of *his* expectations and *her* fears.

The second act takes place in a hotel room. They have spent their first night together. He is idealistic and obsessed with purity, which he sees in Eurydice. Equally smitten by him, she wishes she could match his expectations. She wants him to restore her belief in her own worth. Instead, Orpheus makes her feel as if she can never be pure enough for him. He wants to know more about her. He wants to know the truth but is insufficiently mature to accept it. She avoids his questions;

she only reveals what will hurt him *least*. For she has often slept with others, sometimes under pressure (from her boss, Dulac), and sometimes simply out of kindness. When a letter arrives for Eurydice from Dulac, she is so afraid that he will force her to return to him that she flees—and is killed in a car accident.

Back in the cafeteria, an enigmatic Monsieur Henri tells Orpheus that if he can sit with Eurydice until morning without looking at her, she will return to life. Eurydice appears and as he presses her about her past, he becomes impatient with her constant refrain of 'It's too difficult [to explain]'. Exasperated, he finally turns, and she 'dies' a second time. As she exits, Orpheus' father reappears and acts as if his son had never left him. But Orpheus won't listen. There is a short final act in which Monsieur Henri tries to persuade Orpheus to return to work with his father. But he prefers to die, so that he can join Eurydice in death.

On the one hand, *Eurydice* is a tragicomedy about adolescent longings and misunderstandings, of time and memory, and of idealism and unintentional deceit—a tragedy about the knots that people tie for themselves when they fall in love. And there is an unexpected sub-plot. For behind their pathetic mannerisms, both parents have a keen appetite for *life*—that is, they know that reality is *not* idealistic. Until she met Orpheus, Eurydice understood this. But Orpheus awakens in her a realisation of how far she has fallen from 'innocence' and 'purity'. And it kills her.

Behind this tragicomedy of adolescent love, however, there are political implications as far-reaching as those in Anouilh's later *Antigone* or in Sartre's *Huis Clos* (both 1944). For it suggests that a person's past is analogous to a nation's history. *Eurydice* is the first version of the myth of Orpheus and Eurydice to imply that a nation's self-image might be self-deceiving. Orpheus represents a desire for memory and truth to be compatible. He believes that everyone is the sum of their actions, and what they have done can never be undone. But he also personifies the naivety of believing that a person can be totally 'pure'. Eurydice represents the instinct for an easy life, whether it be that of young women who have flirted with German soldiers during the occupation, or male facilitators and collaborators—that is, all those who prefer to avoid troubling questions by sweeping them under the carpet. The play suggests that a nation needs to take responsibility for the truth not only of its *history*, and its sometimes-shocking mistakes, but also of its *present*—and the moral choices they each uncover.

A few months after Charlotte Salomon began *Life? or Theatre?*, a film was released in the United States which was based on events conceived a year earlier—also in Saint-Jean-Cap-Ferrat. And it represents an unexpected version of the myth of Orpheus and Eurydice.

Casablanca: Orpheus, Self-Pity, and 'Something More Important'

Casablanca (1942) is one of many films devised to rouse American support for the war against Nazi Germany.[38] And yet, a large part of its irresistible appeal comes from it being built around the same metaphors as the myth of Orpheus and

Eurydice: (Rick's) *unbearable loss, impossible longing, descent* (into drink and self-centredness), *misplaced sense of entitlement, determination* (to hurt Ilsa), and (until the very end) a complete absence of *self-awareness*.

The background story. In June 1940, shortly before the Germans march into Paris, Ilsa Lund (Ingrid Bergman) learns that her husband, Victor Laszlo (Paul Henreid), has been killed. Soon after, she meets Rick Blaine (Humphrey Bogart). They enjoy a few days of carefree, 'no questions' happiness. As they are about to take a train south, Ilsa learns that Victor is alive, but wounded. She doesn't hesitate. She writes a quick note to Rick. 'I cannot go with you or ever see you again. You must not ask why. Just believe that I love you. Go, my darling, and God bless you'.

The film begins with two German couriers being killed because they were carrying documents authorising the bearer to be given free passage out of Casablanca. Every expatriate in town wants those letters of transit—even though they are a nonsense (they would have carried no weight with Vichy officials, and even less with their German overseers).

Rick is an Orpheus who, following the unbearable loss of his 'Eurydice', has fallen into depression, an 'underworld' of self-pity and bitterness. He ill-treats other women (Yvonne). He won't let Sam sing 'As Time Goes By' because he associates the tune with Ilsa. He is an Orpheus who *wants* to forget Eurydice but *can't*.

Twenty-five minutes into the film, the inevitable: Victor and Ilsa arrive at 'Rick's Café Américain'. Victor is the much-admired leader of the international underground resistance to Nazi militarism. He is selfless, brave, committed to his cause—and he is married to Ilsa. He embodies everything that Rick *would like to have been*. He needs those letters of transit to continue his work. And they have been entrusted to Rick.

That evening, Rick waits for Ilsa to reappear at his nightclub. He *wants* her to come back, but he is simmering with wounded pride. He gets drunk ('Of all the gin joints in all the towns in all the world, she walks into mine'). Then comes the flashback to the few days that Rick and Ilsa enjoyed in Paris. And as it ends, Ilsa appears at the door. And *all he wants to know is who she left him for* ('Was it Laszlo, or were there others in between, or aren't you the kind that tells?'). Shaken by his despicable question, she leaves.

And yet, he continues to delude himself. The following day, as Victor seeks help from Signor Ferrari (the fly-swatting Sydney Greenstreet), Rick accosts Ilsa at a market stall. He assumes that she ran out on him because she did not want to live a life 'hiding from the police, running away all the time'. He taunts her: 'someday you will lie to Laszlo'. She looks at him scornfully. 'No,' she answers coldly, 'Victor Laszlo was [my husband] even when I knew you in Paris'. She walks away, leaving him stunned.

A moment later, she and her husband tell Ferrari that they will only leave Casablanca *together*—and he tells them that he thinks Rick has the missing letters of transit.

We briefly see a better side of Rick. When Laszlo wants to conduct 'La Marseillaise' (to drown out 'Die Wacht am Rhein'), the musicians look at Rick, and he nods agreement.[39] To prevent a young Bulgarian wife from having to give herself to Louis Renault (Claude Rains), he helps her husband to win at roulette so that the husband can buy their exit visas. But when Victor asks to speak with him, he once again becomes contemptible. He refuses to sell the letters of transit at *any* price.

The film contrasts the different characters of Victor and Rick and the very different ways they treat and trust Ilsa. When Ilsa asks Victor what Rick said, he replies: 'He said, 'Ask your wife''. Then he asks her, gently: 'Is there anything you wish to tell me?' She replies that there isn't, and then adds: 'Whatever I do, will you believe that I ...?' He stops her. 'You don't even have to say it. I'll believe.'

As soon as Victor leaves to attend a resistance meeting, Ilsa goes to Rick's to beg him to put his feelings aside for 'something more important'. She assures him that if only he knew the truth, he would feel differently. He replies: 'I wouldn't believe you, no matter what you said'. When she reminds him that the authorities will kill Laszlo if he cannot get away from Casablanca, he retorts 'What of it?' Orpheus is not naturally cruel, but Rick is so bitter he has become vicious.

Then comes the film's anticipated, but improbable surprise. Ilsa admits that she still loves him. She says she hasn't the strength to leave him again. She tells him, 'You have to think for both of us'.

Laszlo loves Ilsa so much that he would prefer to let Rick take her to safety than allow her to fall prey to Major Strasser's cruelties. The contrast with Rick's self-centredness could not be greater. But as everyone remembers, Rick finally acts as Laszlo was prepared to do. He pretends he will leave with Ilsa, but he asks Renault to complete the letters of transit with the names of Victor Laszlo and Ilsa Lund. Critics like to comment on Rick's self-sacrifice and redemption, whereas all that has happened is that he has been shamed into seeing what a cad he has been.

Film scholars like to point out that the censors of the time would not have allowed the film to end with Rick flying away with another man's wife. This may be so, but it is not the whole story. The film is a version of the myth of Orpheus and Eurydice, but because the succession of scriptwriters didn't realise this, they happened upon a solution to a challenge *implicit* in the myth—and vividly explored by Cocteau in both versions of *Orphée*. How can a man who finds himself 'trapped' in a tragic myth avoid its tragic ending?

In *Casablanca*, the figure of Orpheus is shared between two men. Having lost Ilsa, Rick 'descends' into self-absorption. Once committed to the same 'cause' as Victor (including to the same woman), he is now fighting *only* for himself. He must come to terms with his own selfishness. He must learn that 'A kiss is just a kiss / A sigh is just a sigh'—and that neither are a token of entitlement.[40] In contrast, Victor is an Orpheus who finds himself in an 'underworld' where his life is threatened. He knows he must avoid falling prey to Major Strasser. He *must* escape from Casablanca—and yet, his first thought is how to get Ilsa to safety. It is not only because of his importance to the Resistance; it is also because of his unselfishness about Ilsa that Victor earns the right to escape with her.

The viewer may doubt whether the 'beautiful friendship' between Rick and Louis will greatly help the Allied cause, but it is a perfect tongue-in-cheek ending to an important version of the myth of Orpheus and Eurydice. For by dividing 'Orpheus' between two characters, *Casablanca* finds an unexpected solution to the problem at the heart of the myth. At the end, Rick learns what every Orpheus must: to accept that he has lost Eurydice, and that he must move on with his life. And he learns this from his idealised 'better' self: the man he would like to have been.

Twenty years later (at the height of the film's popularity), other versions of the myth will begin to wrestle with this same question—How does a *man* escape the tragic ending of the myth in which he is 'trapped'—and to find equally intriguing solutions.

Conclusion

Improbable as it might seem, during the late 1930s and the Second World War, writers turned to the myth of Orpheus and Eurydice to testify to their concern about the dysfunctionality of the *society* they saw around them, whether in the United States or in Europe. That is, they turned to the myth because it stirred feelings about the loss of a social morality and a yearning for a more respectful and more responsible society.

- Tennessee Williams provides a blistering testament to the relation between economic hardship, the toleration of abusive behaviour, and the plight of women.
- Caroline Gordon re-examines not only her adherence to the views of the Southern Agrarians, but also her personal values.
- Owen Barfield re-imagines the myth as an allegory of self-realisation from 'sleep into self', where *self* is understood as a recommitment to the good of society.
- Alfred Wolfsohn re-imagines it as a paradigm for the recovery of one's authentic voice and personality.
- Charlotte Salomon turns to her own memories to testify not only to the horrific impact of Nazi policies on ordinary people, but also to the cruel and manipulative self-centredness that such dysfunctional policies intensify.
- Jean Anouilh wittily suggests a relation between the difficulties faced by young lovers and the challenges faced by a nation which had long been reluctant to face up to its failings.
- And *Casablanca* is the first version of the myth to insist that Orpheus must snap out of his own self-imposed dysfunctionality and (re)connect with 'more important' concerns.

In 1945, the Second World War came to an end. During the 1950s, uplifted by the widespread determination to rebuild a better world, writers and other artists once again turn to the myth of Orpheus and Eurydice to re-examine the nature and function of art.

Notes

1 T. Williams, *The Theatre of Tennessee Williams: vol. 1: Battle of Angels, The Glass Menagerie, A Streetcar Named Desire,* New York: New Directions, 1971.

2 T. Williams, *The Theatre of Tennessee Williams: vol. 3: Cat on a Hot Tin Roof, Orpheus Descending, Suddenly Last Summer*, New York: New Directions, 1971.
3 T. Williams, 'The Past, the Present and the Perhaps', *Orpheus Descending*, Secker & Warburg, 1958, p. 10.
4 T. Williams, *Memoirs*, London: W.H. Allen, 1976, pp. 172, 175.
5 As *The Fugitive Kind* (1960), directed by Sidney Lumet, and as *Orpheus Descending* (1990), directed by Peter Hall.
6 L. Cowan, *The Fugitive Group: A Literary History*, Baton Rouge, LA: Louisiana State University Press, 1959.
7 D. Davidson et al., *I'll Take My Stand: The South and the Agrarian Tradition* (1930), 75th anniversary edition, Baton Rouge, LA: Louisiana State University Press, 2006.
8 See L. Cowan, 'Preface', to Caroline Gordon, *The Women on the Porch*, Nashville, TN: J. S. Sanders, 1993.
9 C. Gordon, *The Women on the Porch*, Nashville, TN: J. S. Sanders, 1993.
10 See T.E. Tunc, 'Caroline Gordon's Ghosts: *The Women on the Porch* as Southern Gothic Literature', The *Southern Literary Journal* 46 (1), 2013, pp. 78–95.
11 See J.C. Ransom, 'Art and the Human Economy', *Kenyon Review* 7 (4), 1945, p. 686.
12 Steiner was born in the Austrian Empire in 1861. He had a keen interest in human development (*The Philosophy of Freedom*, 1894; *The Education of the Child*, 1907). In his fifties, he founded the Anthroposophical Society (anthroposophy = study of human wisdom). In 1913, its headquarters moved to Dornach (in Solothurn, Switzerland), just south of Basel.
13 O. Barfield, *Orpheus: A Poetic Drama*, ed. J.C. Ulreich, Jr., West Stockbridge, MA: Lindisfarne Press, 1983. Barfield tried to interest Lewis in Rudolf Steiner, to no avail.
14 O. Barfield, *Orpheus: A Poetic Drama*, ed. J.C. Ulreich, Jr., West Stockbridge, MA: Lindisfarne Press, 1983, p. 17.
15 The word *agape* has been given a great many different meanings, including charity: for the meaning used here, see 1 John 4: 7–10.
16 L.E. Hirsch, *A Jewish Orchestra in Nazi Germany: Musical Politics and the Berlin Jewish Culture League*, Ann Arbor: University of Michigan Press, 2010.
17 A. Wolfsohn, *Orpheus, or The Way to a Mask*, tr. Maria Gunther, East Woodstock, CT: Abraxas, 2012.
18 A. Wolfsohn, *Orpheus, or The Way to a Mask*, tr. Maria Gunther, East Woodstock, CT: Abraxas, 2012, pp. 141, 129.
19 More surprisingly, he seems also to have known of Jung's seminar on Kundalini: see A. Wolfsohn, *Orpheus, or The Way to a Mask*, tr. Maria Gunther, East Woodstock, CT: Abraxas, 2012, pp. 6–7, 51; and C.G. Jung, The *Psychology of Kundalini Yoga: Notes of the Seminar Given in 1932*, ed. S. Shamdasani, London: Routledge, 1996.
20 See S. Braggins, *Mystery Behind the Voice: A Biography of Alfred Wolfsohn*, Leicester: Troubador Publishing, 2011; P. Newham, *The Singing Cure: Introduction to Voice Movement Therapy*, London: Rider, 1993, and *Using Voice and Theatre in Therapy: The Practical Application of Voice Movement Therapy*, London: Jessica Kingsley, 1999.
21 The subject of Death embracing a young woman was popular in German Renaissance art: for example, Hans Baldung Grien, *Der Tod und das Mädchen*, Vienna: Kunsthistorisches Museum, *c.*1510. It is the subject of one of Schubert's best-known songs, to a poem by Matthias Claudius (D.531, op.7, no.3, 1817). Schubert adapted its music for the piano part in the second movement of his String Quartet no.14, in D minor, 'Death and the Maiden' (1824).
22 C. Salomon, *Life? or Theatre?* New York & London: Overlook & Duckworth, 2017, p. 805.
23 For details of her life, see M.L. Felstiner, *To Paint Her Life: Charlotte Salomon in the Nazi Era*, New York: HarperCollins, 1994. For a select bibliography: see Griselda

Pollock, *Charlotte Salomon and the Theatre of Memory*, New Haven: Yale University Press, 2018, pp. 528–535.

24 M.L. Felstiner, *To Paint Her Life: Charlotte Salomon in the Nazi Era*, New York: HarperCollins, 1994, p. 141.

25 In addition to the completed work, over a thousand 'draft' and rejected pages have survived, many of them just as powerful as the completed paintings.

26 C. Salomon, *Life? or Theatre?* New York & London: Overlook & Duckworth, 2017, p. 805.

27 In standard German, the word is *Singspiel*. Salomon may have misspelt the word by mistake. Another possibility: that Wolfsohn spoke the word with a hint of an extra syllable 'e', and it was a 'private joke'.

28 See D.C. Buerkle, *Nothing Happened: Charlotte Salomon and an Archive of Suicide,* Ann Arbor: University of Michigan Press, 2013; also, M.A. Kaplan, *Between Dignity and Despair: Jewish Life in Nazi Germany*, New York: Oxford University Press, 1998.

29 The paintings and text are a shocking testament, but the truth about what passed between Salomon and Wolfsohn is not our concern here.

30 Salomon is inconsistent here: if Daberlohn has already shown Paulinka his 'book', he can't still be writing it.

31 "I knew where [the poison] was—... As I write, it is working. Maybe by now he is already dead. [...] As grandfather already fell asleep gently by intoxication with the "Veronalomelette" (Barbital omelette) and as I made a drawing of him—it felt to me as though a voice called out: Theatre is dead!" "Letter to Amadeus Daberlohn", tr. Darcy Buerkle and Mary Felstiner, in Charlotte Salomon, Life? or Theatre? New York & London: Overlook & Duckworth, p. 805.

32 C. Salomon, *Life? or Theatre?* New York & London: Overlook & Duckworth, 2017, p. 801.

33 C. Salomon, *Charlotte: A Diary in Pictures by Charlotte Salomon*, London: Collins, 1963.

34 I borrow this hyphenated word from Marie-Louise von Franz, where she uses it to suggest that self-awareness comes from a *re-collection* of those fragmented aspects of the personality which the subject has difficulty in acknowledging: see *Projection and Re-Collection in Jungian Psychology: Reflections of the Soul*, tr. W. Kennedy, La Salle, IL: Open Court, 1980.

35 I borrow the phrase 'personal myth from C.G. Jung, *Memories, Dreams, Reflections,* 1962, p. 3.

36 P. Vandromme, *Jean Anouilh, un auteur et ses personnages*, Paris: La Table Ronde, 1965, p. 193.

37 J. Anouilh, *Eurydice*, Paris: La Table Ronde, 1941.

38 See L. Jacobs, 'World War II and the American Film', *Cinema Journal* 7, winter 1967–1968, pp. 1–21. *Casablanca* (1942), directed by Michael Curtiz, produced by Hal B. Wallis. The film is based on a play by Murray Burnett and Joan Alison, *Everybody Comes to Rick's* (written 1940), which includes some of its best-known lines ('We'll always have Paris') and songs ('As Time Goes By'). In the play, Lois Meredith is American, in her thirties, and single: she is *not* married to Laszlo. And as the price of his help, Rick gets to sleep with her. No theatre wanted it.

39 The 'battle of the anthems' is borrowed from Renoir's *La Grande Illusion.*

40 Lines from 'As Time Goes By', by Herman Hupfeld, first performed in the musical *Everybody's Welcome* (1931).

Chapter 9

Orpheus as Embodiment of the Creative Impulse

The 1950s

The end of the Second World War left about seventy million dead.[1] So shocking were the casualties, the displacement of people, and the destruction of housing and infrastructure that political leaders resolved to rebuild a better and more equitable world. In many ways, the post-war years are an exception to the rule that political events rarely represent the best of a culture. Helped by the Marshall plan, as Western economies recovered, their governments passed radically new laws concerning education (from primary to tertiary), housing (for those who needed it), health programmes, and welfare for those who were unemployed or sick. These combined with advances in medicine, and compulsory vaccination for polio, measles, and hepatitis. Never had the world seen such rapid political and social advances. Even so, their ambitious nature meant that they required time for their benefits to become apparent. For most of the population, the 1950s were years of economic struggle.

The desire for change prompted the beginnings of the end to colonial adventurism. India and Pakistan won their independence from the United Kingdom (1947), Libya from Italy (1951), and Vietnam from France (1954). But old habits lingered. The colonial powers were often reluctant to forego their supposed rights—not least because, by weakening their own economic base, they were making themselves even *more* dependent on the United States.

For a new world order had emerged from the ashes. The determination of the United States to keep knowledge about nuclear weapons to itself and only to its closest allies inevitably provoked the Soviet Union to develop its own arsenal. It quickly became obvious that international politics were no longer based on nations shifting alliances to check the rise of a superpower ('balance of power'): they were to be dictated by the 'spheres of interest' of the two nuclear superpowers: that is, by two all-controlling protection rackets. Within each 'sphere of interest', individual nations now found it impossible to form alliances to counter the reach of the superpower—and it soon became clear that *both* superpowers intended to keep it that way.

The political optimism that came with the end of the war meant that versions of the myth of Orpheus and Eurydice produced during the 1950s pick up on the concerns *not* of the difficult 1930s and 1940s, but on the concerns of early twentieth-century modernism. That is, most writers and other artists still belonged to the privileged classes.

DOI: 10.4324/9781003519584-12

This chapter looks at a selection of versions of the myth produced during the post-war years, all of which reflect the need to further explore questions about the nature and value of art. It is in four parts. The first part explores the tension between tradition and innovation in two ballets. The second explores two works whose authors had had their confidence in their creative talent shaken and who turned to the myth to help them recover this lost confidence. The third part explores an important new concern: the re-visioning of the myth for a non-European racial group. The last part explores *The Testament of Orpheus*, in which Cocteau returns to the myth to bid a witty farewell to his own creative years.

Orpheus and Ballet: Tradition vs. Modernity

During the Second World War, the loss of Eurydice became a metaphor for the loss of a familiar and much-loved world, and Orpheus' attempt to recover her, the expression of a hope for the return of peace. In 1941, Ninette de Valois, director of the London-based Vic-Wells Ballet (in 1956 renamed the Royal Ballet), mounted a full-length work on the myth, based on Gluck's music. Three years later, in Paris during the Occupation, the young Roland Petit produced *Orphée et Euridice*, a short work to music by César Franck, with costumes by Jean Cocteau.

When peace finally came, the most pressing challenge facing composers and choreographers alike was the need to discover an aesthetic 'language' appropriate to the post-war world. And within a few years of each other, two ballets based on the myth stand at the head of this new chapter in the history of dance. One seeks to *reinvent* tradition for the modern world; the other seeks to *launch* a tradition pertinent to the modern world.

We begin with a collaboration between two gifted Russians, both emigres to the United States, and both of whom owed a huge debt to Diaghilev.

Stravinsky and Balanchine: The Yearning for a New Classicism

Igor Stravinsky is most famous for the vibrant music he provided for three ballets commissioned by Sergei Diaghilev and first performed in Paris by the Ballets Russes (*The Firebird*, 1910; *Petrushka*, 1911; and *The Rite of Spring*, 1913). In the early 1920s, however, he adopted a calmer, neoclassical musical language. *Apollon musagète* (1928) is the first ballet by the young George Balanchine to employ a minimalist décor, simple costumes, and restrained choreography.[2] In 1933, Balanchine moved to the United States where he established the School of American Ballet. Six years later, Stravinsky also settled there.

Soon after the end of the war, Balanchine invited his older friend to compose the music for a new ballet. *Orpheus* (1948) uses a full orchestra, with a harp (representing Orpheus' lyre) given prominence. Except for the brief penultimate tableau (in which Orpheus is killed by Bacchantes), the entire thirty-minute ballet is pitched softly.[3] It was premiered by the Ballet Society, with choreography by

Balanchine, and minimalist, abstract designs by the Japanese American sculptor, Isamu Noguchi. It is in one act, divided into two scenes (indebted to Gluck's opera) and a coda (indebted to Monteverdi's *Orfeo*).

In the first scene, Orpheus mourns beside the tomb of Eurydice. He is so over-whelmed by his unbearable loss that he doubles up, collapses, twists, and writhes. He makes occasional half-hearted leaps. This is ballet, but the protagonist cannot dance.[4] Nor can he play the lyre. Every tentative melody evaporates in its own sense of hopelessness. This is Orpheus for a generation shaken by the war. He is struggling to understand the nature of his loss and to hold onto his own sense of self.

The second scene begins with the *pas des Furies*. An Angel of Death appears. Orpheus *needs* his help not only to guide him to the underworld, but even to play his lyre before the king of Tartarus. Stravinsky wanted the harp to 'sound as dry and choked as a not very resonant guitar'.[5] In other words, it is not Orpheus' demonstra-tion of sublime music (or dance) which persuades Hades to release Eurydice. As in Gluck's opera, it is the pathetic state into which he has fallen.

The emotional core of the work is the *pas de deux* between Orpheus and Eury-dice, performed in front of the lowered curtain. He cannot look at her; she only wants to look at him. They are each consumed by their incompatible emotions. She wraps herself around him. He twists to avoid seeing her. Eventually, he can bear it no more. He tears off his blindfold (or mask) and, as she falls into his arms, she is pulled back under the curtain. Completely broken, he raises his arms in pathetic incomprehension. The Angel of Death reappears and leads Orpheus out of the underworld. A Bacchante enters, but when Orpheus repulses her, other Bac-chantes enter, attack him, and kill him.

The ballet ends with a short coda. To music based on the opening theme, Apollo raises the lyre of Orpheus as a solemn confirmation of the undimmed power of music.

Balanchine was strongly attached to the tradition of classical ballet. And yet, *Orpheus* is not so much a ballet as modern dance—modern dance grieving for the unbearable loss of classical conviction, resolution, and elegance. When the cast gets it right, it is deeply moving.[6] *Orpheus* is about the need to discover a new classicism, a classicism pertinent to the post-war world. It asks both protagonists to embrace the language of modern dance, but *without* forgetting their classical training.

The premiere marked a new birth. Balanchine's company was renamed the New York City Ballet, and for many years, its logo was based on the lyre of Orpheus.

Only a few years later, another ballet on the same myth was produced. It sug-gests that tradition has no place in the modern world—and that modernity must devise its own musical and balletic language.

Pierre Henry and Maurice Béjart: A New Art for New Times

Pierre Henry studied at the Paris Conservatory with Nadia Boulanger and Olivier Messiaen. In 1946, he met Pierre Schaeffer, an electronic engineer, who was fascinated by sound, and scathing of all those who were reluctant to grasp the real conditions of the post-war.[7] He became a pioneer of 'concrete (= actual, pertinent to reality) music'.

Maurice-Jean Berger was the son of French philosopher, Gaston Berger. In the 1950s, while his father was championing the importance of philosophy at French universities, his son—using the professional name of Maurice Béjart—founded his first ballet company.[8] In 1955, he produced his first work to music by Henry and Schaeffer (*Symphony for One Man*). It is the first ballet set to 'concrete (electronic) music'.

Meanwhile, Henry had come to associate the structure of another work on which he was working with the myth of Orpheus and Eurydice. Together with Schaeffer, he revised it as *Orphée 53*, an eighty-six-minute 'opera' composed entirely of electroacoustic music.[9] He later condensed its final movement into a work he called *Le Voile d'Orphée* (The Veil of Orpheus, 27 min). In 1958, Maurice Béjart used a sixteen-minute version of this as the music for the third act of a new ballet.

It is in two parts.[10] And both its musical and balletic language are emphatically modern. Against a backdrop of broad, richly textured sounds, violent percussive moments begin to dominate, suggesting a confused emotional uncertainty. The first part ends as if building toward a light, before giving way to a complex of distant ill-grasped possibilities. The longer second part is a startling concerto for spoken voice, electronic harpsichord, and electroacoustic music. A narrator slowly recites (in ancient Greek) words and passages from the Orphic hymns. A lyrical dialogue gives way to a harpsichord (a solar lyre) suggesting that Orpheus is struggling against powerful, and then increasingly frenzied forces that gradually overwhelm him. Invoking the name of Zeus, he dies a violent and abrupt death.[11]

For this work, Béjart devised dramatic modern dance—and to great acclaim. Two years later, in Brussels, he founded the Ballet du XXe siècle, a company which would help to revolutionise the traditions of ballet.

Balanchine's neoclassical *Orpheus* and the last act of Béjart's *Orphée* are equally (albeit differently) intense, and they share a common conviction that both music and dance must discover a new 'language' pertinent to the new times—but they represent very different approaches to this challenge. *Orpheus* represents the need to revise classical traditions for the post-war world. It seeks reassurance and *continuity*. In contrast, *Orphée* seeks rupture. It suggests that previous traditions have no place in the modern world: that modernity must devise an emphatically *modern* language.

The following part looks at two works whose authors turned to the myth for a very different reason: to re-affirm their shaken confidence in their own identity as artists.

Orpheus and the Creative Impulse

The following pages consider two responses to the myth that further develop concerns earlier explored by Rilke (especially in *Sonnets to Orpheus*) and by Cocteau (in *Orphée*). In both, the author consciously reflects on the importance that creativity has for them, and in both, the author equates their creative ability with their inmost identity. The first is a poem by Muriel Rukeyser. The second is Jean Cocteau's cinematic adaptation of his earlier play.

Muriel Rukeyser: Re-Collecting Eurydice—And Orpheus

The works of the American poet Muriel Rukeyser are stamped by the searing conviction with which she lived her life. She could not act without also wishing to testify to her experience. Written in her early twenties, 'Poem Out of Childhood' (1935) begins: 'Breathe-in-experience, breathe-out poetry'.[12] All her life, she wrote as she lived, with a determination to understand both herself and the world around her.

Her poem 'Orpheus' (1949/1951) was written soon after the birth of a child whose father had abandoned her, and whom she had to raise by herself.[13] It is in three parts.

In the first, she begins with the traditional ending: 'The mountaintop stands in silence a minute after the murder'. As the women (the Furies, the Maenads) flee from the scene, the clouds and the trees look down in horror at the body of Orpheus. Slowly, they once again 'find their voices' and begin to reflect on what has been 'Lost'. The capital 'L' underlines the awfulness of the loss, as if Orpheus had been the only significant quality and his loss signals a complete void.

The moon, however, will not participate in this lament, because for as long as there is a moon and an ocean to be drawn by it, there will be tides to come. Orpheus stirs one last time to bear witness to this. He tells Rukeyser,

'Do more; for this is how it is,' and died again.

That is, he urges her to see him as he is: 'He is the pieces of Orpheus and he is chaos.' He urges 'Eurydice' to turn away from him—or rather, to turn away from that part of *herself* which has been blasted to pieces. She must believe in the tides to come.

In the second section, the poet reflects on the dismembered body of Orpheus. Recalling a poem which she had written some fifteen years earlier ('Effort at Speech Between Two People'), she pleads with visceral urgency:

The wounds : Touch me! Love me! Speak to me!

The wounds are not only the damage inflicted on the body of Orpheus. They are the hurt of all the empty promises that 'Orpheus' has made to her and has failed to keep. Then she remembers the lyre, the music: in other words, Orpheus. And *then* she remembers: *she* is Orpheus. *She* is wounded—and only 'the gift' can 'heal these wounds'.

That is, Orpheus has been killed, but his gift survives in another Orpheus (Rukeyser), who yearns to recover *her* Eurydice—*her* highest value—which is the gift of poetry (Orpheus). The 'Loss' of Orpheus has made her feel as if she has lost her own ability to write. Only by remembering Orpheus will she find regeneration. She imagines herself as Orpheus guiding Jason's quest. And the death of Orpheus becomes a requiem for the power of poetry. Like Charlotte Salomon, she now becomes *Orpheus* in search of her inner Eurydice: herself-*as-poet*.

In the third part, she discovers that Orpheus has died in order that she can become aware of the importance he has for her:

His death is the birth of the god.
He sings the coming things, he sings arrivals.

She is referring to the promise harboured in every experience, whether of the outer world, or of the 'song of the flute in the kitchen'. She feels the tide rising again within her and her body being made 'whole'. Once again she can connect with Orpheus, for his song represents the living joy at the heart not only of her being, but also of her *every* everyday experience. For Orpheus has the ability to translate experience into poetry; he represents the joy which invests her life with meaning.

The poem ends with a 'Song' in which Eurydice is freed from her own prison of pain and dismemberment. She feels re-empowered to return to creative life. Regeneration is usually experienced as an emergence from constraint. But Rukeyser will not deceive herself. She will not *forget* the imprisoning pain, for it too is part of her history, *her* experience. She had to work her way through it—until she felt the joy of her returning self-confidence. It is a powerful proviso.

Some seventeen years later, in 'The Poem as Mask: Orpheus' (1968), Rukeyser reflects on her earlier poem and admits that some moments were contrived. But she insists that her description of the fragmented god, his whole being split open, and her sense of 'Loss' is still as true to her experience now as it had been when she wrote it. But now, at last, she can finally admit the poem's relation to her 'rescued child' and his 'great eyes'. And by doing so, once again she feels the fragments of her being rejoin, and she can hear the music within herself, and more richly. There are better-known twentieth-century versions of the myth—but few more shattering or more poignant than hers.

Rukeyser was a political activist, convinced that 'There is no "out there"'—for the outer world and the inner world are *one*—and every *other* is part of *oneself*. In 1972, at the height of the Vietnam War, at the invitation of a Hanoi peace group, she and Denise Levertov accompanied Jane Hart on a visit to Vietnam.[14] She wanted to meet these people whom her country thought of as the enemy. 'Breaking Open' articulates her convictions.

The conviction that what is meant by the unconscious is the same as history. […] The movement of life: to live more fully in the present [by bringing] this history to 'light' and understanding. […] In facing history, we look at each other, and in facing our entire personal life, we look at each other.[15]

Hostility has no place in the world. For just as every experience is an opportunity to better understand *oneself*, every *encounter* is an opportunity to understand, to re-connect, and to bond with *others*, with the world of which everyone is a part.

Meanwhile, the other side of the Atlantic, Jean Cocteau was still trying to reassure himself that he had it within him to produce a *significant* work.

Cocteau: Orphée (the Film) and the Fear of Artistic Failure

From the mid-1920s, Jean Cocteau enjoyed increasing success in a wide range of genres. During the war, his partner, Jean Marais, joined the Resistance. Opposed to all violence, Cocteau did not. Following the Liberation, reprisals against those suspected of collaboration were vicious. Many writers leaped to Cocteau's defence (including several who had little patience with him, such as the poet, Paul Éluard). He was exonerated, but the recriminations wounded him deeply. He lost twelve kilos and was hospitalised from nervous exhaustion. No sooner had he recovered, than he began working on the film version of *Les Parents terribles* (1948). It was another box office success. He then returned to *Orphée* (the play)—to revise it as a film.

Orphée (the film, 1950) is based on the same tension between a social reality and an imaginal reality as the play. The major difference is the additional characters of the Princess (whose function is to escort Orphée to the underworld) and of Cégeste (a young poet whose writing fascinates Orphée, despite his inability to understand it).[16] And its cast spans a spectrum of talent.[17]

In the opening scene, the Café des Poètes is crowded with animated young people. Orphée is about fifteen years older than they are, and he sits apart, brooding. His poems continue to enjoy success with middle-class readers, but they are scorned by the young. He yearns to 'astonish' them. Meanwhile, Cégeste becomes embroiled in a fight. As the police arrive, he flees and is promptly run down by two leather-jacketed motorcyclists who promptly leave the scene.

Orphée's anxiety about the value of his work is reflected in the imaginal reality (= the underworld). The Princess arrives in a black Rolls-Royce. As Heurtebise (the Princess' chauffeur) lifts Cégeste into the Rolls, the Princess orders Orphée to accompany her back to her home. That is, by wishing that his writing might become more popular than that of Cégeste, Orphée has brought about the younger poet's death. He is drawn into the world of the Princess, toward his own death, which is his fear of his own effacement. *Orphée* is the first version of the myth in which Orpheus is drawn into the underworld *before* the death of Eurydice.

Meanwhile, Eurydice is worried by her husband's disappearance. Orphée returns home, rudely brushes her aside, and goes upstairs 'to sleep'. But his only concern is to explore his obsession. He immediately climbs out of his window and down a ladder (= out of his social reality and into an 'underworld'). He has become fascinated by surreal phrases coming from his car radio. He is convinced they are meant for him. He feels as if, before he discovered them, he and Eurydice were dead without realising it. He thinks he is on the verge of finding a new writing style.

He tells Eurydice that he must go into town to see the police commissioner. On the way, he catches sight of the Princess. When stopped by a group of young women wanting his autograph, he is so impatient to catch up with the Princess that he refuses, rudely. That is, his *obsession* with discovering a distinctive literary voice has taken such a hold of him that he rejects the social success which he craves (the admiration of the young).

Meanwhile, Heurtebise warns Eurydice not to go to see her friend Aglaonice. Eurydice ignores his warning and is promptly run over by the two motorcyclists (who work for the Princess). Heurtebise brings her body back home and tries to persuade Orphée to see her. But Orphée is so pre-occupied with the words coming from the car radio that he refuses to listen. When at last he goes to see her body, he is grief-stricken.

Heurtebise explains that there is only one way for Orphée to 'undo' what he has done: he must walk through the mirror. He then adds: 'But do you want this for the Princess or for Eurydice?' Orphée hesitates before admitting: 'For both.' That is, he cannot decide *which* is more important to him: recovering Eurydice—or braving his 'death' and discovering a new creative voice.

The film has been criticised for portraying Eurydice as uncomplicated, with no other concern than for her husband. This is to miss the point: *Orphée* is not realism. It contrasts psychological priorities. Everything in the film is mirrored. Just as Orphée is contained in his obsession to reinvent himself as a poet, so Eurydice is contained in her love for a man she only half understands. Because Orphée is obsessed with the need for his old poet-self to 'die', the Princess (who personifies this desire) falls in love with him. Because Orphée is more strongly drawn to the Princess (who belongs to the imaginal world), Heurtebise falls in love with Eurydice (who belongs to the social world).

The film explores self-awareness. As it insists, every time one sees oneself in a mirror, it is for the last time. Every glance involves an awareness of both a death and a rebirth of the self. As Heurtebise leads Orphée through the Zone (an 'underworld' composed of memories and the ruins of people's habits), Orphée wonders about its residents. 'Are they alive?' he asks. 'They think they are', Heurtebise replies, 'for nothing is more tenacious than the mistaken assumptions that one assiduously acquires.[18] That is, nothing is more difficult than peeling off one's carefully constructed *persona* (one's 'mask' or social self) and accepting oneself as one *is*.

Heurtebise leads Orphée into a room where a panel of judges are sitting. Orphée is taken aback to learn that they are not there to judge him. They are there to judge the Princess and Heurtebise, who are found guilty of allowing themselves to become personally involved in (and thus distorting) a process which has nothing to do with them. Orphée must be allowed to show how he would act if *not* interfered with. Given that they personify his mistaken attitudes, this implies that he is being required to reconsider his tendencies. He and Eurydice are allowed to return to life, but on condition that he never looks at her again. Heurtebise asks if he can lead them back to Orphée's home.

Back at his home, Heurtebise has a hard time preventing Orphée from looking at Eurydice. A letter arrives which accuses Orphée of being a thief and a murderer. He becomes petulant. Eurydice can take it no longer. She tries to get him to look at her. The first time, she fails; the second, she succeeds—and thus she dies a second time.

Outside his house, a crowd of angry young people are clamouring to know what part he played in the disappearance of Cégeste. Heurtebise tries to prevent Orphée from facing them, but Orphée insists. In the ensuing struggle, by accident, he is shot. As the police arrive, Heurtebise quickly drives Orphée away, guarded by the two motorcyclists. He leads Orphée back through the Zone, where the Princess and Cégeste are waiting. Cégeste is forgotten. But Orphée and the princess declare their love. Then, unexpectedly, she orders Cégeste and Heurtebise to re-project Orphée back in *time*. 'The death of a poet must be sacrificed to render him immortal': 'what has been must no longer be'.

Orphée arrives back in his bedroom and wakes Eurydice. She is delighted to see him looking at her tenderly. She asks whether he has been working, then chides him for not believing in himself. That is, they are happy—as if nothing in the film had happened.

Predictably, the 'happy ending' has been criticised, but perhaps unfairly. It suggests that Orphée has learned to place *belief in himself* above his 'professional' obsession with winning the admiration of the young. That is, he has accepted that he can only write as *he* knows how. Cocteau always insisted that his film has no message. Nevertheless, he did admit that it has a theme: 'The successive deaths through which a poet must pass before he finally becomes [...] the poet/writer that he *is*.[19] And for a writer who had always carefully constructed his social persona to *conceal* his private self, this was a real challenge.

Few films have elicited more varied responses than *Orphée*. From Jack Spicer's ironic references to it in *The Heads of the Town Up to the Aether* (1960–1961), through Adrienne Rich's poem, 'I Dream I'm the Death of Orpheus' (1968), to Philip Glass's two-act opera *Orphée* (1993). But the most intriguing, and possibly the most satisfying, may still be Cocteau's own response: *The Testament of Orpheus* (1960).

Before considering it, however, we need to look at two versions of the myth which enjoy an African-Brazilian setting. They represent the first major versions of the myth to be acted by an entirely black cast—and yet to be targeted at a predominantly white audience.

Black Activism/Black Orpheus

During the prohibition years (1920–1933), the Cotton Club in New York invited several black American performers—including Duke Ellington, Louis Armstrong, and Count Basie—to play for its exclusively white audiences. From coast to coast, white Americans began dancing to music composed and performed by African Americans. And yet, segregation remained as deeply entrenched as ever.[20] The combination of tradition, racial segregation, and prejudice meant that white culture and black culture rarely overlapped.

It was the same in Brazil. In the early 1940s, Abdias do Nascimento, a Black Brazilian, was imprisoned for resisting the segregation laws. On being released, he founded Black Experimental Theatre (*Teatro Experimental do Negro*, TEN). And for the remainder of his life, he worked tirelessly to improve the conditions of African Brazilians.

Meanwhile, a young white Brazilian writer travelled to the North-East of the country, where the shocking poverty changed his political views. Although he became a successful editor of the literary supplement of a local newspaper, like Cocteau, he yearned to write a distinctive work of his own. But unlike Cocteau, he had learned to take an interest in *social* issues.

Vinicius de Moraes: Orpheus and the Intense Passions of the Marginalised (Brazil)

In 1954, Vinicius de Moraes published a verse play, *Orpheus in a Favela: A Rio Tragedy* (*Orfeu da Conceiçao: Tragédia Carioca*). Two years later, it was given its premiere at the Teatro Municipal in Rio de Janeiro. It included songs with music by Antônio Carlos ['Tom'] Jobim (soon to become famous for his *bossa nova* rhythms). The set designs were by Oscar Niemeyer (soon to become famous as the architect of Brasilia). But perhaps most importantly, all its cast were Black Brazilians, and they belonged to Abdias do Nascimento's Black Experimental Theatre.

Orpheus in a Favela is the first major assimilation of the myth of Orpheus and Eurydice into a partly westernised, but non-Caucasian culture. The mixture of violence and lyricism is universal, but the *poetry* of the play is distinctly Brazilian.

The play is set during Carnival, in Conceiçao, one of the sprawling hillside *favelas* (slums) that encircle and overlook Rio de Janeiro. And as Milhaud had demonstrated in *Les malheurs d'Orphée*, in marginalised communities, passions can be unusually intense. The play sticks closely to the traditional story, but with two important changes. The first is borrowed from Shakespeare's *Romeo and Juliet*. Immediately prior to the opening of the play, Orfeu was engaged to Mira. Only recently has he fallen in love with Eurídice. His parents (Clio and Apolo) worry about this, and their anxiety helps anchor the myth in a social reality. The second is the combination of two aspects of Brazilian culture: Carnival and Candomblé (an African/Yoruba religion coloured by Catholicism, as practised in Brazil).

Aristeo is infatuated with Eurídice. When Mira tells him that Eurídice is pregnant by Orfeu, he is roused to fury. The Black Lady (who personifies Death) enters and announces herself to Orfeu. As Eurídice prepares herself to sleep with Orfeu, Aristeo enters and stabs her. Her body is taken away in an ambulance.

The second act is set inside a samba club called 'The Heads of Hell'. Orfeo's guitar forces Cérbero, the club's bouncer, to let him through. When Pluto asks what he wants, he replies 'Eurídice', whereupon Pluto loses his patience. Each member of a group of semi-entranced women begins to claim that *she* is Eurídice. In the final act, when Orfeu repulses Mira, she rouses her friends, who attack him with knives. He dies, calling for Eurídice.

The play touched a deep social chord.[21] Its vinyl soundtrack (including its overture, a soliloquy by Orfeu, and its five songs) became an instant bestseller with white Brazilians.[22] It caught the attention of Marcel Camus, a French film director. Jacques Viot, was quick to realise that what had worked in the theatre might not work on screen.

Jacques Viot and Marcel Camus: Orpheus, Carnival, and Death

Black Orpheus (*Orfeu Negro*, 1958) has an explosive opening.[23] A group of young men are dancing to the rhythm of the samba. As the title sequence rolls, the camera provides a colourful overview of the life of the *favela*. Meanwhile, Tom Jobim sings *Felicidade* (Happiness), which begins 'Sadness never ends. Happiness does' (*Tristeza não tem fim. Felicidade sim*). From the outset, the film is about a poignant and *unbearable loss*.

The plot begins just before Carnival, with Eurídice, a timid young woman from the Brazilian interior, arriving in Rio for the first time and wending her way through bustling streets that are simultaneously friendly and threatening. She has come to visit her cousin (Serafina). Orfeu (the conductor of the streetcar she takes to the *favela*) flirts with her. They arrive at the terminus (in Santa Teresa, a hillside district of Rio de Janeiro), where she asks Hermes, the station master, the way to her cousin's home.

The film makes several other changes to the play—and to the traditional myth. First, two boys who admire Orfeu's skill on the guitar help to underline the importance of music. Second, in a memorable scene, Orfeu is responsible for Eurídice's death, albeit unwittingly. Third, the film elaborates on Orfeu's 'descent into the underworld'. And fourth, both protagonists—first Eurídice, then Orpheus—are stalked by Death, who is dressed in a black costume with a white skeleton painted on it.

Most visibly, the film exploits the local colour of Rio de Janeiro: its contrast between the poverty of the hillside *favelas* and the glorious views they enjoy; the tension between the intensity with which those in the favela lead their lives and the calmer values of Eurídice; the impossibility of a private romance in a space where there is little privacy; the relation between the frenetic, collective, intoxicating joy of Carnival and the violence always threatening from the shadows. And throughout the film, one hears the relentless, irresistible rhythm of the samba—which represents the irrepressible vitality of black Brazilian musical culture.

In Brazil, *Black Orpheus* stirred mixed feelings. Vinicius did not care for it. Its exploitation of stereotypes was roundly condemned, and its success paved the way for the commercialisation of the Rio Carnival. But internationally, it became a cult success. It won the *Palme d'Or* at the 1959 Cannes Film Festival, and, in 1960, the Academy Award (Oscar) for Best Foreign Language Film. The music for the film differs from that of the play. Tom Jobim contributed 'Felicidade' and 'O Nosso Amor', while Luiz Bonfá contributed the vibrant 'Manhã de Carnaval' and the 'Samba de Orfeu'. The soundtrack was another huge success.[24] And Bossa Nova soon swept the world and became the sound of a generation.

Whatever its possible faults, this colourful version of the myth played a small part in helping to change white attitudes toward black people. In March 1963, following the March on Washington for Jobs and Freedom, Martin Luther King addressed the crowd ('I have a dream'). In 1964, the United States finally abolished segregation.

Meanwhile, Cocteau's *Orphée* had also acquired a cult status and inspired several responses. The most important of these was its author's own 'late thoughts' on the myth which had fascinated him all his adult life.

Orpheus and the Riddles of the Creative Imagination

By the mid-1950s, although Cocteau's health was failing. Nevertheless, he continued writing poetry, occasionally painted eye-catching murals, and he enjoyed the company of his friends. In 1960, in his early seventies, he released his last film as director.

The Testament of Orpheus (*Le Testament d'Orphée*, 1960) makes several unexpected contributions to the myth of Orpheus and Eurydice.[25] The most important, perhaps, is its suggestion that every artist has their 'personal myth'.[26] And Cocteau's friends rallied to help him realise this very personal project.[27]

The Testament of Orpheus: *Cocteau Reflects on His Personal Myth*

Cocteau's *Testament of Orpheus* fuses the myths of Orpheus (unbearable loss and impossible yearning) and Oedipus (unwitting transgression and its punishment).[28]

The main actors from *Orphée* reprise their roles: Cégeste (Edouard Dermit), Heurtebise (François Périer), and the Princess (Maria Casarès), but Jean Marais now plays the small part of Oedipus, while Cocteau plays Orpheus—as *himself.* The cameos are played by some of France's best-known celebrities of the time, including Pablo Picasso (painter), Yul Brynner (actor), and Charles Aznavour (actor, singer-songwriter), none of them credited.

The Testament of Orpheus consists of a dream-like journey in which Orphée moves through a sequence of surreal encounters. Each scene represents a 'station' along the road to the poet's *death*—not as a *via dolorosa*, but as *un jeu d'esprit* that poses questions both serious and playful. They include: What is the source of the creative imagination? How do we explain the issues that fascinate us? Do we choose our metaphors, or do they choose us? What exactly defines a work of art? Does a work of art always reflect the artist? Is there any sense in which art can be defined as a kind of 'science'? And is the increasingly celebrity-driven art of the 1950s distracting attention from the serious function of culture? No attempt is made to resolve these questions. At the end, they are all left hanging. But they should resonate strongly for the viewer.

The film has often been dismissed as pretentious. Cocteau, however, is *playing* with serious riddles about the imagination, art, and life. The script refuses to preach, the wit is always self-deprecating, and the film leads to a joyful and life-affirming conclusion.

Cocteau (Orpheus) first appears in eighteenth-century costume, which is a reminder that many eighteenth-century philosophers enjoyed 'playing' light-heartedly with serious ideas: for example, Voltaire in *Candide* (1759) or Diderot in *Jacques le fataliste* (?1760s). He happily concedes that his 'fantasies' may be delusions resulting from having been 'dropped on his head as a baby'. But he has a serious point: to suggest that, as a person's life draws to a close, they must try to find a pattern to the concerns that have fascinated them along the way. For such concerns are like recurrent dreams: they challenge the individual to make sense of them. The function of the professor (who has invented the time-travel device which soon projects Cocteau back into the twentieth century) is to suggest that this is a serious 'scientific' question.

Cocteau, now in his own everyday clothes, is walking along a road. He follows a man-horse (not a centaur; the head of a horse suggests an animal or dream-like intuition) to a Romani camp, which represents the entrance to the 'underworld'. A fortune teller tears a photograph of Cégeste (as he was in 1950) into pieces and passes them to Cocteau, who throws them into the sea. Like Aphrodite in Greek myth, Cégeste (as he is in 1960) rises from the foam, tells Cocteau to bring a hibiscus flower back to life, and then chides him for 'trying too hard' to understand. They set off on their journey, whose purpose is to teach him a lesson in analytical and intuitive self-awareness.

Cocteau enters the Villa Santo Sospir and walks past his own tapestry of Judith and Holofernes.[29] A young girl stands before the tapestry, being questioned by a man (Henri Torrès, a well-known politician and trial lawyer) as if on a television quiz show. The purpose of a slight mistake she makes suggests that people are not defined by their professional persona (whether poet, novelist, filmmaker, or wit), but by a secondary interest—such as a 'crazy' obsession with the fantasies which intrude into and seem to shape their life.

In the next scene, Cocteau tries to draw a hibiscus. Instead, he produces a self-portrait. The implication is that every work of art is a self-portrait of the artist—and that works of art suggest themselves to the artist. Cocteau's irritation with the hibiscus is a joke: its purpose is to underline that the artist is merely a 'vehicle' through which the work is created. Cégeste immediately orders Cocteau (now in academic robes) to show what *he* can do. From the crushed shreds, he re-creates the hibiscus perfectly. Just as an academic can re-create the past, so an artist can 'astonish'—the point being that the 'astonishment' produced by art is as important to civilisation as science.

Cégeste tells him it is time for him to meet the 'goddess'. The next episode takes place in a deserted room with a desk, exactly as in the trial scene in *Orphée*, but in *Testament*, the Princess and Heurtebise are now the presiding judges. Cocteau is reflecting on two of his life-long artistic anxieties. His fictional characters find him guilty not only of giving free rein to his imagination (that is, of not having more pragmatic interests), but also of trying to understand the imagination (which, being impossible, is fraud).

When the Princess asks the professor: 'How would you defend this man (Cocteau)?' He replies: 'He is a poet, that is, indispensable, although for what reason, I cannot say.' For, while science can readily acknowledge the importance of poetry, it cannot explain the workings of the imagination, which Heurtebise refers to as the 'science of the soul'.

The Princess slowly realises that Cocteau is no longer infatuated by her (that is, by an aspect of his creative soul). She promptly *condemns him to life*. As always, Cocteau finds the paradox. He muses: 'Our creations are eager to kill off their parents and break free, yet these creatures of our imagination are curious about their origins.' That is, the art of every generation must be significantly different from that of the previous generation. And yet, every work of art invites the reader/viewer to speculate on the origins of the concern it explores (which includes its relation to the past).

Cégeste urges Cocteau to continue his journey. They find themselves in the garden of the Villa Santo-Sospir, in which a woman (Francine Weisweiller) in late nineteenth-century costume is reading a detective novel. Cégeste describes her as 'a woman confused about the epoch to which she belongs'. The point, of course, is that time and patience are required to resolve a crime—as they are to understand any psychological process, including the over-arching concerns of one's life.

Cégeste and Cocteau *descend* a stairway that overlook the sea. There follows a short but crucial scene. They are on a small yacht called 'Eurydice'. A woman is standing in the bow. Cégeste identifies her as Isolde. That is, Cocteau is likening his quest to the all-consuming longing of a mature woman for a younger man. He is the first 'Orpheus' to identify *himself* with Eurydice, and Eurydice with his twin concerns. Sometimes she is his creative urge (his wind-blown inspiration-cum-yacht) and sometimes she is his younger male partner, Edouard Dermit (Cégeste). The film explores both.

A moment later, they are in the Rue Obscure in Villefranche-sur-mer. When Cocteau's 'double' (also played by Cocteau) passes him without acknowledging him, he thinks he has been snubbed. Cégeste chides him for thinking always of himself: 'You spend your time trying to *be*, which prevents you from living'. This throwaway dig at existentialism (which was very much in fashion at the time) harbours the reminder that living begins not with oneself, but with one's relation to others.

The setting moves to Les Baux-de-Provence, a village in the shadow of an ancient hilltop stronghold in the Alpilles. Cégeste and Cocteau come across a couple of lovers embracing, each writing about their experience, as they feel it, in a notebook behind the other's back.[30] Cégeste describes this as 'intellectual love', suggesting that the age of psychoanalysis has produced an age of narcissism and solipsism. Everyone is so obsessed with their own experience that they can only half-connect with their partner. Cocteau then ruefully observes how a hunger for *names* promotes a vacuous and narcissistic celebrity-oriented culture (a culture, ironically, which Cocteau personified).

Thereupon, Cégeste wishes Cocteau goodbye. He has had 'orders'; he must leave—and Cocteau must face the goddess (and his death) alone.

He finds himself in a waiting room where a court usher (Yul Brynner) repeatedly tells him that someone (variously the Minister/President/First Secretary to his Highness/his Majesty) will see him in only a few minutes. Then the usher, quoting the lines engraved above the door of Hell in Dante's *Inferno*, tells him to 'abandon all hope here', to which Cocteau drily replies: 'I was expecting this.'

He proceeds into a room in which stands a statue of the goddess Minerva, spear in hand, guarded by two man-horses. As if by magic, the hibiscus reappears in his hand. He approaches Minerva (Claudine Auger), who looks down at him curiously, and then up, with complete disinterest. He feels slighted and, as he walks away, she hurls her spear at his back. Throughout his life, Cocteau had offended classical decorum: he now pays the price.

The death of a poet is a romantic theme, and Cocteau stages his with care.[31] It is a subject as gripping as a bullfight (Luis Miguel Domínguín), a subject for the painter (Picasso), for the singer-songwriter (Aznavour), and for the choreographer and dancer (Serge Lifar). Small wonder that these celebrated exponents of their various arts take such interest in his death. And yet, it is only the Romani who mourn him. A voice over says: 'Pretend to weep, my friends, since poets only pretend to die.' In other words, Orpheus as poet is dead! long live Orpheus the poet!

As if in a trance, Cocteau rises to a standing position and strides away, without seeing either the Sphinx, who follows him, or Antigone and the blind Oedipus (whom, in life, he had always wanted to meet) who are coming toward him. It is as if he is saying, like Muriel Rukeyser, 'No more mythologies'.[32] It is time to focus on the *personal*.

He finds himself on a roadside in the Alpilles. He hears two motorcyclists coming toward him. Remembering *Orphée*, he prepares to be run over by them. Instead, two traffic policemen stop, request his I.D., and examine it. As they do so, Cégeste appears from the hillside and pulls Cocteau *inside*: they both disappear. When the policemen look up, they are so surprised not to see him that they drop his I.D., which lands on the road as a hibiscus flower. An open car comes round the corner, crowded with young people, all laughing. As the policemen give chase, the hibiscus is swept away by the wind.

Cocteau's playful abjuration of his art ends by underlining his commitment to life. From henceforth, he will commit himself to his adopted son, Edouard Dermit. The film reminds us that the gender of the myth's protagonists is fluid. In *Orphée*, Cocteau explored his fascination with Cégeste's *poetry*. Although always a private person, Cocteau's *Testament* is his heart laid bare: he testifies to his love for Cégeste as a person. He identifies with Isolde searching for a young male Eurydice/ Tristan. He has become Eurydice determined to enjoy his final years with his young Orpheus.

Throughout his life, Cocteau hated discord. The metaphors that fascinate a person might help them to formulate *their* views, but they are only metaphors. Why argue with those obsessed with other metaphors? To always insist on one's own interpretation of an issue is to behave as predictably and foolishly as the two policemen who, in the final frames, set off to apprehend the young people in the speeding car and to stifle their carefree laughter. Cocteau doesn't lecture on old age; he gives the last word to youth and carefree laughter.

Today, it is impossible to think of the myth of Orpheus and Eurydice without recalling the primary concerns of all four of Cocteau's major works indebted to the myth. Few writers have contributed so many fresh associations with it, including riddles about the origin of the creative impulse, the nature of art, and the relation between art and life.

Conclusions

Versions of the myth of Orpheus and Eurydice produced during the 1950s are pre-occupied with different challenges facing the artist.

- Stravinsky and Balanchine suggest that only by clinging to tradition will the future reveal a new classicism.
- Pierre Henry and Béjart suggest that the post-war world needs to forget tradition and discover radically new creative forms.
- Muriel Rukeyser translates her loss of trust in a partner into a need to re-affirm her own sense of self as artist—and as mother.
- In his film, *Orphée*, Cocteau translates his fear of effacement into a reminder that he can only write as it is given him to write.
- Vinicius de Moraes suggests that music and violence represent the positive and negative poles of the intense passions found in the Rio *favelas*.
- *Black Orpheus* does the same, but it underlines the importance of music.
- *The Testament of Orpheus* represents Cocteau's 'personal myth', in which he plays with questions about art and life, but without insisting that he has found the key to either.

The film was first shown in 1960. Soon after, the myth became associated with fresh concerns, and perhaps appropriately, they were to express themselves in pre-viously little-regarded genres.

Notes

1 Of these, about half were *civilian* deaths in the Soviet Union and China.
2 *Apollon musagète* (= Apollo, Leader of the Muses) was first performed at the Washington Festival in April 1928, with choreography by Adolphe Bolm. Balanchine's version was first performed at the Théâtre Sarah Bernhardt, in Paris, in June 1928. The following year, it was given new costumes by Chanel. Today, the work is usually referred to as *Apollo*.
3 I. Stravinsky, *Orpheus* and *Danses concertantes*, Orpheus Chamber Orchestra, Deutsche Grammophon, 2007 (CD); G. Balanchine, *Orpheus* and *Serenade*, New York City Ballet in Montreal Vol. 1. VAI, 2014 (DVD).
4 J. Randel, 'Un-Voicing Orpheus: The Powers of Music in Stravinsky and Balanchine's "Greek Ballets"', *The Opera Quarterly* 29 (2), 2013, pp. 101–145.
5 I. Stravinsky, *Themes and Episodes*, New York: Alfred A. Knopf, 1966, p. 48n.

6 See, for example, M. Harss, 'New York City Ballet: Apollo, Orpheus, Agon', *Danc-eTabs*, January 23, 2019, a review of a performance with Gonzalo Garcia as Orpheus.

7 See, https://esprit.presse.fr/ressources/portraits/pierre-schaeffer-298.

8 He chose the name after Molière's partner, Armande Béjart, who created the role of Célimène in *Le Misanthrope*.

9 See C. Delhaye, '*Orphée 53* de Pierre Schaeffer et Pierre Henry, aux origines du scandale de Donaueschingen', *Revue de Musicologie* 98 (1), 2012, pp. 171–191.

10 The 16 min. version is available on CD: P. Henry, *Variations Pour Une Porte Et Un Soupir*, et *Voile D'Orphée*, Arles, France: Harmonia Mundi, 1987. Both versions are available on vinyl from a Russian label: P. Henry, *Le Voile d'Orphée*, Doxy, 2010 (originally issued on LP by Philips, 1969).

11 See LP notes by Jacques Lonchampt, Philips, 1969.

12 From *Theory of Flight* (1935), in *The Collected Poems of Muriel Rukeyser*, ed. J.E. Kaufman and A.F. Herzog, Pittsburgh, PA: University of Pittsburgh Press, 2005, p. 3.

13 Muriel Rukeyser, 'Orpheus', in The Collected Poems, pp. 285–296, reprinted by permission of the Muriel Rukeyser Estate. First published in Muriel Rukeyser, Orpheus, with the drawing Orpheus by Picasso, San Francisco: Centaur Press, 1949. A shorter version was published as 'Pieces of Orpheus', in Poetry 74 (no. 6), 1949, pp. 327–330.

14 Jane Hart was married to Democrat Senator Philip A. Hart. See R. Lewis, 'Jane Hart Says Hanoi Ready To Fight On If Talks Fail', *Ann Arbor News*, Nov. 15, 1972, p. 2.

15 From *Breaking Open* (1973), in *A Muriel Rukeyser Reader*, ed. J.H. Levi, New York: Norton, 1994, pp. 249–250.

16 J. Cocteau, *Orpheus* (*Orphée*), New York: The Criterion Collection, 2000 (DVD).

17 The cast includes Jean Marais (Orphée), Cocteau's partner at the time, Edouard Dermit (Cégeste), whom he subsequently adopted and who became his legal heir, Maria Casarès, the first foreign actress to perform at the Comédie française, the young singer, Juliette Gréco, Roger Blin (the journalist), who three years later would direct the premiere of Beckett's *En Attendant Godot*, and the tiny part of the hotel owner was taken by the film director, Jean-Pierre Melville (Le Silence de la Mer, 1949), who went on to direct *Le Samouraï* (1967) and *Le Cercle Rouge* (1970).

18 The phrase is more witty in French: 'Rien n'est plus tenace que la déformation professionnelle.'

19 The ellipsis: 'in that admirable line by Mallarmé, 'Until eternity at last changes him into Himself' (*Tel qu'en Lui-même enfin l'éternité le change*)', from Mallarmé's 'Le Tombeau d'Edgar Poe' (1876/1887), in *Œuvres complètes*, vol. 1, ed. B. Marchal, Paris: Gallimard/Pléiade, 1998, p. 38; qtd. in J. Cocteau, *Two Screenplays*, London: Marion Boyars, 1970, p. ??.

20 The Cotton Club first opened its doors to Black Americans in 1935.

21 In 1999, *Orfeu*, an updated version of the *play* opened in Rio. In 2002, it was filmed, with scriptwriters including Paulo Lins, music by Caetano Veloso, and directed by Carlos 'Cacá' Diegues.

22 V. de Moraes and T. Jobim, *Orfeu da Conceição*, with L. Bonfá on guitar, and R. Paiva as Orfeu (Rio de Janeiro: Odeon, 1956).

23 M. Camus, *Black Orpheus*, New York: The Criterion Collection, 1999 (DVD).

24 *Black Orpheus*, the soundtrack, New York: Epic, 1959 (vinyl).

25 J. Cocteau, *Testament of Orpheus* (*Le Testament d'Orphée*), New York: The Criterion Collection, 2000 (DVD).

26 This was two years before Jung would provide an account of *his* 'personal myth' in C.G. Jung, *Memories, Dreams, Reflections*, 1962 (p. 3).

27 Francine Weisweiller, Yul Brynner, and François Truffaut all helped to finance the film. By 1959, Yul Brynner was already a very successful actor. In contrast, François Truffaut donated a large part of his royalties from his *first* successful film, *Les Quatre Cents*

Coups (1959). Hence, perhaps, Cocteau's dedication of his film to young filmmakers of the New Wave.

28 Cocteau produced three versions of the myth of Oedipus: (1) an adaptation of Sophocles' *Oedipus the King* (1925/1937); (2) a libretto, translated into Latin by Jean Daniélou, for Stravinsky's opera-oratorio, *Oedipus Rex* (1927); and (3) *The Infernal Machine* (1934).

29 The Villa Santo-Sospir, in Saint-Jean-Cap-Ferrat (only a short walk from the *pension* where Charlotte Salomon had painted *Life? or Theatre?*) was the second home of Francine and Alec Weisweiller. In 1949, Francine invited Cocteau and Edouard Dermit to visit. During the next decade, Cocteau decorated the main rooms with large, glowing mythological line-drawings painted directly onto the white walls. For the dining room, he designed a striking, highly stylised tapestry, *Judith and Holofernes*.

30 Cf. Banksy, *Mobile Lovers* (2014), on a door inset in a stone wall on Clement Street in Bristol.

31 For example, Coleridge, 'Monody on the Death of Chatterton' (1790–1834); Wordsworth, 'Resolution and Independence' (1807); Shelley, *Adonais* (1821); Byron died at Missolonghi, in western Greece, in 1824, and was mourned by Greek nationalists; Vigny, *Chatterton* (1835); Lermontov, 'Death of the Poet' (1837).

32 M. Rukeyser, 'The Poem as Mask: Orpheus', from *The Speed of Darkness* (1968), in *The Collected Poems*, p. 413.

Chapter 10

Orpheus Trapped Inside a Tragic Myth

1960–1995

The years between 1960 and 1995 were dominated by the Cold War—a misnomer, for both sides used heated soundbites to remind their own people of their admirable intentions, and to stir distrust, contempt, and fear of the other. Both sides engaged in wars to retain or extend their own influence and in doing so, resorted to abhorrent methods (the Vietnam War, 1961–1975; the Soviet-Afghan War, 1979–1989; the Gulf War, 1990–1991). And yet, against this grim backdrop, many of the ambitions of the post-war years came to fruition: better education, housing, health care, and greatly improved social mobility, with almost every household benefitting from a marked increase in purchasing power.

Meanwhile, Western nations gradually slipped into new 'domestic' wars: wars related to class, generation, culture, and gender—issues that stirred strong emotions. New technologies (transistor radio, television, magazines) gave the young a new and powerful voice, and they were powerfully swayed by the music of their generation. In 1960, written culture (white, privileged, and 'rational') still held sway. By 1995, musical culture (multiracial, classless, and 'emotional') had replaced it. National cultures based on tradition and thought were gradually supplanted by the cultural issues of a group and the strong feelings these issues aroused. The idea of a 'common culture' lost even its tenuous hold, and its place was taken by a tribal individualism.[1] And every tribe was as dismissive of views that differed from its own as an arrogant teenager.

This chapter looks at six of the most intriguing versions of the myth of Orpheus and Eurydice produced during these watershed years. For the first time, most were now written by authors who did *not* come from the privileged classes, and their works belonged to genres with which the conservative mainstream continued to be uncomfortable: science fiction, fantasy, and contemporary opera. And yet these new genres represent an important new chapter in approaches to the myth, for they engage more purposefully than ever before with the question that lies at its heart: How are its protagonists to *escape* its tragic outcome?

Orpheus and Science Fiction

The first magazine devoted to science fiction was founded in the United States by Hugo Gernsback (*Amazing Stories*, 1926). Contributors included Ray Bradbury,

DOI: 10.4324/9781003519584-13

Ursula K. Le Guin, Robert Heinlein, and Arthur C. Clarke. Issues were printed on cheap paper, had garish covers, and they were sold not in bookshops, but at newsstands. In 1952, Aaron A. Wyn founded Ace Books, whose contributors included Isaac Asimov, Philip K. Dick, and Charles L. Harness. Mainstream reviewers and the elitist general reader did not consider that such works merited serious consideration: they were regarded as 'pulp fiction'.[2] It was not until the *late* 1960s that mainstream publishers finally conceded that writers of science fiction were engaging with important issues.

The following pages look at two versions of the myth of Orpheus and Eurydice. Both were originally published in 'pulp fiction' format and, soon after, republished by mainstream publishers. Both are set in a distant future. In both, the people live simplified lives. The first focuses on the nature and complexity of subjective (= psychological) processes. The second, written over *thirty* years ago, explores the development of artificial intelligence (AI) as a worrying new cultural and political concern.

Samuel R. Delany: Orpheus Trapped Inside a Tragic Myth

Following Cocteau's *Orphée*, *The Einstein Intersection* (1967) is the next version of the myth of Orpheus and Eurydice to further explore how difficult it is for the protagonist to escape from his identification with a myth that has a tragic outcome. And yet, this serious investigation unfolds with a dry, laugh-out-loud humour.

Samuel R. ('Chip') Delany was born in 1942 into a well-respected black family from Harlem, New York. He attended the Bronx High School of Science, where he became aware of racial segregation and gender intolerance, and realised he was gay. Even so, in 1961, he married Marilyn Hacker, a white Jewish-American who introduced him to Ace Books, with whom he quickly published eight science fiction novels.[3] He then started his ninth.

The Einstein Intersection is set in a distant future.[4] Following a global nuclear catastrophe, humans have abandoned planet Earth. In their place are two kinds of mutants. The *functionals* are struggling to hold onto their dominance. Owing to the falling number of 'normal' births, borderline cases are now being accepted as functionals. Such children often possess a talent difficult to explain, such as psychokinesis (the ability to move objects with their mind) or telepathy (the ability to communicate with another person simply by volition).[5] If this 'difference' becomes excessive, they are re-designated as *non-functionals* and confined to a 'kage', where they often die prematurely.

Lo Lobey lives in a village. He carries a machete which is also a flute with twenty holes (i.e. he plays it with his hands *and* his feet). As *machete*, it reflects the way he 'hacks' at any obstruction to his assumptions and desires. As *flute*, it reflects his desire to 'create' order in his life. His function is to herd goats with two others. They make a happy (if incongruous) trio until Lobey falls in love with Friza, a hanger-on who is mute. One day, he discovers her dead. It is unclear whether this is from mutation or whether Lobey is somehow responsible.

La Dire, a female elder, tells Lobey that he must 'kill' whatever it was that killed Friza, after which, Le Dorik (who looks after the *non*-functionals) will come for him. Lo Hawk, a male elder, teaches him to hunt, a skill he will need if he is to recover Friza. They set off and soon come upon a monstrous bull with hands who promptly disappears into a maze of underground passages. The comically unheroic Lobey is ordered to follow him inside.

That is, like Orpheus, he descends into an underworld to recover Friza. And like Theseus, he finds himself in a labyrinth, knowing that a wrong turn might be fatal. During his 'battle' with the bull-minotaur, he discovers a room with an old computer called PHAEDRA (an acronym for Psychic Harmony And Entangled Deranged Response Associations). Half-instinctively and half-accidently, he manages to kill the bull. Whereupon the computer tells him that he is in the 'wrong maze' and that he must find a way to 'kid Death' (= playfully *deceive* Death). That is, he must free himself from his own *deranged* responses—including his obsession with Friza and his reluctance to accept his 'difference'.

On the computer screen, he sees the faces of Friza and Dorik, and between them, a red-haired boy with fins, white gills, and row upon row of tiny shark-like teeth. Kid Death is a cross between a young and ruthless gunslinger (Billy the Kid) and a hungry predator. He admits that *he* killed Friza. He now intends to kill Lobey.

On exiting the source-cave, Lobey finds himself in the middle of a battle between carnivorous flowers (the self-indulgence of his obsession with Friza) and dragons (his own 'deeper' instincts). Suddenly, a functional appears (Spider) and quickly forces the flowers to retreat. The dragons belong to a herd he is taking from the Hot Swamp (the origin of instincts) to Branning-at-sea. That is, Spider is a herder of age-old human instincts; he represents an *organising principle* in the human imagination. And he offers Lobey a job as a dragon herder. The dragon-drive represents the 'journey' (psychological process) that Lobey must make if he is to better harness his instincts.

As the herd travels (each of the herders riding a dragon), the reader learns that Lobey absorbs his musical skill from the world, and that, despite his attributes, Spider alone will not be able to protect him from Kid Death—but one of his herders might. Green-eye, who was born without a father, is a thin, black-haired mute with one green eye—and yet, Lobey *hears* Green-eye tell him 'There is no death, only love'.[6] The reader gradually realises that Green-eye is modelled on Christ.

Lobey is so self-absorbed that he feels *entitled* to recover Friza from the underworld. But when he shows no interest in the danger facing Green-eye, his dragon slips, and he finds himself dangling over the edge of a cliff. Friza promptly appears and tries to help him, but Kid Death allows her to crash to her 'second' death. He then tries to tempt Green-eye, to no avail.[7] Lobey lets himself die, but Green-eye brings him back to life, and weeps.[8] He is saddened by Lobey's inability to grasp that the challenge facing him has to do with his own attitudes.

As the dragon herd approaches Branning-at-sea (a dystopian city in which Lobey will have to confront his mistaken obsession), the challenge facing him becomes fused with the events of Holy Week (between Christ's entrance to Jerusalem and his crucifixion and resurrection).[9] He meets Pistol, who quickly becomes irritated by his arrogance. He sees a poster of The Dove, a young woman with a childish smile, who embodies that impossible 'something' (whether good, bad, or wild) for which everyone longs because it embodies an aspect of their own desire. The posters are for a survival programme designed to prevent functionals from developing obsessive fantasies by urging them to have as many partners as they can (to ensure a maximum mixing of genes, thus slowing mutation).

Spider invites Lobey to think of mythology in terms *not* of story, but of how he *feels* when he brushes against a myth. For myths are *not* fixed. The world needs Green-eye because he can *create* from nothing (faith)—and Green-eye needs Lobey because Lobey/Orpheus can invest events with meaningful order (music).

Lobey finally realises that even if he can reach Friza, he does not know what he will encounter. Spider (now as Minos, gatekeeper to the underworld) smiles: 'Now I can let you through'. Lobey goes to The Pearl, a nightclub, to meet Pistol. He is greeted by The Dove, who helps him to recognise that his obsession with Friza might be self-destructive. In his mind's eye, he sees Green-eye hanging from the tree outside.

As he runs from The Pearl, he realises that it is built over Branning-at-sea's kage. But because he continues to think of Friza, PHAEDRA reproaches him: 'Why bother to look for her? Whatever illusion you devise, you will *always* leave alone. Seek outside the frame of the mirror. Beg at the tree.' Lobey is hurled out of the nightclub, where he finds Green-eye, exactly as he had imagined. He plays to him, begs for resolution, but when nothing happens, he plunges his machete into Green-eye's thigh.[10]

Lobey's 'deranged' hopes have been shattered. He goes to a beach. Kid Death appears, determined to appropriate Lobey's musical skill and then kill him. He orders Lobey to play. As Lobey plays his flute, he hears a whip repeatedly striking Kid Death. Finally, Spider announces: 'It's over'.[11] Lobey is shocked—but is still unable to grasp what has happened. He is not clear what choice he made 'between the real—and the rest'. It is left to the reader to decide what, if anything, he has learned.

Like Virgil's epyllion, *The Einstein Intersection* is about the need to understand the relation between an individual's situation (their social reality) and their 'fantasy' (their imaginal reality). It explores the intersection between the recognition that the observer influences the thing they perceive (Einstein on relativity) and the acceptance that, in any closed mathematical system, there are always events which can be neither proven nor disproven (Gödel on incompleteness).[12] That is, although subjective factors influence our every experience, it is impossible to fully demonstrate this—which makes it hard to accept that they might, or do.

The Einstein Intersection won the Nebula Award for the best Science Fiction novel of the year, a prize awarded by *writers* of science fiction. It represents a radically new way of exploring the myth and the psychological process it describes.

Delany reworks the myth to illustrate the 'deranged' nature of Lobey's obsession with Friza. The novel suggests that a myth (the mythic imagination) is both experiential and dialogical, and that every decision Lobey makes changes the remainder of the myth. But his most surprising contribution is the suggestion that, to avoid the tragic implications of the myth, Lobey needs *help*—and he receives this from two unexpected characters—distinct, but related. This is the first version of the myth to associate it with an *organising principle* in the imagination (Spider; the Jungian Self) and the Christian myth about atonement (Green-eye). The novel represents a psychological process leading from pathological narcissism to an intimation of the need for greater self-awareness.

Five years after its publication, another American writer turned to the myth of Orpheus and Eurydice to explore the *fear* that Western nations might be sliding toward authoritarian government. Although his novelette includes no specific references to the myth, it is the first version of the myth to explore the anxiety stirred by increasing dependence on computers and, more specifically, on AI.

Poul Anderson: Orpheus and the Threat from AI

Poul Anderson, who was born to Scandinavian parents in Pennsylvania, began writing while studying physics at the University of Minnesota. In 1947, he published two novelettes that are amongst the first works to reflect a keen anxiety about nuclear weapons.[13] They explore the fate of America following a *Third* World War.

He was in his mid-forties when he wrote 'Goat Song' (1972), a novelette first published in 'pulp fiction' format. Three years later it was reprinted by a mainstream publisher.[14] It is set in the future. Civilisation has grown so complex that human beings have surrendered government to an all-controlling computer called SUM. Human beings wear bracelets which connect them to SUM, which constantly processes the information it receives. It holds the details of their 'soul' and, after death, it promises them resurrection at an unspecified future time. But like Gradgrind (in Dickens' *Hard Times*, 1854), it can only process facts and measurable data. Despite its use of the word 'soul', it has no understanding of either feelings or mystery.

The events are narrated by a character called Harper, who lives on the 101st floor of a highly desirable tower block. He can appreciate the *use* of computers in modern life. But he is worried about the loss of interest in imaginative literature—and he is shocked by the growth of narcissism. Individuals have become so obsessed with 'their own precious private consciousnesses' that they cannot relate to each other. They submit to 'neuroadjustment' and turn to drugs to achieve 'wonder'. In contrast, Harper finds 'wonder' in poetry. And he believes that myths hold 'truths' and that they shape individual experience.

The plot follows the Augustan myth of Orpheus and Eurydice surprisingly closely. Harper's beloved is bitten in the foot by a snake and dies. He now seeks her resurrection. His friend Thrakia, with whom he refuses to sleep, considers his 'sexual monomania' to be 'morbid'. 'Goat Song' also borrows from the myth of Persephone. SUM has granted the Dark Queen eternal youth so that she can help him to control humanity. One Autumn, she is on her way 'home' to SUM when

Harper confronts her. He begs her to plead with SUM to grant that his beloved be resurrected. She tells him there can be no exceptions—until he plays a song. Shaken by the feelings it expresses, the Dark Queen agrees to take him to SUM.[15]

She leads him into an underworld of machines and missile launchers. They cross a river into a world with an oppressive absence of light. He comes before SUM, which is programmed to be interested in 'human psychophysiology' and is curious about his 'sexual monomania' and his 'atavistic, superstition-oriented personality'. In desperation, Harper offers to become SUM's 'prophet' if only his 'girl' be returned to him. SUM imposes the condition. Harper is almost at the gate when he turns. His beloved is snatched away, and he finds himself outside in the freezing cold, homeless and insane.

He sings 'Tom o' Bedlam' and the dirge from Shakespeare's *Cymbeline*.[16] He begins to plan how SUM might be destroyed. He spends his last months trying to rouse as many as he can to help him to overthrow SUM. He loses touch with reality. The Dark Queen reappears and is sorry to see the state into which he has fallen. But when he cuts the bracelet from his wrist, she demands his arrest. He is allowed to live as an exile. The story ends with him going to meet some women (an evident reference to the Maenads who tear Orpheus to pieces).

'Goat Song' won Anderson his fifth Hugo Award, the highest accolade for a writer of science fiction, and deservedly. Whereas Orwell had worried about totalitarian political control, Anderson is worried about the impoverishment of individual feelings, consciousness, and culture. He is worried that humans will forget to ask meaningful questions. The story foresees a world in which people become the 'slaves' of a technology which *they* have created. It explores a possible danger of over-dependence on computer technology and especially of AI.[17]

That is, it attaches a new and prescient concern to the myth of Orpheus and Eurydice. It represents a chilling vision of a world in which all our responses have become so conditioned by social engineering that we lose the two most precious aspects of our humanity: our ability to respond to the concerns of others, and to reflect on the 'mystery' of the imagination that has made human culture so diverse and so endlessly enriching.

We come now to a work which many contemporary composers and scholars of music regard as one of the outstanding examples of latetwentieth-century opera.

A Postmodern Orphic Opera

Harrison Birtwistle was born in 1934 and studied the clarinet at the Royal Manchester College of Music. Early works include the chamber opera, *Punch and Judy* (which explores the violence of humans who behave like puppets) and *Monodrama* (which is based on an early form of Greek tragedy in which a single actor assumes several dramatic roles). They quickly attracted critical attention. In the late 1960s, the Royal Opera invited Birtwistle to compose a work for them. A commission was signed—but owing to the abstract and complex nature of the two subjects he proposed (Chronos, Faust), discussions stalled.

Zinovieff and Birtwistle: The Over-Ambitions of Postmodern Myth

In 1970, Birtwistle became interested in the myth of Orpheus and Eurydice. Three years later, Glyndebourne Opera took over the commission from the Royal Opera and invited him to write an opera on the myth. Peter Zinovieff promptly devised the libretto, which is heavily indebted to Jung, and Birtwistle drafted the orchestral music for its first two acts. But the scale of the planned work was greater than the old Glyndebourne opera house could handle.[18] English National Opera (ENO) took on the commission, but then hesitated to promise a firm date for the premiere.[19]

Meanwhile, Birtwistle became Music Director at the National Theatre, where he contributed to several productions directed by Peter Hall. For Aeschylus' *Oresteia* (1981), he devised pulsating rhythms for the chorus; and the production was celebrated for its use of masks designed by Jocelyn Herbert. Encouraged by the reviews it received, ENO finally gave Birtwistle the promise he needed. He quickly added the electronic music (realised by Barry Anderson in association with IRCAM) and completed the third act.[20]

The Mask of Orpheus was premiered in May 1986, by English National Opera, with designs and costumes by Jocelyn Herbert. It consists of *three* loosely connected versions of the myth, each of which represents a different aspect of the same three characters (Orpheus, Eurydice, and Aristaeus). This requires a stage with three levels, one above the other.

- The upper stage tells a *human story*, and all three characters are represented by singers wearing a half-mask. Orpheus the 'man' lives too much in his mind.[21] Aristaeus and Eurydice represent different aspects of his personality. Aristaeus represents his 'shadow'; that is, tendencies of which he is unaware, and with which he has not yet come to terms.[22] Eurydice represents different aspects of his 'anima'; that is, of his unconscious image of womanhood.
- The central stage tells the story of Orpheus as 'hero'. As *heroic figures*, the characters are represented not by singers, but by mimes or actors in full masks (or by small puppets). And the heroic story often differs dramatically from the human story.
- The lower stage tells the story of how the 'myth' came to be formulated. And as *mythic characters*, they are represented by large puppets or dolls whose 'voices' are sung by singers offstage and are amplified.[23]

In short, although there are only three main characters, they are represented by *nine* very different figures, several of which might be on stage at the same time.

At various intervals, these three narratives are frozen while a mimed enactment of *another* myth briefly 'comments' on a specific moment in the myth of Orpheus. These other myths are of two kinds: myths about Dionysus (his birth; Lycurgus; Pentheus) and myths about love (Adonis and Venus; Hyacinth and Apollo; Driope,

Lotus and Priapus).[24] But they are given so little time that it is probably impossible to represent them sufficiently clearly for their implications to be understood by the audience.

The entire opera is composed of fragments of scenes which unfold according to carefully structured abstract patterns such as the repetition of an event presented from an opposite point of view, ritualistic ceremonies, a contrast with another myth, even the movement of the tide as on an imagined shore. Most of the opera is sung in English, but some parts are sung in an invented language devised from the phonemes contained in the two words, 'Orpheus' and 'Eurydice'.[25]

Traditionally, an opera tells a story set to music. *The Mask of Orpheus* does not. It rests on a postmodern suspicion of claims about a single narrative with a specific meaning. Neither Birtwistle nor Zinovieff had any interest in traditional narrative. They wanted to explore the implications of what they saw as tensions within the component parts of the myth of Orpheus and Eurydice—Zinovieff in relation to myth; Birtwistle in relation to music.

Birtwistle drew from his friend's libretto *only* what caught his imagination. His opera is shaped by abstract musical concerns which successive textual moments suggested to him. Stage directors of opera usually seek to 'realise' the concerns of its narrative. For *The Mask of Orpheus*, Birtwistle suggested that they would be better advised to work not from the text, but *from the music*. And his musical language is anything but easy to translate into 'poems': that is, into a persuasive and intriguing staging. For he is interested not in story, but in time, in number patterns, in reversal, in repetition, and in cyclicality.

The Mask of Orpheus harbours an exuberant delight in the creative possibilities harboured by musical language. It reminds the audience that myth and music are languages, and that every language is a closed system. To understand language, one must learn to play with it. And as every live performance has confirmed, the opera is mesmerising and (for all its possible weaknesses) makes a powerful impression.[26]

But our concern here is with the treatment of the myth. The self-indulgence of the conception and, more importantly, the difficulties it poses for staging need no underlining. To call the libretto overblown is understatement. More problematically, it identifies the tragic narrative of the myth with cyclicality. It suggests that once 'inside' the myth, there is no escaping it. Zinovieff and Birtwistle both read and referred to Jung, but they appear not to have grasped the key to his ideas: that most dreams, fantasies, and myths harbour a life-affirming function. They imply a possible way forward. In other words, to be stuck inside a recurrent dream or tragic myth is to have repeatedly failed to learn from its implications.

The Mask of Orpheus represents an overwhelming musical experience. Its attempt to tell 'the whole story' of the myth of Orpheus and Eurydice is altogether less successful.

Eight years later, Birtwistle would team up with a different librettist and produce a second and altogether more successful opera on the same myth. But before we come to it, we must consider the work which brought them together.

The Head of Orpheus in Contemporary Fantasy

The following pages explore three unexpected versions of the myth of Orpheus and Eurydice: the first is a *novel*, the second an *opera*, the third, a short story told in *comic* strips. They can all be described as 'fantasy', and they all end with a significant insight, whether psychological or political, or both.

We begin with a novel, strongly influenced by Jung, in which a protagonist's 'social' reality is unexpectedly disrupted by experiences/events that unfold in an 'imaginal' reality.

Russell Hoban: The Head of Orpheus Corrects the Myth

Russell Hoban was born in 1925, the son of Jewish parents from the Ukraine who settled in the United States, near Philadelphia. In the nineteen sixties, he and his first wife collaborated on several children's books (most famously, *The Mouse and His Child*, 1967). In 1969, following their separation, he settled in London, where he began writing for adults. Like Cocteau, he had a life-long fascination with the myth of Orpheus and Eurydice. The whimsical and loosely autobiographical *Kleinzeit* (1974) represents the first of three extended responses to the myth.[27] Our concern here is with the second.

The Medusa Frequency (1987) is a wacky fantasy novel with a dazzling pace and language.[28] Almost every other sentence makes one smile or even laugh out loud ('I came awake as I always do, like a man trapped in a car going over a cliff'). Its hero is Herman Orff, who is forty-nine, lives in a 'lost outpost' in west London (Fulham) and earns a living by distilling literary classics (*Treasure Island, War and Peace*) for comic books. He yearns to write a successful novel. His first two novels having bombed, he is paralysed by writer's block. On his desk, he keeps three reproductions of Vermeer's *Girl with a Pearl Earring*, which remind him of Luise von Himmelbett (= of the heavenly bed) with whom he lived for two years, who then left him, and for whom he continues to yearn.

There is a backstory. Thirteen years earlier, Istvan Fallok, a composer of electronic music, began a two-year relationship with Luise. When it ended, she lived with Herman Orff, a writer, also for two years. When they broke up, she began a relationship with Gösta Kraken, a filmmaker, which also lasted two years. All three men continue to be haunted by memories of her. All three are also obsessed with Vermeer's painting, *Girl with a Pearl Earring*. They all associate both Luise and Vermeer's *Girl* with Eurydice. And their associations with the myth are determined by their choice of art-form.

The Medusa Frequency is a first-person novel told by Herman Orff, who is so immersed in his private concerns that he allows both his professional and personal life to fall apart. He has successive hallucinations of the head of Orpheus, which tries to 'correct' his mistaken notions about the myth of Orpheus and Eurydice. That is, just as Virgil adapted the myth to comment on the challenge facing Aristaeus, so Hoban reworks the myth to comment on the challenge facing Herman

Orff—which is to understand why he was unable to hold on to Luise, and why he has been unable to come to terms with his triple fixation (with Luise, with Vermeer's *Girl*, and with Eurydice).

The narrative begins late one night with Herman Orff sitting helplessly at his computer (a 1980s model with green script). Nothing comes to him. He types: 'What are you afraid of?' He receives the reply 'NNVSNU TSRUNGH'. He *knows* that he typed these words, but he assumes that they are messages from the Kraken, a deep-sea monster who was born in terror and is always thinking of Eurydice.[29] For as he wryly notes, 'At three o'clock in the morning Eurydice is bound to come into it'. He is reminded of a *netsuke* of a Japanese fishergirl being embraced by a giant squid trembling at the 'actuality' of her beauty.[30]

To help overcome his writer's block, Orff submits himself to EEG (electroencephalogram, a device designed to identify *abnormal* wave patterns in the brain). He recalls a holiday with Louise, and of her saying to him that the underworld is not just a place for the dead: 'What we call world is only that little bit of each moment that we know about—underworld is everything else that we don't know but we need it'.[31] But, like Delany's Lobey, Orff has no idea what he *needs*.

While walking along the river Thames, he hears a voice crying 'Eurydice!'. It comes from a slime-covered stone, but he *sees* it as the head of Orpheus, rotting and eyeless. The head explains that the traditional story is wrong—that his mistake was not to turn *around* too soon; it was to turn *away* too soon. Eurydice left him because *he* lacked fidelity. Orff is reminded of Luise baking. He vaguely realises that he felt insufficient fidelity to the smell of her fresh brown bread; that is, to their shared life together.

Orff becomes drawn to Melanie Falsepercy (False Persephone), but, true to form, remains more interested in his own concerns. An old cabbage, which he sees as the head of Orpheus, tells him that he and Eurydice enjoyed their life together until they began to feel as if they had become entangled in a myth of which neither wanted to be any part.

When Melanie calls to say she is working and cannot see him, he turns to the Vermeer *Girl* to discover that her 'virtue' has evaporated. And yet, when he turns on the radio, he hears her say 'Come and find me'. He takes the ferry to The Hague only to learn that Vermeer's painting is on loan to an exhibition in America. He comes across Gösta Kraken, who is similarly disappointed, but Gösta's postmodern chatter irritates him. He quickly moves away and, while looking at a painting of a Brazilian landscape, he has a waking fantasy of Luise rising and becoming the Medusa.[32] As he sets off for the station to catch the train home, he sees Luise, catches up with her, and he learns that she is happily married.

Back home, he begins THE STORY OF ORPHEUS. A football bursts into his home. He sees it as the head of Orpheus, furious with him for trying to translate life into art. The head bites his arm and tells him that one cannot go looking for Eurydice because one will never find her. When Orff tells him that he saw the Medusa, the head becomes wistful: 'I never found her', he regrets.

Reluctantly, Orff agrees to consider writing the screenplay for Gösta's next film, which is to be called 'Eurydice and Orpheus'. He is invited to a restaurant to discuss this. But when his starter (a half-grapefruit) arrives, Orff sees it as the sliced-off top of the head of Orpheus, upside down, as if he were meant to spoon out its brain. He promptly wraps it in a napkin and runs for the exit.

Back home, the head tells him that the myth is composed *only* of fragments, and everyone arranges these fragments in the light of their individual concerns. The trick is *not* to allow the fragments to become a story with a tragic ending. As soon as the story 'found them', Eurydice *had to* leave Orpheus (and to settle with Aristaeus), because 'Eurydice is the one who cannot stay'. And the long and painful punishment given to Orpheus is to be able to love only 'Eurydice lost'.

When the producer phones to ask him why he left the restaurant the way he did, Orff becomes confused, suffers an angina, and wakes up in hospital. Slowly he recovers. Returning home, he determines to begin a novel called *The Seeker from Nexo Vollma*. He receives a well-wishing 'goodbye' note from Melanie. But the only outlet he can now find for his 'novel' is as a comic strip on the back of cereal packets.

Although those interested in Hoban's work regard *The Medusa Frequency* as one of his finest achievements, it was not widely successful. It is difficult to understand why. All previous versions of the myth identify creativity with one or other of Orpheus' twin gifts: music and poetry. In contrast, following Maurice Blanchot, Hoban identifies creativity with the determination to recover something *lost*.[33] *The Medusa Frequency* asks, 'Is not all art a celebration of loss?'. But whereas Blanchot focuses on the nature of *writing*, Hoban recognises that the challenge facing his protagonist is not to focus on the loss (cf. Virgil), but to develop a greater interest in the woman he loves, and a fidelity to *her*.

Medusa is usually associated with being turned into stone. Hoban sees her as something that *prevents* Orff from becoming 'swallowed' by his own fantasy projections about a lost love. The novel ends with him looking at Vermeer's *Girl* and no longer seeing her as either Luise or Eurydice—but as Medusa, 'flickering and friendly' and trusting him with the idea of Vermeer's *Girl* (but now only as a *painting*). Although left open, the suggestion is that he *may* have finally understood why Luise left him and come to terms with his triple fixation.

Hoban is the first writer since Halévy and Offenbach to imagine *both* protagonists of the myth wishing that they had never become 'trapped' inside its narrative; that is, to realise that identifying with the myth has seriously messed with their lives.

Harrison Birtwistle so enjoyed *The Medusa Frequency* that he wrote to Russell Hoban. They soon agreed to collaborate on an opera. The result is a modern masterpiece.

Hoban and Birtwistle: Unbearable Loneliness, Impossible Longing

The Second Mrs Kong was premiered by Glyndebourne Touring Opera in October 1994.[34] The title refers to *King Kong*, the classic RKO film of 1933.[35] The first Mrs Kong is Ann Darrow, for whom the monster develops a tender longing.[36] The *second* Mrs Kong is Pearl as she appears in Vermeer's painting, *Girl with a Pearl Earring*.

Hoban's opera is unlike any other. Neither protagonist represents a *living* person. Kong does not represent the fifty-foot-high gorilla-like monster of the film. Hoban (and the programme) defines him as 'the *idea* of Kong'. It would be more accurate to suggest that he represents the two *feelings* ascribed to Kong in the later scenes of the film (his bewilderment at finding himself in New York and his tender love for the relatively diminutive Ann Darrow). Similarly, Pearl does not represent the young woman who posed for Vermeer. She represents the *feelings* of a young woman awakening to a sense of her aloneness, and her longing for an ideal male other. That is, both protagonists embody feelings of unbearable loneliness and of an impossible longing for an ideal other. It is the first version of the myth of Orpheus and Eurydice to define it as a tragedy of incompatible but deep-rooted feelings. The opera is about why such archetypal feelings can never be consummated.

The other major characters represent figures from ancient myth (Anubis, Orpheus, Inanna). The minor characters are a parody of contemporary types (a crassly materialist film producer, a bogus guru)—and they are all *dead*.

The opera begins in a misty gloom. As the dead appear on stage, Anubis, the jackal-headed boatman of Egyptian mythology (the conductor of souls to the underworld) commands them to re-live their memories. As the hubbub of fragmentary memories deteriorates into nonsense, Anubis tells Vermeer: 'Feed on your dream of love, and I'll feed on you'.

Vermeer steps inside 'the place of memory' (for him, Delft, *c*.1665) and Anubis reminds him: 'No matter how many times you remember, it always ends the same'. Vermeer quickly rejects four women who want to model for him. But when he sees Pearl collecting for the church, he is thunderstruck. All his adult life he has been haunted by a face that he has never seen. It is the face of Pearl. He persuades her to model for him. He gives her a jacket, turban, and a pearl earring, as well as a mirror (which is not in Vermeer's painting).

Meanwhile, in the world of shadows, a messenger arrives with a 35-mm film can for Mr Kong, who is struggling to understand what 'idea' he represents. Pearl looks at the mirror and sees: 'In the shadows of the future waits a *king* who never was.' Through a succession of Chinese-whisper mis-hearings, this is gradually transformed into her waiting 'for my Kong'. She suddenly becomes aware of Vermeer, and asks, 'Who are you?' to which *both* Kong and Vermeer answer 'Nobody'. Hoban has reworked the theme of the artist and his model to suggest that the artist is only a medium whose task is to explore the *nature* and *reality* of what fascinates them.

As Kong watches the train derailment from the 1933 film, his memories become confused ('a jungle painted all on glass', a sensation of being 'very, very high and falling, falling'). Although he *knows* that he has no material substance, he longs to hear Pearl's voice again.

The second scene is set in a stockbroker's high-tech penthouse, with a computer and a giant screen. It opens with a parody of the commodification of Vermeer's painting. Pearl then sings of being 'lost and lonely in the shadows of the future'. She idly plays with the computer keys, and her choices are projected onto the screen. She presses 'Classics'—and the ending of *King Kong* appears on the screen. She is confused. 'This is *not* the Kong whose voice I heard'. The Mirror reassures her that 'the wild and wordless, lost and lonely child of all the world is not dead!'

Pearl sits at the computer keyboard and sings: 'O Kong, here am I, only a picture of a picture, only the image of a girl long dead.' She tries to find Kong through the website of a stockbroker on the recently invented World Wide Web. Her efforts unfold on the giant screen in a brilliant confusion of her awakened longing and stockbroker-speak. It begins with Pearl typing 'Pearl here ... Where is Kong?' and receiving the reply 'What shares?'—to which she promptly replies 'Not shares. I want all of him'. When told to 'Try world of shadows', she is answered by Kong's voice offstage. He is afraid. She assures him that she will not let him die. He is taken aback by her interest. She admits to being unbearably lonely. They declare their love. Vermeer's painting of *Pearl* is the first Eurydice-figure to actively *search* for Orpheus.

Whereupon Kong turns to Orpheus: 'Pearl loves me. I must find her'. He knocks Anubis down, pulls Orpheus into Anubis' boat, and they move off—*into a fog*.

Act two explores the incompatibility between deep-rooted inner longings and reality. It begins with the entrance of Kong and Orpheus, still in Anubis' boat. Orpheus is inconsolable. He has just turned and lost Eurydice for ever. He sings 'Lost! Lost! Lost and lonely in the shadows.' His despair begins to affect Kong who now begins to doubt whether Pearl exists, whether he does, and even whether there is a world. Immediately, they are attacked by four temptations: Doubt, Fear, Despair, and Terror. Orpheus begs Kong to listen to them; Kong refuses to do so. In the ensuing struggle, Terror tears off Orpheus' head, but Kong remains undeterred: he is convinced that somewhere beyond 'this dark sea', Pearl and happiness are waiting for him.

As Kong and the Head of Orpheus resume their quests, a second boat appears. Anubis and the other dead have come to see where Kong's determination will lead him. They pass through the customs barrier between the world of shadows and the world of the living. As they come to the latter, fresh doubts assail them both. When they see a telephone box, the head of Orpheus helps Kong to telephone Pearl. He gets through. He tells her he is coming. She asks him to be careful.

Immediately, a character representing the Death of Kong bursts into the telephone box and drags Kong out. The dead place bets on the outcome. Inanna hopes Kong will be killed so that he will return to her in the World of Shadows. Just as in an action movie, Kong is about to be killed when he reminds himself that he is an idea, and thus has no physical reality. He kills the Death of Kong. As he sets off to find Pearl, Inanna complains that she has never won anything that *she* wanted.

The finale is set in the penthouse flat. Pearl is anxious. She feels 'so nowhere and so not at all'. When she looks at her mirror, she cannot find her own reflection. When Kong arrives, she is 'not ready'. But when he knocks again, she opens the door, and they instantly recognise the other. They both ask whether they look the way the other imagined them. They both say they do. Pearl tells Kong 'You look like what you are—my own true love'.

Both have longed for this moment. Pearl looks at the mirror: 'Please say that our happiness begins!' But the Mirror replies: 'No. This is the moment when reality begins. You cannot have each other [...] you will be together and apart forever'.

Kong and Pearl reach for each other, but they cannot touch. The dead try to intercede on their behalf, to no avail. The Mirror explains: 'It is not love that moves the world from night to morning ... It is the longing for what cannot be. The world needs the power of your yearning, the power of your love that cannot be fulfilled'. The opera ends with Kong and Pearl repeatedly reassuring each other that they remember when they first fell in love.

The Second Mrs Kong unfolds entirely in an imaginal world. It explores the difference between feelings that *can* be met and feelings that *cannot*. To confuse the latter (archetypal feelings) with the feelings that a person has for another in a *social* reality is to repeat the error of Virgil's Orpheus. Hoban's libretto is the first version of the myth to illustrate and explain the distinction between myth and reality: that is, to underline *why* individuals ought to think twice about longing for a mythic (imaginal) character or identifying with a mythic structure.

The opera represents both a wonderfully zany and a deeply poignant version of the myth of Orpheus and Eurydice. In terms of its libretto, it is a far more coherent, persuasive, and important work than *The Mask of Orpheus*. At a concert performance at the Royal Festival Hall in 2004, the voices were 'discreetly amplified', which allowed most of its surreal text to be appreciated. And as Andrew Clements wrote, Birtwistle 'clothes it with some of his most ravishing and richly scored music'. It is 'one of the great operatic achievements of our time'.[37] It is also one of the most psychologically insightful versions of the myth.

For the last section in this chapter, we turn to a work by a young English writer, which also features the head of Orpheus—and its primary concern is emphatically *political*.

Neil Gaiman: Orpheus and Political Idealism

Neil Gaiman grew up in the south of England. He became a journalist, while also working for the British Fantasy Society. In 1984, he published his first short story. Partly by accident, he soon established himself as a writer for comic books. Karen Berger, an editor at DC Comics in New York, invited him to re-imagine a new Sandman series in which each story, although self-contained, would contribute to a distinct imaginary world. From 1989 to 1996, issues of *The Sandman*, each containing one or more stories, were published at approximately one-month intervals. They quickly achieved a cult following.

Gaiman's Sandman has several names, including Morpheus, Oneiros, and the Shaper of Form, but he is most often called Dream. He is depicted as tall, thin, with hollow cheeks, a mop of black hair, and consumed by inner concerns. He is one of the seven Endless that shape human nature (the others are Desire, Delirium, Destruction, Despair, Destiny, and Death).

'Thermidor' (1991; in the French Revolutionary calendar, *Thermidor* is the name of the hottest month: equivalent to mid-July to mid-August) is pencilled by

Stan Woch and inked by Dick Giordano.[38] It is set during the last five days of the 'Reign of Terror': that is, in late July 1794. And it cleverly adapts the final scene of the Augustan myth—the head of Orpheus floating down the Hebrus—for a story about the use of the guillotine during the French Revolution.

In late June 1794, Dream appears to Johanna Constantine (a young English woman from an earlier *Sandman* story about how places change, but people's characters do not).[39] He asks for her help. She agrees on the condition that he gives her something which it is in his power to give. The story is about how Dream engineers, and how Johanna and the head of Orpheus bring about the fall of Robespierre.

Johanna travels to Paris. On the 6th Thermidor (24 July), disguised as a French country woman, she is stopped by two French soldiers who force her to show them what she has in the sack she is carrying. It is a severed head. Shocked, they allow her to pass—but, on arriving home, the head (which is of course the head of Orpheus) warns her that Robespierre will soon be looking for her.

The following morning, Saint-Just appears at Johanna's door. Although they had once enjoyed a brief affair, he orders soldiers to search her rooms and he threatens to torture her. Unable to get her to tell him anything, he takes her to the prison in the Luxembourg Palace. On their way to her cell, they pass the cell of Thomas Paine, who complains that the revolution has perverted his writings.

The story is built around the juxtaposition of the views of Thomas Paine and those of Robespierre. Paine was born in Thetford (Norfolk, England). In 1774, in his late thirties, he emigrated to America. In January 1776, he published *Common Sense*, a pamphlet which strongly supported the independence of the thirteen colonies. Its success helped to trigger the Declaration of Independence (July 1776). Another of Paine's pamphlets, *The American Crisis* (from which Gaiman quotes), was read aloud to George Washington's army on the eve of the Battle of Trenton (26 Dec 1776).

In 1787, Paine returned to London. *Rights of Man* (1791), which strongly defends the rights of *all* against the hereditary rights of a few, was so great a success that the British government sought out the most vocal of those who supported Paine's views and imprisoned them.[40] Paine fled to France and, *in absentia*, was convicted of seditious libel, a hanging offence. In France, he was welcomed and (along with Hamilton, Washington, and Franklin) awarded honorary French citizenship. At the National Convention, he was made the representative for the Pas-de-Calais. He voted *against* the execution of Louis XVI, and his sympathies for the moderate Girondins earned him the enmity of Robespierre and the *Montagnards* (Jacobins).[41] In 1793, the creation of the Committee of Public Safety gave Robespierre autocratic power: it was not long before he introduced a Reign of Terror. In December, Paine was arrested, imprisoned in the Luxembourg Palace, and one day (by accident) almost executed.

Like many other political tyrants, Robespierre held some laudable political views. He believed in reason. He was opposed to slavery. He wanted to abolish inherited privileges, to promote direct democracy, and to ensure that everyone was equal before the law. He also wanted to unify a seriously divided nation. Many of his political objectives he shared with Paine. But he was an idealist *and* a fanatic. Robespierre was not a tyrant *because* of his views or his intentions, but because of what Gaiman calls his 'visionary' tendency—that is, the fanatical means he adopted to achieve his ends. This is the 'perversion' to which Thomas Paine refers in 'Thermidor'.

Robespierre, whose spies have told him everything, appears in Johanna's cell. He has guessed the identity of the head, and as a 'visionary' believer in Reason, he is determined to destroy this relic of myth. He gives Johanna time to decide. That night, Dream appears to her in her sleep and, as he ponders what to do, his raven Jessamy suggests that he get his son (Orpheus) to sing. Dream gives Johanna a drink which will allow her, after she wakes, to remember what he told her. Meanwhile, Robespierre has guessed where the head must be.

The following morning, Robespierre and Saint-Just take her into the foul-smelling room where the corpses of the executed are awaiting transportation to the lime-pits. They ask her to identify the head of Orpheus. She picks it up, covers her ears, and tells it to 'sing to them'. The head sings of the anger of mobs, and of freedom and love. The other severed heads join in chorus and sing of how leaders always seek to raise themselves above others and to manipulate them. Saint-Just, Robespierre, and the guards are transfixed. Johanna quickly escapes, with the head.

The following day, in a speech before the National Convention, Saint-Just falters and falls silent. Robespierre finds himself lost for words, and he is laughed at. That night, he and his faction are arrested. The following day (10th Thermidor; 28th July), both men are guillotined, and with them, the Terror 'dies'. Three months later, Thomas Paine is released from prison.[42]

Johanna returns the head to the priests on the island of Naxos. She never sees Orpheus again, but he keeps his promise: occasionally, he appears to her in her dreams. And if it were within her power, she would love to sing the song that his head sang to Robespierre to *all* those in authority.

Although only a few pages long, 'Thermidor' represents a memorable contribution to the myth of Orpheus and Eurydice. It contrasts the progressive political thinking of Thomas Paine with the repressive 'visionary' fanaticism of Robespierre. It is the first retelling of the myth to invest the *song* of Orpheus with political implications. And it is a reminder that the strongest defence against creeping authoritarianism, which can so easily metamorphose into tyranny, is the power of the free and creative imagination. Myth, it suggests, represents one of the key languages of the imagination, and myths present themselves to the imagination for the purpose of exploring humanity's deepest concerns—including their political concerns.

A month after its publication, Gaiman released a further *Sandman* story: 'The Song of Orpheus'. Although based predominantly on *Ovid's* account of the myth, like both Augustan versions, its primary concern is to correct the hero's inappropriate attitude. When Orpheus insists on trying to recover Eurydice, Dream is *unable* to help his son. That is, like Hoban, Gaiman insists that the function of a dream is to promote not fantasy, but *life*. Indeed, his entire *Sandman* series is a defence of myth and storytelling as an expression of an ethical psychology.[43]

Conclusion

Cocteau's *Orphée*—both the original play (1926) and the film (1950)—were the first versions of the myth of Orpheus and Eurydice in which the male protagonist expresses a need to 'escape' from a mythic pattern in which he feels 'trapped'. Versions of the myth produced between 1960 and the 1990s further explore this need. That is, they engage with the implications of their author's fascination with a myth that ends in tragedy. And once again, they span a surprising range of concerns, from the political to the psychological:

- Both Delany and Hoban explore a male protagonist's need to escape from a myth in which he feels trapped. At the end of *The Einstein Intersection*, Delany leaves it uncertain what Lobey has learned, if anything. In contrast, by the end of *The Medusa Frequency*, Orff has learned that he lost Luise because he was never able to focus on *her* need for *his* commitment.
- *The Mask of Orpheus* is an anomaly. Its music may be mesmerising, but in terms of its libretto, it *accepts* that the tragic pattern is cyclical.
- *The Second Mrs Kong* also ends in tragedy, but with very different implications. For Kong and Pearl represent archetypal feelings and yearnings that can *never* be realised.
- Neil Gaiman reflects on how ostensibly admirable political views can easily metamorphose into fanatical and ruthless policies.
- Meanwhile, and long before it became a widespread worry, Poul Anderson had reflected on the threat that AI might pose to both human nature and human culture.

The Millenium was fast approaching. It is time to look at a selection of recent and contemporary versions of the myth—and they all further explore the need for the protagonist to come to terms with 'reality': that is, to grow in self-awareness.

Notes

1 For example, H. Rosenberg, 'The Herd of Independent Minds', in his *Discovering the Present*, Chicago, IL: University of Chicago Press, 1973, pp. 15–28.
2 Pulp (as popular) fiction has probably always existed. It goes back to at least the sixteenth century (cheap ballads), and it thrived in the late-nineteenth and early-twentieth centuries.
3 Delany and Hacker (who became a respected poet, editor, translator, and academic) separated, occasionally lived together, divorced in 1980, and yet remained close friends.
4 S.R. Delany, *The Einstein Intersection*, New York: Ace Books, 1967; London: Gollancz, 1968.
5 In clinical trials, to date, neither has been demonstrated.
6 This recalls two passages: 'When our mortality is clothed with immortality, then … Death is swallowed up' (1 Cor. 15:54) and 'the greatest of (those qualities which last for ever) is love' (1 Cor. 13:13).
7 Cf. the temptation of Christ, Matthew 4: 1–11.
8 Cf. John 11:17–44.

9 See Luke 19–24.

10 Cf. the soldier who thrusts his spear into Christ's side, from which flows blood and water—the first *sign* that although 'dead', Christ still *lives* (John 19: 34).

11 Christ's last words on the cross: *Consummatum est* = it is over, finished, accomplished (John 19: 30).

12 See A. Einstein, T*he Principle of Relativity* (first formulated 1905). London: Methuen, 1923; K. Gödel, *On Formally Undecidable Propositions of Principia Mathematica and Related Systems* (1931), tr. B. Meltzer, ed. R.B. Braithwaite. New York: Basic Books, 1962.

13 'Tomorrow's Children', written with F.N. Waldrop, and 'Chain of Logic', published in *Astounding Science Fiction*. A slightly earlier work to explore the possibility that humanity might be eradicated by the atomic bomb is Max Frisch, *The Chinese Wall (Die Chinesische Mauer*, 1946).

14 'Goat Song' was first published in *The Magazine of Fantasy and Science Fiction*, Mercury Press, February 1972. It was republished in P. Anderson, *Homeward and Beyond*, New York: Doubleday, 1975.

15 The words of this 'song' are by Charles Wolfe. According to Wolfe's first editor, they were composed to bring out the feeling intrinsic to an 'air' (tune) which became popular in seventeenth -century Ireland (see 'Gramachree' at *tunearch.org*). Wolfe, however, denied the words had any biographical origin: see *Remains of the Late Rev. Charles Wolfe, A.B.* 6th ed., London: Hamilton, Adams, 1836, pp. 32–34.

16 None of broad range of poems quoted in the story is attributed.

17 From the 1950s, there was a keen interest in AI: e.g., J. McCarthy et al., 'A Proposal for the Dartmouth Summer Research Project on Artificial Intelligence', August 31, 1955.

18 In 1934, the old opera house had only 300 seats; in 1977, the seating was increased to 850, but the backstage area remained rudimentary. The current opera house, with 1,200 seats and a sophisticated backstage area, opened in May 1994.

19 See J. Cross, *Harrison Birtwistle: 'The Mask of Orpheus'*, Abingdon, Oxon: Routledge, pp. 31–40.

20 IRCAM = *Institut de Recherche et Coordination Acoustique/Musique* (Institute for Research and Electronic Sound and Music) is a Paris-based institute dedicated to research in electro-acoustical music.

21 See M. Hall, *Harrison Birtwistle*, London: Robson Books, 1984, pp. 124–125.

22 We can either ignore our dreams, forget them, or according to Jung, try to learn from them (by adjusting our attitudes in the light of their implications).

23 Birtwistle regretted that this 'fundamental idea' was not realised in its first production: see M. Hall, *Harrison Birtwistle*, London: Robson Books, 1984, p. 150.

24 Zinovieff (who liked to mystify every aspect of his libretto) called them, respectively, the 'Passing Clouds of Abandon' and 'Allegorical Flowers of Reason'.

25 The listener must guess what the words might mean. In the programme, the commands of Apollo—*Ofofarif! Dreid!* and *Rufi!*—are translated as 'Remember!', 'Speak!' and 'Love!'

26 To date, the work has received only two fully staged productions, both by the English National Opera. The first (1986) underlined ritual and Orphism; the second (2019), arguably travestied them: see A. Clements, 'The Mask of Orpheus: Travesty of a production', *Guardian*, 20 October 2019. In April 1996, it was also given a successful 'semi-staged' performance by the BBC Symphony Orchestra at the Royal Festival Hall, London (which was recorded and issued on CD by NMC).

27 See M.I. Rumbold, *'Freelance Mystic': Individuation, Mythopoeia and Metafiction in the Early Fiction of Russell Hoban*, MA dissertation, Rhodes University, South Africa, 2007.

28 R. Hoban, *The Medusa Frequency*, London: Jonathan Cape, 1987.

29 The Kraken is a figure from ancient Norse mythology. Tennyson's 'The Kraken' (15 lines, 1830) is about a creature lurking at the bottom of the sea and waiting for the moment it will assume a clearer form. Reference to Eurydice may have been prompted by the film, *The Clash of the Titans* (1981), in which Andromeda is terrified by a sea monster (until rescued by Perseus).

30 The motif is more familiar from Hokusai's painted woodblock print, *Tako to Amo* (Octopus and Pearl Diver), first published in a collection of *shunga* (erotic art) in 1814. Its accompanying text underlines that *both* the octopus and the pearl diver derive pleasure from their experience. Hoban wittily confuses trembling and terror.

31 The influence of Jung is evident: see, for example, C.G. Jung, 'The Relations between the Ego and the Unconscious', in *CW* 7 (*Two Essays on Analytical Psychology*), (1917/1928/1934), 1977, par. 204/p. 125.

32 Frans Post, *View of Itamaracá Island in Brazil*, 1637 (Mauritshuis).

33 See Maurice Blanchot's short theoretical essay on *le regard d'Orphée* (1955) which, following its translation into English, was widely cited: 'Orpheus's Gaze', *The Space of Literature*, ed. and tr. A. Smock, Lincoln: University of Nebraska Press, 1982, pp. 171–176.

34 The following summer, it was given a fuller staging at Glyndebourne (East Sussex, England).

35 The film draws on various works, including Arthur Conan Doyle's *The Lost World* (1912) and Madame Leprince de Beaumont's classic rendering of 'Beauty and the Beast' (1756).

36 An early draft for *The Medusa Frequency* features Perseus and Fay Wray. In January 1985, Hoban gave a reading of this work-in-progress at the National Poetry Centre, London. See 'Perseus and Fay Wray', sound recording, British Library (C15/271).

37 A. Clements, 'The Second Mrs Kong', *Guardian*, Thursday 11 November 2004.

38 'Thermidor' was first published in August 1991. Today, it is most easily available in N. Gaiman, *The Sandman*, vol. 6: *Fables and Reflections*, 30th Anniversary Edition, New York: DC Vertigo, 2019. The *penciller* is responsible for the basic design of a page: the shape and size of the panels, the setting and design of each panel, the pose and facial expression of each figure. The *inker* is responsible for 'finishing' the outlined design in India ink, using pen and brush.

39 N. Gaiman, 'Men of Good Fortune' (*Sandman* #13). New York: DC Vertigo, 1990.

40 See E. Vallance, 'The Reign of Terror', chapter 10 in *A Radical History of Britain* (2009), London: Little, Brown, 2009, pp. 255–282; also, K.R. Johnston, *Unusual Suspects: Pitt's Reign of Alarm and the Lost Generation of the 1790s*, Oxford: Oxford University Press, 2013.

41 The *Montagnards* (= people from the mountains) were radicals, so called because they sat on the highest benches in the National Assembly.

42 In his later years, Paine ruffled many feathers. He openly attacked Washington, he criticised the Jay Treaty (1794/1796), and *The Age of Reason*, which argued for Deism, was criticised by Christians. He became an isolated, but unrepentant figure. He died in New York, in 1809.

43 A little over a year later, Gaiman wrote a final story in which Orpheus features ('Brief Lives', 1992–1993), a long story about Delirium spread over several issues. Many hundreds of years after having abandoned his son (and even though he knows he is breaking the rules), Dream returns to Naxos to grant his son's wish and to kill him. The priests who had guarded him bury him and are disbanded. The mortal (legendary figure) becomes myth.

Chapter 11

Orpheus and Eurydice, Confronting Reality and Self-Awareness

1995–2020

In 1995, the world economy was reaping the benefits from the end of the Cold War, reduced WTO tariffs, cheap labour from China, and the rapid rise of new players (the Gulf States, the Tiger economies, BRICS). For 3,000 years and more, capitalism had driven both economic and social progress. But now its global reach, excesses, and shenanigans were beginning to undermine the cohesiveness of Western societies.

Digitalised stock markets, overpowerful holding companies, and grasping intellectual property rights had changed the nature of world business. Greed and speculation were in overdrive. Swollen egos were drunk on easy money and entitlement. Global trading was out of control. Predictably, it brought a succession of financial crises.[1] With every crisis, governments were forced to borrow, the 'borrowed' money was quickly siphoned up by the same canny institutions and individuals who had helped to create the crisis, while the less-well-off had to tighten their belts. As a result, despite the mind-boggling sums of new wealth being created, in many Western countries, the 'filtering down' of this wealth was slowing. Billionaires were sprouting up like mushrooms in Autumn, and yet, even in *wealthy* nations, between 15% and 30% of the population were struggling with basic everyday needs.[2] The gap between the 'haves' and the 'have nots' was beginning to widen.

Meanwhile, political discussions on radio and television were being modelled on the *worst* of political practices. Guests were allowed only two or three minutes (the length of a pop song) to answer questions about complex issues, which resulted in every issue being reduced to the reiteration of a vacuous, party-approved soundbite. Instead of drawing out the respective merits of different views, presenters assumed that their job was to embarrass each speaker in turn. With the predictable result that Western societies became increasingly disenchanted with their politicians—and political differences became toxic. On both sides of the Atlantic, Western societies were becoming bitterly divided.

Western leaders were failing the people they represented. By focussing on the economic benefits of financial services, they had long neglected many other sections of the economy. They were failing to pursue the educational policies necessary to ensure the healthy evolution not only of social attitudes, but also of different

DOI: 10.4324/9781003519584-14

communities. They were failing to engage meaningfully with a long list of global challenges, the most urgent of which were outdated financial and intellectual property laws, excessive levels of debt, climate change, and international migration. And by the combination of their reluctance to engage in talks with those whom they saw as their enemy and their hawkish public pronouncements, they were actively abetting global tensions. Western nations were losing their way.

This final chapter looks at seven versions of the myth of Orpheus and Eurydice written during these difficult years. Unsurprisingly, their primary concern is the challenge to engage with *reality*. The first part looks at three versions of the myth written by men, all of which explore the difficulty 'Orpheus' has in understanding the needs of 'Eurydice'. The second, looks at three versions written by women, and they illustrate different ways in which Eurydice bravely confronts a reality which she would have preferred not to have had to face.

Orpheus and the Inability to Accept Reality

The following pages explore three works, all of which explore unbearable loss, impossible longing, an overdeveloped sense of entitlement—and foreground a male protagonist's difficulty in dealing with *reality*, whether because of his ingrained narcissism, his moral weakness, or his deep-rooted dissociative tendencies. And yet, they are all very funny.

Woody Allen: Orpheus on the Psychoanalyst's Couch

Allan Stewart Konigsberg (born 1935) is a talented playwright, screenwriter, and film director. At nineteen, he changed his name to Heywood (Woody) Allen. In the 1950s, he became a stand-up comedian, quickly establishing his longstanding persona: that of a writer befuddled by everyday experience. Although he wrote films on a broad range of subjects, he is perhaps best known for his series of works that explore broken relationships: they include *What's New, Pussycat?* (1965), *Annie Hall* (1977), and the time-travelling fantasy, *Midnight in Paris* (2011).

Deconstructing Harry (1997) hinges on the eponymous hero's attempts to recover a lost love, even from 'hell'. Its protagonist is Harry Block (Woody Allen), a successful writer who has made a mess of his personal life.[3] He is neurotic, narcissistic, and his third marriage has recently collapsed. He is seeing his sixth analyst, and he is trying to understand why he has the same obsessive fixations as he had in adolescence. He has a vivid fantasy life combined with an increasingly tenuous hold on reality. He drinks, pops pills, and feels a need to seduce every woman he sees. Now in his early sixties, he is suffering from writer's block—and he is about to lose the latest young woman in his life.

There are two parallel plots. One borrows from and parodies Ingmar Bergman's *Wild Strawberries*.[4] It tells the story of a car drive to Harry's old school where he is to be honoured for his achievements as a writer. He is accompanied by a friend (who dies of a heart attack on the way), his son (whom he 'kidnaps' from the care of a friend of his second wife), and a hooker called Cookie (whom he has only recently met). The other plot is about Harry's inability to let go of his relationship with Fay (Elisabeth Shue).[5] She has fallen in love with Harry's best friend, Larry (Billy Crystal), and they are about to get married. As in every Woody Allen film, his cast give brilliant cameo performances.

As he drives toward his old school, he repeatedly phones Fay to persuade her to cancel her marriage. On the way, he is flooded by memories of stories he has written based on his relationships with his three wives and other partners. In all of them, the male protagonist represents an aspect of his own tendencies: for example, Mel (Robin Williams) is constantly 'out of focus' (as Harry is toward the end of the film). The conversations and tiffs with his various partners are predictably comic, but also grating.

Like Herman Orff in *The Medusa Frequency*, Harry falls in love easily, but he has difficulty building a lasting relationship. In his novels, he portrays his ex-wives and friends in amusing, but often demeaning situations. He notes their every flaw. He sees their every weakness. He parodies them mercilessly. And yet he cannot see why they should feel offended by him having depicted them in this way. When Fay announces that she is going to marry Larry, he cannot understand either why or when he lost her. He had not even noticed her absence, just as he never properly noticed her when she was present. Now, finding that she is no longer available for him when *he* needs her, he yearns to have her back.

Toward the end, Harry finds himself in an elevator going down into the depths of the earth. At the bottom is Hell, where Larry presides over a nightclub filled with clichéd devils and near-naked women. Harry tells him that he is prepared to kidnap Fay to get her back. Larry laughs and reminds him that he is not the kidnapping kind. Whereupon the police arrive to arrest Harry for kidnapping his son. He is thrown into jail and told that he is in 'deep trouble'. Fresh from their wedding, Larry and Fay arrive and offer to bail him out of jail in exchange for his blessing. He grudgingly gives it and returns home.

Harry returns to his apartment and consoles himself for Fay's loss by reassuring himself of the love of all his fictional characters. He imagines the staff of his old school reminding him that he has not yet been honoured and showing him, instead, his own 'characters' applauding him. This recalls the spellbound animals lying at the feet of the forlorn Orpheus. In the final scene, Harry is writing, presumably about the events in the film.

In *Wild Strawberries*, Isak Borg *learns* from his experience. By the end of the film, his views have mellowed. In contrast, Harry Block learns nothing from his experience. He still cannot understand his responsibility for the hurt that both his behaviour and his writing have caused. *Deconstructing Harry* ends as it began, its hero so wrapped in his own concerns that he cannot comprehend either the distress or the happiness of others.

Meanwhile, another filmmaker had been exploring the relation between writer's block and an emotional block. He too set it within an 'analytic' frame—and his work harbours an intriguing version of the same myth.

Sliding Doors: *Orpheus and the Fear of Losing Eurydice*

Peter Howitt (b.1957) enjoyed his first successes as an actor in television. *Sliding Doors* (1998) was his first major film as both scriptwriter and director.[6] Although it never mentions the myth, it represents the first version of the myth in which the plot hinges on Orpheus' *fear* of losing Eurydice.

The trailer insists that *Sliding Doors* is about Helen (Gwyneth Paltrow): 'What if one split second sent your life in two completely different directions?'. But, as in all works written by a male author, there are good reasons to wonder whether it might not be more pertinent to an aspect of *male* psychology. These pages argue that its events all reflect a dilemma pertinent to Gerry (John Lynch)—and that the film represents an unexpected version of the myth of Orpheus and Eurydice.

Sliding Doors begins with quickly alternating scenes. Helen leaves Gerry, her partner, to go to work, where she learns that she has been fired. As she leaves, in the elevator, she accidentally drops an earring. A stranger, James (John Hannah), picks it up and returns it to her. Meanwhile, Gerry lets Lydia (his *previous* girlfriend, who wants back into his life) into Helen's flat and they make love. And as they do, Helen takes the underground (subway) home. She arrives on the platform just as the sliding doors of a train are closing. The film runs backwards for a few seconds, then does a 'second take'. This time, an *imaginary* Helen squeezes inside the closing doors and, without recognising him, sits next to James.

As the train pulls out, the *real* Helen is left standing on the platform, where she learns that the next train has been delayed. As she leaves the station, she is mugged, and is taken to a hospital to have the cut above her eye treated. By the time she arrives home, Lydia has left. Unable to find another job in PR, and because she is willing to support Gerry, she takes on two menial jobs: delivering sandwiches to offices during the day, and in the evenings, working as a waitress. At home, although she wonders whether Gerry is having an affair, she tries to believe his reassurances. Lydia, however, is determined to have Gerry back. She persuades Gerry to lie to Helen and to spend a weekend with her in Dorset. Meanwhile, in London, Helen faints while working as a waitress. She phones Gerry in Dorset, but he hangs up before she can tell him that she is pregnant.

Meanwhile, the *imaginary* Helen arrives home unexpectedly early and discovers Gerry in bed with Lydia. Outraged by his betrayal, she promptly leaves him and moves in with her best friend. Anna takes her to have her long, brown hair cut short, dyed blonde, and given a striking new styling. Predictably, Helen and James soon become friends. He encourages her to set up her own PR business, and she is invited to organise the grand opening of a restaurant. The *real* Gerry turns up at the opening and begs the *imaginary* Helen to come to their apartment so he can persuade her to come back to him.

Soon after, the *real* Helen finally discovers that Gerry is still seeing Lydia. She learns of a possible job in PR. When she arrives for the interview, to her horror, she is met by Lydia and Gerry, who is an unwitting party to this final humiliation. Helen rushes out of the apartment and falls down the stairs. She is taken to hospital. She survives her fall but loses her baby. When Gerry pleads to be forgiven, she sends him packing.

Meanwhile, the *imaginary* Helen has learned that James is married. She feels betrayed. But James frantically searches for her in the gloom of a rainy London evening (the underworld) to let her know that he is amicably separated from his wife. Delighted, she crosses the street to phone Anna, without looking, and she is run over by a van. Later, she dies in hospital.

As the *real* Helen leaves the hospital, she accidentally drops an earring in the elevator. A stranger, James, picks it up and returns it to her. They look at each other as if they think they *might* have met before, but can't remember when. The final verses of the song, *Tenderness on the Block*, assure the audience that this time 'She'll find true love'.[7]

Although the film did well at the box office, critical reception was mixed.[8] Some took exception to the suggestion that when a woman finds herself in a bad relationship, all she needs to do is to remember that true love lies 'just around the corner or in the next lift (elevator)'.[9] But the film may not reflect *her* fantasies.

Helen's character is a stereotype. The *real* Helen bravely endures working at two jobs. She becomes suspicious of Gerry only because he is always blustering ('I asked a simple question. There's no need to become Woody Allen'). Her character is not developed beyond such comic ripostes and a stifled joy on learning that she is pregnant. In similar fashion, the *imaginary* Helen may have more sparkle and resilience, but her character is not developed beyond a worry that she knows very little about James. Despite convincing performances from Gwyneth Paltrow, neither Helen has any 'depth' of character.

In contrast, the challenge facing Gerry is repeatedly underlined. Whenever he thinks that the *real* Helen might discover that he is cheating and that she might leave him, he hurries to his local pub to speak with his best friend. Their conversations parody a psychoanalytic session. On one occasion, Russell asks him, 'Would you like my opinion?' Gerry is worried. 'Will I like it?' he inquires. Russell retorts, 'Of course not, it would be based on reality'.

They have four meetings, and all their conversations hinge on Gerry's fear of losing Helen. The first comes while he is still living with the *real* Helen. He wants to end his affair with Lydia, but he can't find a way to do so. Russell warns him that events 'ungoverned' by him will bring things to a head in a way which he might not like. The second meeting is shortly before the trip to Dorset. Russell berates Gerry for his treatment of Helen, describing him as 'a morality-free zone'. The third meeting comes after the trip to Dorset. An over-excited Gerry tells Russell that he finally ended the affair with Lydia (in fact, she leaves him, albeit only briefly). At the fourth meeting, when he is worried that Lydia might be pregnant, Russell tells him: 'You've just lost'.

James likes to quote the catchphrase 'Nobody expects the Spanish Inquisition!' (from *Monty Python's Flying Circus*, 1971), suggesting that disaster always strikes when it is least expected. At the outset, it refers to Helen. But as the film unwinds, the character to whom it most obviously applies is Gerry.

The film is shaped by Gerry's character and behaviour in the *real* events. He causes Helen hurt not by design, but by weakness. This is compensated ('corrected') in the *imaginal* reality. James is kind and honest, he knows what he wants, and he has 'backbone' (cleverly symbolised by his favourite sport of rowing). In relation to Gerry, he represents both a type whom Gerry would like to be (cf. *Casablanca*), and a type whom Gerry is afraid will steal off with *his* Helen (cf. Helen of Troy). In the real plot, Helen is too willing to believe Gerry. In the imaginal reality, with James' help, she recovers her self-worth.

Sliding Doors is not held together by a 'what if' question. In psychological terms, it is held together by Gerry's inability to send Lydia packing and to commit himself to Helen. The film explores the metaphors central to the myth of Orpheus and Eurydice. It begins with Gerry being *afraid* he will lose Helen/ Eurydice; it includes two 'descents' into an *imaginary* world (underworld) to try to prevent this; and it ends with him losing the 'Eurydice' whom he really loves. The story of James and the *imaginary* Helen is not only a 'romantic comedy'; it represents Gerry's *fear* of what *might* happen if he does not free himself from Lydia. The ending suggests that the male protagonist finally realises his mistake. 'Gerry' might have lost Helen; but 'James' (his better self) may be able to 'find true love' with her.

Both *Deconstructing Harry* and *Sliding Doors* explore a male protagonist's lack of self-awareness and his resulting difficulty in facing reality. Written at the same time, another version of the myth explores the same concern, but against a much larger canvas.

Salman Rushdie: Orpheus, Dysfunctional Relationships, and a Dysfunctional Society

Salman Rushdie was born in Bombay into a well-educated family of Kashmiri-Muslim origin shortly before the partition of India and Pakistan and their independence (1947). He studied History at Cambridge. While working as a copywriter, he began writing fiction. His first novel was little noticed. His second enjoyed a huge success. *Midnight's Children* (1981) engages with the difficulties of India's early years, the challenges facing the country, and its political shenanigans. His subsequent novels were equally ambitious and entertaining.

His sixth novel, *The Ground Beneath Her Feet* (1999), turns to the myth of Orpheus and Eurydice to explore how the Western world has become fundamentally unstable.[10] It begins with an account of an earthquake in which an idolised rock singer (Vina Apsara/Eurydice) is swallowed by the earth and disappears. It spans events beginning in India in the nineteen thirties, through England during the sixties and seventies, to America in the eighties and nineties. It has an irresistible, exhilarating, and relentlessly tongue-in-cheek 'runaway bus of a narrative', whilst also providing a blistering take on the relation between political upheavals, devious business practices, and the confusions of youth and their 'alternative' answers to every question. Each cameo fuses into the next. The credible blurs into the fantastic, and vice versa. The reader is constantly and deliberately disoriented by the excess of whacky incident and whimsical commentary.

There are three main characters. One is associated with Eurydice; two with Orpheus. They are all friends, and they all come from families whose inability to cope with the ever-changing economic reality of the times has rendered them hopelessly, but also comically dysfunctional.

The Eurydice is Vina Apsara, who is born Nissy Shetty in the United States. Her father is jailed for malpractice. When her next family are brutally murdered, she is taken in by a distant relative who abuses her. When she resists, she is sent to India, to another distant relative: Piloo Doodhwala (once Shetty).

The first Orpheus is the narrator. Rai (Umeed Merchant) is born in Bombay in 1947 into a privileged family, formerly Hindu, now non-practising Muslim. In 1956, when he is nine, on Juhu Beach, he sees the twelve-year-old Nissy Shetty in a stars-and-stripes swimsuit: it is 'instant infatuation' and a 'lifelong enslavement'. Her guardian (Piloo Doodhwala), offended that Rai offered an apple to her and not to his own daughters, thrashes her and throws her onto the streets. She turns up at Rai's home, because his parents are also 'Shettys' (= Merchants). They take her in, whereupon she declares that she wants to be called Vina Apsara.

Rai's parents are struggling with the changing reality of Bombay. His father turns to gambling, loses heavily, and hangs himself. His mother is cheated by Piloo Doodhwala and, soon after, she dies of a brain tumour. When their house burns down, someone suggests that Vina was responsible (which she wasn't). She flees to London, and then to New York.

The second Orpheus is Ormus Cama, who is the younger of twins born in 1937. His father, Sir Darius Cama, is an Anglophile Parsi, fraudulent lawyer, and yet easily misled by others. When the older twin dies, his mother (Lady Spenta) is so shaken that she neglects her other sons (Cyrus and Virus), as well as Ormus, who is into his teens before the family become aware of his gift for music. He is nineteen when he sees Vina in a record store. They instantly become infatuated with each other—and both are 'consummate mythologizers of themselves'. On Vina's sixteenth birthday, they sleep together for one night. He proposes; she vows that she will always love him, but that she will not be faithful. They do not sleep together for another decade.

As his family slides into ever more embarrassing difficulties, Ormus claims that his music comes to him from his dead twin. That is, he is a musical shaman whose music expresses an unbearable sense of dispossession and a longing to recover a part of a lost inner self. When Vina disappears, he slips into a 'parallel universe'. Yul Singh, the head of a New York record company, happens to hear him play 'Yesterday'—a song to which Singh has the rights, which has not yet been released, and yet which Ormus claims to have written.

Lady Spenta, now a widow, is rescued from financial embarrassment by a friend who invites her and her family to go to England. On the plane, Ormus meets John Standish, who runs a pirate radio station and becomes infatuated with him. In 1967, following a car accident, one of Standish's sons is killed, the other is brain-damaged for life, and Ormus finds himself in a deep and lasting coma. In 1970, his song 'It shouldn't be this way' is finally released and becomes an international hit. Vina flies to Bombay to find Ormus, spends the night with Rai, then flies to London, where she bends over Ormus, whispers 'It's me', and he wakes. Although he gradually recovers, only his right eye sees the real world; the left eye sees a 'parallel' universe. Vina invites him to go to America with her.

In the United States, they are controlled by Yul Singh, their manager. They front a group called VTO. Its first album, released in 1971, turns them into the greatest of the supergroups. Ormus' songs release something primal in the listener, while Vina becomes one of the first sacred monsters of the counterculture and the age of confession. They finally marry. She is still in the prime of life. He is prematurely old and frail, both physically and mentally. Even so, their success continues. As Ormus becomes increasingly dysfunctional, he begins to see what others cannot. He begins to 'thunder' against 'hedonism, self-indulgence, and desire'. His songs 'excoriate a generation lost in space'. He deplores a culture of 'grown-up children'. But his followers cannot grasp that he is referring to them. They idealise the very tendencies he seeks to condemn. His intended message is lost in the Dionysiac frenzy produced by the combination of his music and Vina's voice.

Meanwhile, Rai has become a photographer. He goes wherever 'Mighty America' falls hard on 'the back yards of the world'. He descends into the 'hell' of the world's trouble spots, including Vietnam, and emerges with shocking images of military and political brutality. Then, with blistering irony, in a series of photographs which he entitles *The Trojan Horse*, he records how the victorious Vietnamese are 'overrun by American corporations'. But all the while, he hopes and prays that one day—instead of appearing and disappearing as and when it suits her (usually to complain about Ormus)—Vina will leave Ormus and settle with him.

In 1988, Vina releases her first solo album. On tour, she visits Mexico and is indignant when Rai shows up. The following day, there is an earthquake in which she is 'swallowed'. All around the world the expression of grief is overwhelming.[11] And Rai's photograph of her becomes the face of the catastrophe.

Ormus is devastated. He seeks Vina everywhere. He becomes obsessed with a twenty-year-old Mira Celano, who impersonates her and who sings 'like sunshine in a ruined church'. Ormus takes her on a world tour (1994–1995). But he finally admits that Vina is dead. By the time he returns to New York, he has died 'inside'. One winter day, he is shot by another Vina impersonator.

Although Vina's death shakes Rai to the core, he soon realises that they had little in common. Quite by accident, he gets to know Mira and is relieved to discover that she has no patience with fads, dysfunctional fantasies, alternative realities, or now-you-see-me, now-you-don't relationships. They get together. Mira and her daughter, Tara, become his 'islands' in the 'storm' of life.

The novel's predominant concern, however, is not its foreground, but its *background*. The main characters are types who never quite become individuals. The first part is set against the seismic changes that unfold in India between 1937 and the mid-1960s (the Congress Party, calls for independence, different loyalties during the Second World War, partition and independence, the resulting social upheavals, and the need to adjust to rapidly changing economic and political realities, especially in cities such as Bombay). The second part spans events between the mid-1950s and the early 1990s, moving freely between India (stumbling from one political crisis to another under Indira Gandhi), England (in the throes of a 'youthquake', where the young are giddy on drugs and rock culture), and the United States (lurching from the Cuban missile crisis, through the Vietnam War, the Lebanese troubles, and the Gulf War).

Rai had wanted to believe in the 'American dream' or, rather, in 'the America of dreams'. Instead, he becomes increasingly appalled by its reality—by its ruthless, exploitative, and self-seeking politics and business, mimicked in both India and England. The story of Ormus and Vina is but a metaphor for a disturbingly dysfunctional and unstable world. No other version of the myth of Orpheus and Eurydice touches on such a wide range of issues or explores so many cleverly interlocking concerns.

We have looked at three recent versions of the myth by *male* authors. It is time to consider three recent versions written by *female* writers.

Eurydice and the Acceptance of Reality

The final part of this study turns to three works, in all of which a female protagonist comes up against a reality that challenges her to the core—and yet, in all three works, she faces this reality with courage and integrity.

We begin with the first version of the myth to explore the pain of being thrust into an 'underworld' by a rapidly advancing cancer.

Kathy Acker: Eurydice and Her Struggle against Terminal Cancer

American writer Kathy Acker (Karen Lehman) was born into a wealthy but troubled Franco-German Jewish family which settled in the United States between the wars. She studied classics at Brandeis University and at the University of California, San Diego. Like Muriel Rukeyser, she saw writing as the struggle to express and understand her concerns, and she was convinced that such concerns were also important to society. By her mid-twenties, she began to be seen as one of the most audacious writers of punk culture. She was determined 'to go to as many extremes as possible'. Her works delight in shock, in sexuality, and in subversion. They mix ostensible reality with dream. They are powerful, in-your-face, and often violent. In discussion, however, she would listen to others both respectfully and attentively.

In April 1996, in California, she was diagnosed with breast cancer. Terrified of chemotherapy, she underwent a double mastectomy, but the cancer had already spread to her lymph nodes. Exasperated with the 'cancer industry', she sought help in alternative therapies. 'I was this one thought: I knew I wanted to live'—and she continued to live as *she* wanted. In September 1997, while performing in *Pussy,*

King of the Pirates, she collapsed on stage.[12] She moved to London, where in 'The Gift of Disease', she described her experience with harrowing objectivity.[13] Her health deteriorated. She returned to California. Still lucid and debating with others to the last, she died in Tijuana, in Mexico, in November 1997, age fifty.

'Eurydice in the Underworld' (1997) is a short story: the last work she published before her death. It is closely based on the events prior to and following her mastectomy.[14] It juggles with chronology and with genres (drama, poetry, diary). It blurs the line between reality and fantasy. It makes ironic and playful references to other literary works, including *The Lady of the Camellias*. It explores the instability of apparently stable relationships. It challenges the arrogant certainties of medicine and psychoanalysis. It undermines the notion that the self is definable. But above all, it reworks a harrowing personal experience.

From H.D. to Margaret Atwood, several women had turned to the myth of Eurydice and Orpheus to describe the pain of betrayal. Kathy Acker is the first to turn to the myth to describe the experience of finding herself alone as she faces the imminent *loss* of what she holds dearest—life.

The first half is in the form of a play. The opening scene unfolds the day *after* Eurydice's operation for breast cancer. She feels as if she has been violated. YOU (Eurydice), sitting on a bed surrounded by soft-toy animals, is violently sick. OR (Orpheus) feels helpless: he can only sing to her and to the animals lying at her feet. When YOU is told that chemotherapy will increase her chances of survival by only ten percent, she becomes frightened. She clings to life in the only way available to her. She and OR make love. Re-emboldened, OR sings of his determination to accompany YOU into death.

But Acker rejects the male fantasy of Orpheus descending into the world of the dead. OR is told he cannot accompany YOU into the underworld: the operating theatre, 'a room designed to suck up human life'. In a section entitled 'the third station (death)', she describes EUR's feeling of chilling alienation as she is prepared for the operation. And with biting irony, she notes that while EUR goes into surgery, OR uselessly searches for his 'Eurydice' in the hospital grounds.

The second half of the story unfolds *after* her death in a sequence of first-person narratives which explore the fragility of human relationships. 'Diary written by Eurydice when she's dead' describes a journey in dream-like sequences that comment on her anxieties and fears. In 'the courtroom of the dead', she is desperate either to escape being judged or to negotiate her fate. She sleeps during the day. At night, in her dreams, memories of what she has read become confused. In 'the school of the dead', she finds herself in a school dorm ('the usual *Jane Eyre* shit'). She is in a kitchen where, against all her moral instincts, she murders someone. Images come to her: images of betrayal, of shock, and of a longing for survival and love. She cannot understand why her lover has hurt her deeply. She retreats inside her feelings and finds herself making love to a guy who embodies her own desire.

She deliberately misrepresents Plato (who claimed, not that Orpheus *never* loved Eurydice, but only that he did not love her sufficiently to *die* for her).[15] She remembers Blanchot writing 'Eurydice is the extreme to which Orpheus's *art* can attain'.[16]

To which she replies: 'How can writing matter?' The only important thing is life. And the reality of life is that even the strongest bonds are fragile. Our bodies can intertwine; our minds cannot. We live, as we die, alone. In the short section, 'letter from Orpheus found after his death', Orpheus tells E that although he loved her, he was always unhappy with her. She is not the girl for him; he feels angry toward her. In her reply, E reflects on how she always resented having to give up her own time, time for her *writing*, to help him. Only in their love making could she feel at one with him.

The story concludes with the thoughts of Orpheus after he has returned to 'the realm of the living'. He admits that watching YOU die made him nauseous. He resents her for not understanding male weakness, and for not saving *him* from his addictions. His last reflection is chilling: that he is glad to have met U because now he knows he can love again.

Orpheus is pitiful in his self-centeredness; Eurydice, in hers. This is the reality of human nature, such as we know it. Acker is writing about *her* experience. In the Augustan myth, Orpheus almost wills his own death. In Acker's rewriting, Eurydice struggles against her fate as bravely as she can—and then releases Orpheus so that he can live and love again—and life and love were *her* highest values.

Four years after its publication, another American turned to the myth to explore an even more unexpected issue. Sarah Ruhl's *Eurydice* is the first version of the myth of Eurydice and Orpheus to explain the incompatibility of the protagonists in relation to the kind of 'language' they each understand.

Sarah Ruhl: Eurydice as a Father's Daughter

Sarah Ruhl (b. 1974) is an American playwright from Illinois. Her mother held a PhD in Language, Literacy, and Rhetoric; her father had a deep love of literature and words. Both encouraged her appreciation of writing. At Brown University, Paula Vogel turned her thoughts to drama, and her early plays enjoyed increasing success.

Eurydice (2003) was first performed at the Madison Repertory Theatre in Wisconsin.[17] It unfolds in a succession of cameos, each created by an intriguing mix of language and mime. Orpheus and Eurydice are in their late teens, but they behave slightly younger than they are. The underworld resembles 'the world of *Alice in Wonderland* more than it resembles Hades'. Some moments are contrived and slip into the cutesy; others illustrate its author's keen sense of theatre. But for our purpose here, the importance of the play stems from two intriguing concerns: the first is its exploration of the part that *nurture* plays in moulding personality. The second is its contrast between different ways of relating to the world (through language, words, and ideas and through music, melody, and harmony).

Although designed to be performed *without* an interval, the printed text identifies three 'movements', each of which is divided into distinct scenes.

The First Movement opens on a beach. Although Eurydice and Orpheus are infatuated with each other, neither understands the other. From her father, Eurydice has learned to love books and to enjoy discussing the merits of the different ideas they express. She finds ideas interesting; she enjoys comparing them. But she has no ear for either rhythm or melody. Orpheus lives in a world of music which, he insists, just *is*. He can express himself only in gestures and vague analogy. He cannot grasp that an idea or an opinion might be 'interesting' in itself. In short, neither can relate to the issues of importance to the other. And yet, despite these differences, they become engaged.

Meanwhile, in the underworld, Eurydice's father (who is dead, but, unusually, has retained his memory) tries to send her a letter for her wedding day. The play explores Eurydice's *intuition* that she and Orpheus do not have enough in common to marry—and her *fear* that they may never be able to resolve their differences.

At her wedding party, Eurydice misses 'interesting' people with whom she can talk. She slips away for a drink of water and is approached by a 'Nasty Interesting Man' who tells her he has a letter from her father. He makes unwelcome advances, leaving her torn between wanting to know what her father wrote to her and her desire to rejoin her husband. Still holding the unopened letter, she escapes, trips, and falls down the stairs to her death.

On arriving in the underworld, Eurydice behaves like a spoiled brat. She assumes that life there will be much the same as above ground. She expects service. She mistakes her dead father for a porter. She asks him to take her (empty) luggage to a hotel. She soon learns that the language of the dead is as soft as that of stones. Separate spaces are forbidden in the underworld, but her father slowly creates a room for her, made entirely from string. He reminds her of language. He tells her family anecdotes and talks about what she liked to do as a child (sit under a tree which she associated with him). All the while, the three Stones (who function as a Chorus) try to prevent their communication.

Meanwhile, amongst the living, Orpheus struggles to express how much he misses Eurydice. She does not receive the first letter he sends ('Dear Eurydice, Symphony for twelve instruments. Love Orpheus'). She receives the next ('I'm going to find you'), but she has forgotten what a letter is. She stands on it, shuts her eyes and thinks 'there's no place like home'. Remembering what she enjoyed, Orpheus lowers the *Complete Works of Shakespeare* into the underworld for her, but she has forgotten what a book is. Her father (re)teaches her how to read from *King Lear*. They try to sing, but neither can hold a tune.

Third Movement: Orpheus enters the underworld. He appears to be singing, but he is making no sound. Even so, his 'song' makes the Stones weep. The lord of the underworld (played by the same actor as the Nasty Interesting Man, but as a child) tells him to start walking home. Eurydice might follow, but if he turns to check, she will disappear.

Her father repeatedly encourages her to join her husband. In mime, as if at a wedding, he leads her to join Orpheus. He reminds her that she must not turn. But as soon as she begins walking toward Orpheus, she misses her father and turns to look at him once more. The Stones persuade her to turn *again*—and to follow Orpheus. She does, and as she approaches him, she calls his name.

Whereupon, *he* turns, and tells her that she could never keep rhythm. As she is drawn back into the underworld, she is surprised that the Stones look happy to see her. Orpheus tells her not to look at them, but to think of the time they have enjoyed together. She sees everything grey, like her home. He tries to catch her attention. They begin to walk away from each other. She has died a second death.

Meanwhile, her father dismantles the string room and then, encouraged by the Stones, he dips himself in the river of forgetfulness. Eurydice re-enters and wonders where her room is. She finds her father lying on the ground, having lost his language and memory. The lord of the underworld (who is now a larger-than-life child) orders her to become his bride. She replies that he is too young. She then writes a letter to Orpheus, and another letter to his next wife, with well-meant advice (which recalls the ending of Kathy's Acker's short story). She then dips herself in the river of forgetfulness and lies down next to her father. Orpheus enters. He has died and lost his memory. He finds Eurydice's letter, but not knowing what to do with it, he stands on it, closes his eyes (exactly as Eurydice had done when she received his letter), and tries but fails to understand what he should do.

Sarah Ruhl's play is the first version of the myth to concentrate on the importance of interests acquired and developed in early years, especially those she associates with her father, who died some eight or nine years earlier. She is *not* exploring a psychoanalytic (Elektra) complex. She is reflecting on the importance that *language* and *ideas* hold for her.

Eurydice is drawn back to her father and to the underworld because its greyness reminds her of her grey-painted home. What is at issue, however, is a distinction between the familiar (greyness) and the unfamiliar (colour). Eurydice's infatuation with Orpheus represents an instinctive yearning for the richness that music and its emotional colours—its *other*ness—might contribute to her life. The play explores how ingrained modes of being and perception are so strong that often they prevent a person from understanding and engaging with the strangeness of the 'other', and the resonance this strangeness harbours. It is about the difficulty of learning to engage with the *reality* of the other, and with the deeper concerns implicit in *their* language, whether music or words.

Eurydice was well received and secured widespread acclaim. Some fifteen years after its initial success, Ruhl adapted her play as the libretto for Matthew Aucoin's three-act opera *Eurydice*, jointly commissioned by Los Angeles Opera and the Metropolitan Opera, New York, and first performed in 2020.

We remember that Virgil's *Georgics* reflect on the challenges that face a smallholder. Perhaps fittingly, our study concludes with a work by an American singer-songwriter who grew up on a smallholding in Vermont.

Anaïs Mitchell: Eurydice in Hadestown

Anaïs Mitchell was born into a Quaker family. Her parents, once hippies, bought a small farm and taught themselves the skills of eco-conscious husbandry.[18] Her father also taught creative writing at Middlebury College; her mother was a social worker with a special interest in vulnerable families. In 2002, aged twenty-one, Anaïs Mitchell travelled to Mexico, and the combination of soul-destroying poverty and the exploitative business practices that she saw there triggered an early version of the song 'Way Down Hadestown'.

This became the seed of a project on which she continued to work while establishing herself as a singer-songwriter.[19] In 2006, she moulded a handful of songs which she associated with the myth of Orpheus and Eurydice into a one-act folk opera.[20] Ten years later, a revised and expanded version premiered at the off-Broadway New York Theatre Workshop.[21] In 2019, a further revised version opened *on* Broadway—and it promptly won eight Tony Awards.[22]

Hadestown is a sung-through folk-rock musical (i.e. even the dialogue is rhymed, metered, and set to music). It is set in a modern world (but also suggestive of the 1930s Depression) of debilitating poverty and brutal exploitation. It has catchy words and tunes, and vibrant orchestrations. It begins *and* ends with a reminder that the subject is 'a sad song'.

In the first act, Hermes urges Orpheus to speak with Eurydice. Orpheus promptly proposes to her, assuring her that their marriage would result in an everlasting spring which would bring the world 'back into tune'. Summer arrives. Eurydice is no longer lonely, and Orpheus feels as if he is holding the world in his arms. But summer is soon over.

In the fall, Hades (an exploitative entrepreneur) reclaims Persephone. She loves him, but only half-realises that Hadestown is a cruel and abusive sweat factory—a 'hell on earth'—surrounded by walls. As winter sets in, Eurydice is drawn into it for the economic security it offers ('Way Down Hadestown'). Orpheus realises that Hades and Persephone have forgotten 'the song of their love' (he creates an unnatural world; she turns to drink). Eurydice accepts work in Hadestown. On learning that she has 'died', Orpheus sets off to recover her, while the Fates wonder at his presumption. Meanwhile, Hades reminds Eurydice that she has papers to sign.

Persephone tempts the Workers to drink; they soon have nothing to live for; and Eurydice realises that she will soon end in the same hopeless oblivion. Orpheus arrives and assures her that she will recover her freedom, but Hades is quick to remind him that she signed a contract of her own accord. When the Fates tell him his quest is hopeless, Orpheus almost abandons his purpose. Then the Workers rally to his cause. So does Persephone. When Orpheus sings of the love that Hades once bore for Persephone, and of how easily man is tempted by financial greed, Hades and Persephone become reconciled. The Fates advise Hades to include the condition. The Workers ask Orpheus and Eurydice to show them the way out. But when the Fates sow doubt in Orpheus, he turns.

Hermes explains that this is how the old song ends, although it invites re-singing, as if one day it 'might end' differently, for despite 'the way it is', Orpheus can make you see 'how the world could be'. He urges everyone to sing the 'love song' and the return of 'spring'. The show seems to end. Then, as if it were a spontaneous 'encore', Persephone and the cast honour all those who sing when the world is darkest.

Hadestown is the first version of the myth to foreground the debilitating nature of poverty, the shameless exploitation of poorly paid workers, and the perils of drink and drugs—themes which had long been the subject of folk music and jazz. It calls on workers—and by extension, the audience—to unite and engage in dialogue which might, one day, bring about an end to these divisive social and political ills. Its lyrics are heartfelt, its music is irresistible, and the orchestrations are compulsive.

Even so, it is not without its problems. It makes an insufficient distinction between the social and the imaginal worlds. The 'upper' world is represented by cold and hunger. The 'lower' world (*Hadestown*), by an easing of the hunger, but at the price of unacceptable social exploitation. This may represent the plight of the poor in the current world, but it blurs the reason for turning to a myth that ends in tragedy. The musical would like to 'escape' the tragic ending, but it has not envisaged how this might be achieved.

Conclusion

During the twentieth century, writers and other artists continued to associate the myth of Orpheus and Eurydice with a wide range of new concerns—and many of the most interesting of these are by American writers, including women.

In the early twentieth century, H.D. produced the first distinctive version of the myth of Eurydice and Orpheus, while Yvan Goll turned to the myth of Orpheus and Eurydice to explore the yearnings of the underprivileged; Milhaud, to explore the fears of the marginalised; Kokoschka, to explore the perils of self-absorption; Malipiero, to illustrate the effect of collective dissociation on society; and Rilke and Cocteau, to reflect on the artist's need to transform themselves if they want to produce a significant work of art.

In the difficult 1930s and 1940s, writers turned to the myth to testify to the effect of social dysfunctionality on women (Williams, Gordon); to illustrate their hunger for new ways of being that might invest their life with greater meaning (Barfield, Wolfsohn); to reconsider the harm that can come from not *listening* to others, and to make sense of the pain and confusions that have shaped a young woman's life (Salomon); to reflect on the failures of nationhood (Anouilh); and to demonstrate the need to overcome one's individual concerns in the face of more important issues (*Casablanca*).

During the post-war years, they turned to the myth to further explore the need for art to represent both its time and its society, and to reflect on the relation between tradition and modernity (Stravinsky, Henry); to better understand the nature and importance of the creative impulse (Rukeyser, Cocteau); to illustrate the intense passions that characterise marginalised communities, and the tension between beauty and violence in a Brazilian slum (Vinicius, Viot); and to testify to the concerns that have shaped an artist's life as he abjures the art for which he became best known (Cocteau).

In the 1960s, writers of science fiction turned to the myth to explore the need to escape the feeling of being 'trapped' inside a tragic narrative (Delany) and to reflect on the threat that AI poses to both culture and individual relationships (Anderson). One fantasy writer turned to the myth, first to explain why the traditional myth was 'wrong', and then to identify the poignant heart of the myth (Hoban), while another did so to explore the harm that can be done by political fanaticism (Gaiman).

The last quarter of a century has seen a spate of new versions of the myth. In the final chapter, we looked at six of these, all of which explore a flawed perception of reality—and we noted a perhaps revealing difference between those written by men and those written by women.

All three versions of the myth by male writers foreground the difficulties that a male protagonist has with facing reality: they are so focussed on their own concerns that they cannot relate to their partner. In two of these, the protagonist mistakes his reluctance to lose a partner for 'love' (*Deconstructing Harry*, *Sliding Doors*). In contrast, *The Ground Beneath Her Feet* explores the extent of the dysfunctionality that characterises the post-war world—a world in which everyone lives in a parallel universe of their choosing, with the result that no one shows any interest in their 'reality', and self-awareness becomes an effete pretension.

In contrast, all three versions of the myth written by women show the protagonist's determination not only to brave or to better understand the dysfunctional reality in which she finds herself, but also to discover the resilience she needs to move on in her life. As she grapples with the unforgiving reality of her imminent death, Kathy Acker demonstrates an unflinching self-awareness. Sarah Ruhl's *Eurydice* represents a whimsical but serious reflection on the influence of *otherness* in a young woman's life, its origins in the language she owes to her father, and both the difficulties this has caused her and the meaning with which it has invested her life. In contrast, Anaïs Mitchell's *Hadestown* is all heart. It turns to the myth to testify to its author's repugnance at the exploitative practices upon which 'vampire capitalism' rests.[23]

This study has argued that a myth is not to be identified with a 'story' that circulated in antiquity. It is a 'structure of metaphors'—and for as long as this structure of metaphors continues to resonate, writers and other artists will rework it to express new concerns. A myth is represented by the 'sum' of all the different concerns that become associated with it up to a given moment: for our purpose here, until the early twenty-first century.

What makes the myth of Orpheus and Eurydice so intriguing is that the combination of metaphors that define it—*unbearable loss, impossible longing, misplaced entitlement, descent,* and *darkness* (first associated with the myth in ancient Greece), and *self-indulgence, despair,* and *self-awareness* (which were added later by Virgil)—can trigger an unusual range of associations. This explains the startling range of concerns that have been found at its heart during the last two and a half thousand years. It explains why this myth has been re-imagined more often than any other 'Greek' myth. And why it has been re-imagined not only in such strikingly different ways, but also why different responses to it explore such radically different concerns.

Notes

1 Most obviously, the Asian financial crisis (1997), the global financial crisis (2007–2008), the European sovereign debt crisis (2009), and the stock market crash (2020).

2 In the United States, families in the top 1% of distribution hold more than one-third of total wealth, families in the bottom 50% hold only 2% of total wealth, and some 37.9 million live in poverty ('Trends in the Distribution of Family Wealth, 1989 to 2019', US Congressional Budget Office, 2022; and 'National Poverty in America Awareness Month: January 2023', US Census Bureau, 2023). In the United Kingdom, the wealth held by the richest 1% of households is greater than for the entire bottom 80% of the population, and 13.4 million live in poverty ('Household total wealth in Great Britain: April 2018 to March 2020', Office for National Statistics, UK, 2022; 'Overall UK Poverty Rates', Joseph Rowntree Foundation, 2023). The international situation is even more shocking. Strong economies, such as the United States—with a federal debt, in 2023, of $32.6 trillion—can continue to grow by borrowing colossal sums at relatively modest rates. Whereas developing economies must pay higher rates to borrow far more modest sums. As a result, 40% of the world population (3.3 billion people) are living in countries whose debt interest payments are greater than what they can afford to spend on health or education. On average, African countries pay eight times more for borrowing than the wealthiest European economies, and four times more than the United States ('UN Warns of Soaring Global Debt', New York/Geneva, The United Nations, July 12, 2023).

3 W. Allen, *Deconstructing Harry*, Burbank, CA: Fine Line Features, 1997 (DVD). Before taking the part of Harry, Allen approached Elliott Gould, Dennis Hopper, Dustin Hoffman, and Albert Brooks, who all declined: see Bradford Evans, 'The Lost Roles of Albert Brooks', *New York* (magazine), June 30, 2011.

4 Such a journey is also central to Allen's earlier film, *Stardust Memories* (1980), which for the most part parodies of Federico Fellini's *8½* (1963).

5 Her name recalls Fay Wray, the actress who plays Ann Darrow in the classic version of *King Kong*.

6 P. Howitt, *Sliding Doors*, Los Angeles, CA: Miramax, 1998 (for the DVD) and Eye, Suffolk, UK: ScreenPress Books, 1998 (for the screenplay).

7 The music for the film is well chosen. It includes 'Turn Back Time' (Søren Rasted, Claus Norreen) performed by Aqua (MCA Records, 1996); 'Coming Up for Air' written and performed by Patty Larkin (Windham Hill Records, 1997), and 'Tenderness on the Block' (Warren Zevon, Jackson Browne, 1978), performed by Patty Larkin (High Street Records/Windham Hill Group, 1997).

8 For example, Roger Ebert gave it 2/4 stars, and was critical of the screenplay.

9 A. Errigo, 'Sliding Doors Review', *Empire* (online, 2000; https://www.empireonline.com/movies/reviews/sliding-doors-review/).

10 S. Rushdie, *The Ground Beneath Her Feet*, London: Jonathan Cape, 1999.

11 Rushdie had planned Vina's death long before the death of Princess Diana in August 1997. He was probably thinking of the response to the deaths of Janis Joplin (Oct. 1970) and John Lennon (Dec. 1980).

12 A rock operetta based on her novel (*Pussy, King of the Pirates*. New York: Grove, 1996), which re-contextualises *Treasure Island*, performed by The Mekons with Kathy Acker, *Pussy, King of the Pirates*, Chicago, IL: Touch and Go Records, 1996. The live performance was on 20 September at the Museum of Contemporary Art in Chicago.

13 K. Acker, 'The Gift of Disease', *The Guardian*, 18 January 1997; see also, J. McBride, 'The Last Days of Kathy Acker', *Hazlitt*, July 28, 2015, URL https://hazlitt.net/feature/last-days-kathy-acker; and C. Kraus, 'Cancer Became My Whole Brain: Kathy Acker's Final Year', *The New Yorker*, August 11, 2017.

14 K. Acker, *Eurydice in the Underworld*, London: Arcadia Books, 1997.
15 Plato, *Symposium* (179*d*), in Plato, *Lysis, Symposium, Phaedrus*, ed. C. Emlyn-Jones and W. Preddy. Loeb Classical Library. Cambridge, MA: Harvard University Press, 2022, pp. 164–167.
16 M. Blanchot, 'The Gaze of Orpheus,' in *The Space of Literature*, tr. A. Smock, Lincoln: University of Nebraska Press, 1982, pp. 171–176.
17 Sarah Ruhl's Eurydice was first published in *Divine Fire: Eight Contemporary Plays Inspired by the Greeks*, ed. C. Svich, New York: Back Stage Books, 2005. It was later published separately in the U.S. (by Samuel French, New York, 2008) and in the U.K. (by Methuen, London, 2010).
18 See Don Mitchell's early novel, *Thumb Tripping*, New York: Little, Brown, 1970, which became a film in 1972; also, D. Mitchell, *The Nature Notebooks*, Lebanon, NH: University Press of New England, 2004; M. Allen, 'The Road to *Hadestown* with Vermont's Anaïs Mitchell', *Yankee* (New England), Dec 2019/Jan 2020.
19 A. Mitchell, *Working on a Song: The Lyrics of 'Hadestown'*, New York: Plume/Penguin Random House, 2020, p. 83; also, 'The Hell with Broadway: The Story of Anais Mitchell's *Hadestown*', *Rolling Stone*, June 1, 2019.
20 A. Mitchell, *Hadestown*, New York: Righteous Babe Records, 2010, CD.
21 A. Mitchell, *Hadestown: The Myth, the Musical*, 'Live Original Cast Recording' (New York: Warner Music Group, 2017, CD).
22 A. Mitchell, *Hadestown: Original Broadway Cast Recording*, New York: Ghostlight Records, 2019, CD.
23 For vampire capitalism, see: K. Marx, *Capital: A Critique of Political Economy*, vol. 1, tr. Ben Fowkes, London: Penguin/New Left Review, 1976, p. 342; and P. Kennedy, *Vampire Capitalism: Fractured Societies and Alternative Futures*, London: Palgrave Macmillan, 2017.

Index

Note: Page numbers followed by "n" denote endnotes.

For Product Safety Concerns and Information please contact our EU
representative GPSR@taylorandfrancis.com
Taylor & Francis Verlag GmbH, Kaufingerstraße 24, 80331 München, Germany

www.ingramcontent.com/pod-product-compliance
Lightning Source LLC
Chambersburg PA
CBHW070330270326
41926CB00017B/3828

9 781032 857305